This book is an important collection of articles providing a multifaceted look at the various factors that India has to deal with to assure continuing success in its development strategy. The authors provide a comprehensive assessment of the numerous challenges we face not only in economic management but also in ensuring our national security and managing foreign policy in a rapidly changing world. This is a much-needed addition to the literature on this subject.

*Montek Singh Ahluwalia*
Former Deputy Chairman, Planning Commission

India confronts diverse and formidable challenges to its security and economic resurgence. We need to marshal our genius and resources and work unitedly to ensure the nation's all-round progress. I commend Lieutenant General Kamal Davar for his pioneering and dedicated effort to synergise the views of so many eminent Indians in this path-breaking anthology, very aptly captioned *Securing India's Rise*.



*General N.C. Vij*
Former Chief, Army Staff

An outstanding anthology with contributions from some of the best minds in the business, compiled and edited by Lieutenant General Kamal Davar, possibly our finest military strategist. For India to emerge as a great nation, we need not only military might but also skilled diplomacy and smart power in dealing not only with insurgencies within but also with our formidable neighbours in the east and west.

*A.S. Dulat*
Former Chief, Research and Analysis Wing

In recent years, India, which is situated in a troubled neighbourhood, has been confronted with diverse challenges to its national security, internal cohesiveness, and social and economic well-being. Lieutenant General Kamal Davar, one of India's leading strategic thinkers, has done yeoman service by editing this much-required anthology, *Securing India's Rise*, which collates the views of 19 eminent Indians suggesting measures to augment India's Comprehensive National Power. A must-read for Indians from all walks of life.

*Ambassador Gopalaswami Parthasarathy*
Chancellor, Central University, Jammu

*Securing India's Rise*, edited by eminent strategic thinker and the first director general of India's Defence Intelligence Agency Lieutenant General Kamal Davar, encapsulates the perspectives articulated by 19 accomplished Indian thought leaders. The contributors have been instrumental in shaping India's strategic thought and steering its destiny. It is a must-read for policymakers, scholars, military fraternity, academia and informed citizens. I am sanguine that the book will provide readers with the much-needed nuanced understanding of the challenges and opportunities that beset India in its resurgence and transition to a great power.

*Major General B.K. Sharma (Retd)*
Director, United Service Institution of India

The anthology *Securing India's Rise*, edited by one of India's renowned military professionals Lieutenant General Kamal Davar, is indeed a much-needed review of the significant constituents of Comprehensive National Power. Collating the considered views of 19 distinguished authors is no easy task, and we need to pay serious heed to the balanced recommendations of these notable contributors for India's security and progress.

*Lieutenant General Harwant Singh*
Former Deputy Chief, Army Staff

With an impressive set of experts drawn from different domains, *Securing India's Rise* will be a valuable addition to the slim literature on the concept of Comprehensive National Power and will be relevant to both policymaker and the layperson.

*Commodore C. Uday Bhaskar*
Director, Society for Policy Studies

India's rise to superpower status is not yet a certainty. Smart policy is needed in the formulation of which an eclectic band of original thinkers need to be harnessed. This is what Lieutenant General Kamal Davar has done in *Securing India's Rise*. The book is an essential read for those who are aware of the distance to be travelled before the potential of India becomes a fact.

*Professor Madhav Das Nalapat*
Vice-chairman, Manipal Advanced Research Group

# SECURING INDIA'S RISE

# SECURING INDIA'S RISE

*A Vision for the Future*

Edited by

Lieutenant General Kamal Davar

B L O O M S B U R Y

NEW DELHI • LONDON • OXFORD • NEW YORK • SYDNEY

BLOOMSBURY INDIA
Bloomsbury Publishing India Pvt. Ltd
Second Floor, LSC Building No. 4, DDA Complex, Pocket C – 6 & 7,
Vasant Kunj, New Delhi 110070

BLOOMSBURY, BLOOMSBURY INDIA and the Diana logo
are trademarks of Bloomsbury Publishing Plc

First published in India 2021
This edition published 2021



ISBN: PB: 978-93-54350-48-1; e-Book: 978-93-54350-54-2
2 4 6 8 10 9 7 5 3 1

Typeset in Manipal Technologies Limited

Printed and bound in India by Thomson Press India Ltd.

To find out more about our authors and books, visit www.bloomsbury.com and sign up for our newsletters

*This book is dedicated to my parents, freedom fighter and humanist Dr M.C. Davar and Lilavati Davar, who instilled in their children an unfailing love for Mother India and respect for the human values it represents.*

## CONTENTS

*Foreword* by Dr Karan Singh xv
*Acknowledgements* xviii

Introduction 1
*Lieutenant General Kamal Davar*

1 Law and the Idea of India 9
*Dr Shashi Tharoor*

2 Positioning India in a Shifting Geopolitical Terrain 30
*Ambassador Shyam Saran*

3 National Security Decision-making Process in India and Its Trajectories 46
*General V.P. Malik (Retired)*

4 India and the Maritime Dimension 68
*Admiral Arun Prakash (Retired)*

5 Facing China's Challenges Robustly 91
*Professor Srikanth Kondapalli*

6 India's Economic Challenges and Countering China 114
*Mohan Guruswamy, Distinguished Fellow, United Service Institution of India, New Delhi*

7 Revisiting India's Nuclear Doctrine 125
*Bharat Karnad, Emeritus Professor*

8 India–Pakistan: The Way Forward 142
*Ambassador Sharat Sabharwal*

9 India and the Two-front War 164
*Lieutenant General D.S. Hooda (Retired)*

10 India's Relations with West Asia and Energy Security 185
*Ambassador K.C. Singh*

11 The Shifting Borders of Conflict 204
*Dr Ajai Sahni*

12 Non-traditional Neighbourhood Challenges Impacting Indian Security 222
*Tilak Devasher*

13 Combating Left-wing Extremism 243
*Prakash Singh, IPS*

14 India's Approach on Jammu and Kashmir after Revoking Article 370 262
*Lieutenant General Syed Ata Hasnain (Retired)*

15 Emerging Security Scenarios and Role of Intelligence 288
*Vikram Sood*

16 Indian Journalism: The Fourth Pillar of Our Democracy? 307
*Seema Mustafa*

17 COVID-19: Global Challenges and Indian Responses 319
*Manish Tewari*

18 A New Frontier: Digital Insecurity and India 342
*Samir Saran and Akhil Deo*

19 Education—A New Thrust 362
*Brigadier Sukhjit Singh (Retired)*

*Epilogue* 379
*Notes* 401
*About the Editor and Contributors* 437

# FOREWORD

India, along with the rest of the world, is facing a very difficult time. On the one hand is the serious economic downturn that began well before the Covid-19 pandemic. Then came the pandemic at the end of 2019, with its attendant challenges, lockdowns and 'unlock-downs', and millions of migrant workers having to walk hundreds of kilometres back to their villages. The virus itself has already killed over 1,50,000 Indian citizens; half a million infected cases have been reported and the severe pressure on our limited medical facilities is revealing the inherent weaknesses in our country's health infrastructure. Added to all this are the disturbing confrontations with the Chinese military in Ladakh, where even though we are more than holding our own so far, we can see a continuing threat to national security to contain which massive outlays of additional funds are required. Even with all this in mind, we must, nevertheless, strive to secure India's rise on the global stage during and after the Covid-19 pandemic.

It is interesting that all our foreign disputes revolve around the modern state of Jammu and Kashmir (J&K), which my intrepid ancestor Maharaja Gulab Singh founded in 1843. This was possible at that time because the Dogra forces led by such legendary commanders as General Zorawar Singh extended the borders of India all the way to Central Asia (Gilgit-Baltistan) and Tibet (Ladakh). This extension of India's territory was achieved at a great cost with the sacrifice of the lives of brave Dogra soldiers drawn from Jammu and Himachal Pradesh. These are the extensions that are now being challenged by Pakistan and China. We have already lost control of Gilgit-Baltistan and large sections of Ladakh such as Aksai Chin, as a result of which, almost half of the area of the 85,806 sq miles is no longer under our control. Not only have we lost this territory but both the interlopers are continuing their hostile activities to further trouble India on both fronts. In fact, the bifurcation of the state last year and the Home Minister's statement in Parliament that we are pledged to recapture Aksai Chin has given China the excuse to up the ante in Ladakh, while Pakistan with its fatal attraction for Kashmir, continues its nefarious activities on the western front.

Lieutenant General Kamal Davar, with his distinguished military record of 41 years in the Indian Army—during which he was wounded in action as a young officer in 1965, served in virtually all theatres of military operations in India and commanded the entire Ladakh sector—is eminently suited to edit this significant anthology. The present volume brings together a truly impressive range of scholarship, which includes writings from Members of Parliament, retired senior military officers, distinguished members of foreign service, political and military analysts and economic experts. Many of the contributors are personal friends and I can vouch for their ability and integrity.

Taken together, these essays give us multiple insights into the problems that we face, and the ways in which we can overcome them. We have a long and unique history going back several thousand years to the Vedas, and down through the long and tortuous corridors of time, India has seen many ups and downs. We have produced some of the greatest kingdoms in human history, some of the greatest philosophers, architects, mathematicians and administrators. However, we have also suffered many centuries of subjugation and humiliation. In 1947, India emerged, for the first time, as a Sovereign Democratic Republic stretching all the way from the great Himalayas down to Kanyakumari where three great oceans meet at the feet of Mother India; but even after Independence, we have seen both military defeat in 1962 and subsequently, victory in 1971.

All of this points to the fact that if we make diplomatic or military miscalculations, we will inevitably pay the price, whereas if our planning and implementation are impeccable, we will achieve victory. The essays in this book will surely help us understand the intricacies of the present situation that India finds herself in so that we will, hopefully, avoid past mistakes whether in the military, economic or diplomatic fields. I commend Lieutenant General Kamal Davar for editing this valuable anthology.

Dr Karan Singh
Former Member of Parliament and Minister,
Government of India

## ACKNOWLEDGEMENTS

After the publication of my book *Tryst with Perfidy* on the Pakistani deep state nearly three years ago, I had been rather impatient to write the next one! Though many security-related and strategic themes came to mind, the title 'Securing India's Rise' just caught hold of my imagination, goading me on to prepare an all-embracing, holistic look at India's current state, and ponder over various issues which may contribute to its growth in the foreseeable future. The choice before me was to attempt writing it exclusively on my own or request eminent Indian thinkers to contribute a chapter each on a subject of their expertise. I chose the latter option to enable this anthology to become, hopefully, far more meaningful for its readers with the thoughts of the luminaries who I managed to bring together.

I would like to express my gratitude to the illustrious and renowned scholar-statesman Dr Karan Singh for writing the Foreword. Nineteen other eminent and distinguished Indians, from former Union Minister Shashi Tharoor, former Army Chief General Ved Malik, former Naval Chief Admiral Arun Prakash, former senior diplomat Shyam Saran, former Union Minister Manish Tewari, former R&AW Chief Vikram Sood, veteran Indian Police Service Officer Prakash Singh, senior Army officers Lieutenant General Ata

Hasnain and Lieutenant General D.S. Hooda, former Ambassadors K.C. Singh and Sharat Sabherwal, distinguished soldier Brigadier Sukhjit Singh, MVC, former Special Secretary R&AW Tilak Devasher, counter-terrorism expert Dr Ajai Sahni, academic Professor Srikanth Kondapalli, President of the Observer Research Foundation Samir Saran and his young associate Akhil Deo, veteran economist Mohan Guruswamy, strategic affairs expert Bharat Karnad and senior media personality Seema Mustafa, have all contributed their invaluable ideas for ensuring India's rise. I remain eternally grateful to each one of them.

Working from the salubrious climes of Kasauli, Himachal Pradesh, through the COVID-19 pandemic period, I was greatly assisted by the brilliant young researcher Chayanika Saxena, especially with her attention to detail and IT skills. I am also grateful to former Deputy Chairman Planning Commission Montek Ahluwalia, Brigadier Sukhjit Singh, MVC, Ambassador Shyam Saran and my brothers, Yogeshwar and Praveen, for their suggestions in compiling this anthology.

All throughout the editing of the book, my wife Madhu exhibited great patience while my sons-in-law Sanidhya and Rishi, my daughters Tania, Malvika and Aprajita, and my grandchildren Arnav and Ahana all provided adequate support, in their own way. My thanks too to Bloomsbury India for publishing this anthology, which I hope will be of some use for my beloved country as it rightfully strives for a deserving seat at the global high table.

# Introduction

## LIEUTENANT GENERAL KAMAL DAVAR

Having worn the nation's sacred olive green uniform for 41 years with great pride and unending joy, matters of national security have naturally loomed large, perhaps the foremost, in my life. My concern, as an ordinary citizen, on the myriad and complex issues that constitute the vast mosaic of this matter of great import have continued unabated, even well after my retirement from the Indian Army. I have thus persisted passionately with an abiding interest in security issues concerning our beloved motherland, India, that is, Bharat.

My life's inspiration was, and remains, the thought that India, a young nation state, but with roots in one of the world's oldest surviving and great civilisations, has much to contribute to the well-being of not only its own people but also the world at large. Like most Indians, I too cherish a world view that looks beyond the frontiers of this ancient, noble land.

That India is situated in one of the most geopolitically stressed and impoverished regions of the world would be an understatement. Nevertheless, over a billion people, who—notwithstanding their economic woes or social status—proudly call themselves Indians, have sacrificed, suffered and contributed since India's tumultuous independence on 15 August 1947 to the nation's growth and security. India, by every standard, has vastly progressed since gaining its freedom from the British yoke and is now on the threshold of becoming a global player. Yet, today's world and specifically our immediate region, bestrewn with numerous differences and fault lines, present our nation with many formidable challenges to its territorial integrity, political stability and economic resurgence. The study of some of these challenges and measures to overcome them is, thus, the focus of and thrust for this publication.

I would like to express my deep sense of gratitude to the 19 eminent Indians from various fields who have spent a lifetime in the service of the nation and have contributed a chapter each, writing on the area or subject of their specific interest or expertise. I am sanguine that their views, if taken into consideration and implemented, will go a long way in 'Securing India's Rise'—the title of this anthology.

To Dr Karan Singh, one of India's most respected and erudite philosopher-statesmen, I tender my deep gratitude for writing the Foreword for this book. The descendant of the former ruling dynasty of India's restive state J&K, Dr Karan Singh remarks in his Foreword, 'it is interesting that all our foreign disputes revolve around the state of Jammu and Kashmir (J&K), which my intrepid ancestor Maharaja Gulab Singh founded in 1843', which is indeed an inalienable truth. Importantly, the baggage of history bequeathed to us by the departing British rulers in August 1947 continues to weigh heavily on our shoulders, and most of our strategic problems continue to persist despite many conflicts and efforts at peace-making with at least two of our immediate neighbours. We need to correct, once and for all, these strategic mistakes inherited from the British.

A single book simply cannot cover all that ails India in a comprehensive manner nor discuss at length each and every issue that will contribute to securing its rise. Thus, the limitations of space have left a few issues unaddressed. Nevertheless, 19 outstanding essayists have shared their invaluable thoughts which, if implemented, can certainly assist in contributing to India's success in the foreseeable future. The views of these luminaries to enhance India's Comprehensive National Power (CNP) thus merit serious attention.

It is worth recapitulating the contours of the drivers of CNP which enhance national security in all its manifestations. CNP is the sum total of a nation's natural resources, its economic strength, military capabilities, the just rule of law, scientific and technological prowess, the robustness of its industrial base, population, education and medical infrastructures, governance and, importantly, internal cohesion and unity. If embellished by enlightened, selfless leadership backed by a resolute political will, the progress and prosperity of any nation will, in all likelihood, ride an ascending trajectory. However, as is commonly known, most nations suffer from many pitfalls, thus falling short of becoming ideal nation states and India too is no exception. We have thus miles yet to traverse to attain our national objectives and wipe the tears of the last Indian in our long queue of want, deprivation and despair. Concurrent to our efforts to improve the lives of the majority of our 1.35 billion people, we have to ensure our territorial integrity while simultaneously also dealing with the 'sieges within', which have a propensity of appearing from time to time.

India is the world's largest democracy, the second most populous nation, with the fourth-largest armed forces in the world; till last year it was also one of the fastest globally growing economies. Unmistakeably, it is universally acknowledged to be an emerging global player and one of the world's 'powerhouses' in the making. It shares around 15,000 km of land borders with some not-so-friendly neighbours and has 7,500 km of coastline that also needs to be constantly protected. Will India's rise, in keeping with its still untapped vast potential and the world's expectations of it becoming a major power in the 21st century, address effectively its burden of regional and global responsibilities? Or will India be content in plodding along and be merely reactive in its strategic moorings?

India confronts more than just formidable challenges to its security and well-being. Though India is among the top three powerful nations in Asia, with China and Japan as the other two, an overly hegemonic and assertive China has left no stone unturned to put diverse obstacles in India's path towards progress. To keep India boxed in South Asia is a clear objective of its India policies. Aided and equally abetted by its near-enslaved protégé, Pakistan, China's famed 'string of pearls' stratagem and its 'salami slicing' tactics have been eating at India's vitals.[1] For decades, China has also been aiding and abetting insurgent movements in India's north-east region and supporting Naxal extremists in India's 'Red Corridor'. However, the current confrontation between the two Asian giants in Eastern Ladakh, the most serious face-off between the two since the India–China Conflict of 1962, has all the makings of a serious flare-up that may extend even to the waters of the Indo-Pacific. Where does India stand today in its security preparedness vis-à-vis China while the asymmetry between the two nations continue to grow?

On the other hand, Pakistan, born from the same womb as India in 1947, has consistently followed pronounced anti-India policies since its traumatic birth. Apart from initiating the conflicts of 1947–48, 1965, 1971 and the Kargil Conflict in 1999, Pakistan has continually been unabashedly sponsoring terrorist activities in J&K and in the Indian hinterland. The raison d'être of Pakistan since its independence in August 1947 appears to be to harbour an implacably visceral hostility towards India. Pakistan following an unchanging, self-destructive and myopic anti-India politico-strategic formulation hardly leaves any room for optimism regarding India–Pak relations in the near future. Weapons of mass destruction and terrorism make an apocalyptic cocktail and India must factor in the alarming possibility of nuclear materials falling into the wrong hands in Pakistan. With China's near complete economic domination of Pakistan—primarily as a result of the emergence of the over US$60 billion China–Pakistan Economic Corridor and the construction of the Gwadar Port in Balochistan—a military collusion of convenience between these two nations against India has been virtually formalised with consequential ominous portents for India. In addition, will Pakistan ever shed its maniacal obsession for J&K and learn to live in harmony and thus prosper as a peaceful neighbour?

Issues such as India's foreign policy to match the prevailing international dynamics, our energy security compulsions, re-visiting our nuclear doctrine and shaping viable policies vis-à-vis our likely adversaries merit deliberate attention. Does India possess the requisite decision-making capabilities related to defence at the apex levels apart from adequate intelligence capabilities, which has been found wanting in a few previous occasions when the nation was taken by surprise as in the 1962 and Kargil conflicts and the 2008 Mumbai blasts among other events. A true democracy requires the presence of a free and unbiased media—do we possess this attribute? India has been the victim of terrorism engineered by the Pakistani deep state for decades as also afflicted by left-wing extremism (LWE) inflicted by Naxals. Though India has substantially attained the ability to counter terrorism and LWE, the problem persists since Pakistan will continue to pursue its K-2 (Kashmir–Khalistan) policies to 'bleed India by a thousand cuts'. Over the last few years, Pakistan has also enjoyed China's unstinted support.

The Indo-Pacific region has now become the most strategic global expanse through which over 60 per cent of the world's trade transits. With China disdainfully disregarding all internationally based freedom of the seas conventions, including a rules-based maritime order, India too has been drawn into the Indo–Pacific political contentions. India needs to further strengthen its navy to safeguard both its western and eastern seaboards, whilst simultaneously improving its capabilities to successfully conduct a two-front war. The latter is more than a likely possibility now given the current face-off with China in Eastern Ladakh.

Like the rest of the world, India too has been gravely afflicted by the Chinese-origin virus that has caused the COVID-19 pandemic, which has wrecked the economies of countries apart from causing thousands of deaths globally. Thus the bitter lesson for all, including India, is to be prepared for combating such future bio-warfare instances. As a nation, how prepared are we? How well is India shaping up in educating its impoverished masses or preparing itself to survive the challenges for developing a workforce fit for a future hi-tech world? These too are some of the other significant issues.

With many eminent personalities offering their suggestions through this anthology, it is my fervent hope that governments, both at the Centre and in the states, study their recommendations. Educational institutions, the media, NGOs and all citizens working for national betterment may also find much merit in the recommendations set forth in this compilation.

From an old soldier to my beloved motherland, I offer this work with a prayer that the suggestions of these estimable scribes may help contribute in *securing India's rise.*

1

# Law and the Idea of India[1]

## DR SHASHI THAROOR

I recently delivered a speech on 'Law and the Idea of India' and it was in many ways a fitting theme given the current state of our nation. But the 'Idea of India' has become a highly contested concept these days. The Idea of India—though the phrase is Tagore's—is, in some form or another, arguably as old as antiquity itself, and numerous are the proofs of the aspiration for cultural unity that appear throughout the history of our civilisation.

I have written in my book *An Era of Darkness* about how the notion of Bharatvarsha in the Rig Veda, of a land stretching from the Himalayas to the seas, contained the original territorial idea of India; and how the travels of Adi Sankara at the cusp of the 10th century, establishing his *mutths* (centres of learning) in Srinagar, Dwarka, Puri and Sringeri, helped knit together the spiritual idea of India within its 'sacred geography'. Lest some see this as a purely Hindu idea, Maulana Azad, too, has written of how Indian Muslims on the Haj were all seen by the Arabs as 'Hindis', whether they were Pathans or Tamizhs. So the idea of India as one civilisation inhabiting a coherent territorial space and a shared history is timeless.

However, the Idea of India as a modern *nation* based on a certain conception of human rights and citizenship, vigorously backed by due process of law and equality before law, is a relatively recent and strikingly modern idea. Earlier conceptions of India drew their inspiration from mythology and theology. However, the modern Idea of India, despite the mystical influence of Tagore, and the spiritual and moral influences of Gandhi ji, is a robustly secular and legal construct based upon the vision and intellect of our Founding Fathers, notably (in alphabetical order!) Ambedkar, Nehru and Patel. The Preamble of the Constitution itself is the most eloquent enumeration of this vision. In its description of the defining traits of the Indian republic, in its conception of justice, of liberty, of equality and fraternity, it firmly proclaims that the law will be the bedrock of the Idea of India.

To my mind, the role of constitutionalism in shaping the Idea of India is the dominant strand in the broader story of the evolution and modernisation of Indian society, especially over the last two centuries. Every society has an interdependent relation with the legal systems that govern it, which is both complex and, especially in our turbulent times, continuously and vociferously, contested. It is through this interplay that communities become societies, societies become civilisations and civilisations acquire a sense of national and historical character.

It is no surprise then that while the ancient and the medieval worlds largely celebrated kings and conquerors since the Age of Enlightenment, many of the great people who changed the course of their nations and the world for good, and sometimes worse, have been lawyers—I just need to mention the name 'Dr B.R. Ambedkar (MA, PhD, MSc, DSc, *Barrister-at-Law*, LLD, DLitt)' to illustrate this point! These men, and increasingly women, had the vision and the intellect to anticipate the problems and challenges that all civilisations in the modern era have had to confront. In the process, they found the best check-and-balance mechanism in the book of law, referred to as the Constitution, for combating these plagues to protect the interests of all our people in equal measure.

The story of humanity over the last few hundred years has been the story of the spread of democracy, rapid industrialisation and urbanisation, increasingly accompanied by globalisation of trade and commerce, and the increasing impact of science and technology on human society and culture. This diversity of challenges can only be addressed if we agree on the ground rules of how we disagree and negotiate change. Of course, some societies have confronted these challenges sooner and better, while others have delayed their hour of reckoning at their own peril. I would suggest that the Indian experience in tackling these challenges so far has been of the middling variety. It would have been far worse if not for the Idea of India, most eloquently championed by Jawaharlal Nehru, and enshrined in the political and legal system created and protected by our Constitution and its architect, Dr Ambedkar.

It is often said that any truism about India can be immediately contradicted by another truism about India. The country's national motto, emblazoned on its governmental crest, is *Satyameva Jayaté*: Truth Alone

Triumphs. The question remains, however: whose truth? It is a question to which there are at least a billion answers—if the last census hasn't undercounted us again.

But that sort of an answer is no answer at all, and so another answer to those questions has to be sought. And this may lie in a simple insight: the singular thing about India is that you can only speak of it in the plural. There are, in the hackneyed phrase, many Indias. You may be familiar with the American motto, 'E Pluribus Unum'—out of many, one; if India were to borrow it in dog Latin, it would read something like 'E Pluribus Pluribum'! Everything exists in countless variants. There is no single standard, no fixed stereotype, no 'one way'. This pluralism is acknowledged in the way India arranges its own affairs: all groups, faiths, tastes and ideologies survive and contend for their place in the sun. At a time when most developing countries opted for authoritarian models of government to promote nation-building and to direct development, India chose to be a multi-party democracy. And despite many stresses and strains, including 22 months of autocratic rule during a 'state of Emergency' in 1975–1976, when even habeas corpus was suspended and even during our current difficult times, a multiparty democracy—freewheeling, rumbustious, corrupt and inefficient, perhaps, but nonetheless flourishing—India has remained.

One result is that India strikes many as maddening, chaotic, inefficient and seemingly unpurposeful as it muddles its way through the second decade of the 21st century. Another, though, is that India is not just a country, it is an adventure, one in which all avenues are open and everything is possible. The British historian E.P. Thompson wrote,

> India is perhaps the most important country for the future of the world. All the convergent influences of the world run through this society.... There is not a thought that is being thought in the West or East that is not active in some Indian mind.[2]

That Indian mind has been shaped by remarkably diverse forces: ancient Hindu tradition, myth and scripture; the impact of Islam and Christianity; and two centuries of British colonial rule. The result is unique. Many observers abroad have been astonished by India's survival as a pluralist state. But India could hardly have survived as anything else. Pluralism is a reality that emerges from the very nature of the country; it is a choice made inevitable by India's geography and reaffirmed by its history.

This means that the Idea of India is itself very unusual in today's world. Talking about Indian nationhood reminds me of the probably apocryphal story of two law professors arguing about a problem. When one suggests a practical solution to the dilemma, the other counters: 'It may work in practice, but will it work in theory?' Indian nationalism is not based on language (since we have at least 22 or 35 Indian languages, depending on whether you follow the Constitution or the ethnolinguists). It is not based on geography (the 'natural' geography of the subcontinent—framed by the mountains and the seas—was hacked by the partition of 1947). It is not based on ethnicity (the 'Indian' accommodates a diversity of racial types in which many Indians have more in common with foreigners than with other Indians—Indian Punjabis and Bengalis, for instance, have more in common with Pakistanis and Bangladeshis, respectively, than they do with Poonawalas or Bangaloreans). And it is not based on religion (we are home to every faith known to mankind, and Hinduism—a faith without a national organisation, no established church or ecclesiastical hierarchy, no Hindu Pope, no Hindu Mecca, no uniform beliefs or modes of worship—exemplifies as much our diversity as it does a common cultural heritage). So Indian nationalism is the nationalism of an idea, the idea of an ever-ever land—emerging from an ancient civilisation, united by a shared history, sustained by pluralist democracy under the rule of law.

This land imposes no narrow conformities on its citizens: you can be many things and one thing. You can be a good Muslim, a good Keralite and a good Indian all at once. Where Freudians note the distinctions that arise out of 'the narcissism of minor differences', in India we celebrate the commonality of major differences. To stand Michael Ignatieff's famous phrase on its head, we are a land of belonging rather than of blood.

So the Idea of India is of one land embracing many. It is the idea that a nation may endure differences of caste, creed, colour, culture, cuisine, conviction, costume and custom, and still rally around a democratic consensus. That consensus is around the simple principle that in a democracy under the rule of law, you don't really need to agree all the time—except on the ground rules of how you will disagree. The reason India has survived all the stresses and strains that have beset it for nearly 70 years, and that led so many to predict its imminent disintegration, is that it maintained consensus on how to manage without consensus. Today, some in positions of power in India seem to be questioning those ground rules, and that sadly is why it is all the more essential to reaffirm them now. What knits this entire Idea of India together is, of course, the rule of law, enshrined in our Constitution.

Jawaharlal Nehru's opening remarks when he moved the motion at the newly established Constituent Assembly on 13 December 1946 gives us a view of the immense pressure and responsibility on the lawmakers to ensure that they responded fittingly to the situation and did justice to the task of Constitution-making. They had to preserve the 'past' idea of India and march towards the 'future' idea of India. Nehru said,

> We are at the end of an era and possibly very soon we shall embark upon a new age; and my mind goes back to the great past of India to the 5,000 years of India's history, from the very dawn of that history which might be considered almost the dawn of human history, till today. All that past crowds around me and exhilarates me and, at the same time, somewhat oppresses me. Am I worthy of that past? When I think also of the future, the greater future I hope, standing on this sword's edge of the present between this mighty past and the mightier future, I tremble a little and feel overwhelmed by this mighty task. We have come here at a strange moment in

> India's history. I do not know but I do feel that there is some magic in this moment of transition from the old to the new, something of that magic which one sees when the night turns into day and even though the day may be a cloudy one, it is day after all, for when the clouds move away we can see the sun later on.

We are perhaps once again at a 'strange moment in India's history'. But if we stay in the past, we should also recall Dr Ambedkar's concluding remarks to the Constituent Assembly in his 'The Grammar of Anarchy' speech on 25 November 1949. He informed us of the maladies of India and the ideal Idea of India, to be ensured by the rule of law. In a magisterial expression of India through the prism of politics, law and social hierarchies, he said,

> In politics we will be recognizing the principle of one man one vote and one vote one value. In our social and economic life, we shall, by reason of our social and economic structure, continue to deny the principle of one man one value. How long shall we continue to live this life of contradictions?

Ambedkar's eloquent assault on discrimination and untouchability, for the first time cogently expanded the Idea of India to incorporate the nation's vast, neglected underclass.

The working instrument of our democracy is the Constitution of India. It is the basic framework of our democracy. Under the scheme of our

Constitution, the three main organs of the State are the Legislature, the Executive and the Judiciary. The Constitution defines their powers, delimits their jurisdictions, demarcates their responsibilities and regulates their relationships with one another and with the people. But the most important contribution of the Constitution to the Idea of India was that of representation centred on individuals. As Madhav Khosla explains in his brilliant new book of legal history, *India's Founding Moment*, the political apparatus of establishing a constitutional democracy in postcolonial India—a land that was 'poor and illiterate; divided by caste, religion, and languages; and burdened by centuries of tradition', involved an attempt to free Indians from prevailing types of knowledge and understanding, to place citizens in a realm of individual agency and deliberation that was appropriate to self-rule and to alter the relationship that they shared with one another.

The founders of the Republic chose—as the Chairman of the Constitution's Drafting Committee, Dr Ambedkar, recognised—to impose a liberal Constitution upon a society that was not liberal. They saw the principles of liberal constitutionalism—the centrality of the state, non-communal political representation and so on—as responsive to the challenges posed by the burden of democracy. In keeping with contemporary liberal thought, they committed India to a common language of the rule of law, constructed a centralised state and rejected localism, and instituted a model of representation whose units were individuals rather than groups. The key objective, according to Khosla, was to 'allow Indians to arrive at outcomes agreeable to free and equal individuals'. That was not easy.

Constitutions are, of course (and Ambedkar explicitly made this point), tools to control and restrain state power. The challenge lies in reconciling restrictions on state power with popular rule—to prevent temporary majorities (since in a democracy, a majority is temporary, though some people forget that) from completely undoing what the Constitution has provided. Khosla suggests that the founders of the Indian republic held a conception of democracy that went beyond majority rule and rejected, in Ronald Dworkin's notable phrase, 'the majoritarian premise'. They subordinated politics to law. As Dr Ambedkar put it, the rights of Indian citizens could not 'be taken away by any legislature merely because it happens to have a majority'. The struggle for Indian independence was after all not simply a struggle for freedom from alien rule. It was a shift away from an administration of law and order centred on imperial despotism. Thus was born the idea of 'constitutional morality', meaning 'the commitment to constitutional means, to its processes and structures, alongside a commitment to free speech, scrutiny of public action [and] legal limitations on the exercise of power'. This was how freedom was intended to flourish in India.

Of course, Dr Ambedkar realised it is perfectly possible to pervert the Constitution, without changing its form, by merely changing the form of the administration to make it inconsistent and opposed to the spirit of the Constitution. Ambedkar argued that constitutional morality 'is not a natural sentiment. It has to be cultivated. We must realise that our people have yet to learn it. Democracy in India is only a top dressing on an Indian soil which is essentially undemocratic.' He insisted that the directive principles—an unusual feature of the Indian Constitution—were necessary because although the rules of democracy mandated that the people must elect those who will hold power, the principles confirmed that 'whoever captures power will not be free to do what he likes with it'.

At the same time, the Constitution wanted Indians to have a new understanding of authority. They would be liberated through submission to an impersonal force that saw them as equal agents and that liberated spirit would make possible socio-economic transformation. This was important because to leaders such as Jawaharlal Nehru—whose vision of democracy entailed equality and a decent standard of living for all—the establishment of a free and democratic India required the substitution of the economic power of a few rich individuals by a form of state control that could end poverty, reduce unemployment and improve material conditions.

It is striking that the Constituent Assembly rejected separate electorates, weighted representation and reservations on the basis of religion. Only days before Indian independence and the Partition of British India, Sardar Vallabhbhai Patel, in his capacity as Chairman of the Advisory Committee on Minorities and Fundamental Rights, wrote to the President of the Assembly, Rajendra Prasad, to explain why separate electorates had been rejected. Differentiated citizenship on the basis of religion, Patel argued, had already been tried in the colonial era and had led to Partition.

The answer lay in moving away from a representative framework that recognised identities that were regarded as stable and fixed and toward a model of citizenship centred on the political participation of individuals. Such a model would allow the categories of majority and minority to be constantly defined and redefined within the fluid domain of politics and it would thereby offer the greatest form of security.

This fundamental difference of opinion continues to haunt our politics today. The nationalist movement was divided between two sets of ideas, held by those who saw religious identity as the determinant of their nationhood and those who believed in an inclusive India for everyone, irrespective of faith, where rights were guaranteed to individuals rather than to religious communities. The former became the Idea of Pakistan, the latter the Idea of India. Pakistan was created as a state with a dominant religion, a state that discriminates against its minorities and denies them equal rights. But India never accepted the logic that had partitioned the country: our freedom struggle was for all, and the newly independent India would also be for all.

On the other hand, the Hindutva idea of a Hindu Rashtra, espoused today by the Bharatiya Janata Party/Rashtriya Swayamsevak Sangh, is the mirror image of Pakistan—a state with a dominant majority religion that seeks to put its minorities in a subordinate place. It is particularly striking in the context of today that the Constitution-makers explicitly rejected the notion of religion playing any role in citizenship, arguing that each individual voter exercised agency in the democratic project and should not be reduced to the pre-existing loyalties of religious affiliation. 'For India's founders, one could not be a political agent unless one's political identity was self-created.' The Constitution granted representation not to one's predetermined identity (religion) but to one's individual expression of agency. That was why the individual vote was so important. Democratic politics cannot be reduced to the advocacy of pre-set interests; interests instead had to be expressed through politics. 'The very constitution of one's identity as a citizen,' Khosla explains, 'was itself a form of freedom.'

The adaptability of the Constitution to the ever-changing realities of national life has effectively made it a vehicle of social change.

Equally important, the above process has been substantially facilitated by our Parliament, the institution conceived for that very purpose by the Constitution. The Constitution created itself as a self-generating and self-correcting entity, a living document that allowed for its own amendment to meet the changes of the times, subject to the Doctrine of Basic Structure, again an invention of the judiciary. In a way, it reflected the confidence in the people of this land to make adjustments and rise to meet every new challenge to our society. During the past nearly seven decades of Independence, the Constitution, which came into force on 26 January 1950, has been amended over 100 times by Parliament, a creature created inter-alia for that very purpose by the Constitution. The small-minded may consider the high number of amendments as one of the weaknesses of our Constitution, but those with a broader vision would understand that it is actually a sign of its inherent strength—a strength that derives from its ability to be flexible without the risk of self-destruction. It has the exemplary inbuilt ability to adjust to the needs of the times and the fact that this is enabled through a thoroughly democratic and representative process has been the key to its effectiveness in moving our society forward in a democratic and, more broadly, inclusive manner.

During the journey of the constitution, there have been innumerable instances which have either corroded or preserved or nurtured the Idea of India. The Founding Fathers of our freedom passed the baton of constitution and law to the next generation. Much progress has taken place under the purview of one of the Founding Fathers of the nation, Pandit Jawaharlal Nehru. The first amendment in 1951 abolished zamindari (though, against the right to property) and placed reasonable restriction on speech while the seventh amendment in 1956 laid the foundation of states on linguistic lines. The creation of states, union territories and their autonomy brought many of the north-eastern states and new territories to the Indian union, and provided legitimacy to extending the Idea of India in these territories.

During the Emergency, the 42nd amendment involving various articles brought two key principles of India formally into the Constitution—'Socialist and Secular'. The Idea of India is inseparable from these ideas, the dark period of their birth notwithstanding, which is why no subsequent government has undone them. The various amendments to the constitution (23rd, 45th, 51st amendments, among others) have tried to make the Idea of India more inclusive as we tried to bring the vulnerable sections into the mainstream. Activist judges have taken the Constitution beyond strict legislation to promote human rights and welfare in a series of landmark judgements. As one of the largest democracies, we struggled to provide education to all Indian children; the landmark 86th amendment was passed in 2009 'conferring on all children in the age group of 6 to 14 years the right to free and compulsory education'. The Right to Information Act passed in June 2005 is another hallmark of how the law guides and derives value from the Idea of India. Accountability and disclosure of information is the demand of the Indian population and today the law enshrined in the Constitution of our land emphatically acknowledges their right to do so—under the right to life under Article 21, the court recognised the right to know that is indispensable in a participatory democracy.

It must be said, however, that the Victorian-era Penal Code, drafted by Macaulay without consulting any Indians in 1837, and enacted by the British in 1861, is full of iniquities that undermine the quality of the rule of law in our country and make the Code ripe for amendment if not overhaul. Many of the provisions of the Code have ceased to apply in Britain itself, but we carry on this unfortunate colonial legacy in India. These include the pernicious sedition law, Section 124A, which is daily misused by state governments and the lower courts despite decades of Supreme Court rulings that sedition should only apply to incitement to violence; the notorious Section 377, discriminating against a section of our society for their sexual orientation, which stayed on the statute books till the Supreme Court finally read it down two years ago; and a host of examples of gender bias against women. The latter have been to a great extent remedied by a series of progressive judgements by the Supreme Court. Whatever the arguments over individual provisions, I fully support our former Rashtrapati President Pranab Mukherjee's appeal in 2016 to scrap the colonial-era Penal Code and write a new one reflecting our experience and needs as an independent nation. It is a call I hope every one of us will rise to before long.

In the last decade, the Anna Hazare movement raised the question of the role of civil society in determining legislative priorities in our democracy. The Lokpal Bill was essentially introduced by the government in response to the strength of numbers in the streets. As a Member of Parliament I wonder sometimes what our role is supposed to be, with our law-making functions being encroached upon by civil society on the one hand and the judiciary on the other!

There is no doubt that today's lawmakers face new and tougher challenges than ever before. The rapid advancement and penetration of information technology, improving social indicators, the change in demography, the growing economic prowess of our nation, the rise of new global threats and our ever greater international integration all impose new constraints on the sovereign function of law-making, even as they also allow new opportunities.

The civil society protests of recent years add a fresh challenge. In a democracy, there are specific rights accorded to citizens by the state to help them exercise their political freedoms: freedom of speech and political association and related rights allow citizens—in other words, members of civil society—to get together, argue and discuss, debate and criticise, protest and strike (and in Kerala—only in Kerala!—to declare hartals inconveniencing the general public) and even go on fasts and hunger strikes, in order to support or challenge their governments. This is an essential part of promoting governmental accountability between elections: no one can seriously argue that a citizen's democratic rights begin and end with the right to choose his government through voting alone. Indeed, as Amartya Sen so brilliantly pointed out with reference to India in his *The Argumentative Indian*, it is through such discussions and engagement that a deliberative democracy is created. There is often a useful distinction between law and legitimacy: the greater the extent to which ordinary people are engaged with, concerned by and empowered to determine their own political destiny, the more they accept the decisions of the state institutions and the more legitimate the law becomes to the people.

So to that extent, civil society does and should have an influence on lawmaking. But that is not the same thing as saying it should have a direct role. In Switzerland, for example, ordinary citizens can actually bypass the elected legislature and write laws by voting for them in referenda that are organised by the state and whose outcomes are recognised by the government as having the full binding force of law. That is not the case, however, in most other democracies, where civil society's impact is confined to the influence it is able to bring to bear on the elected lawmakers through the shaping of public opinion, effective lobbying, media campaigns and mass movements.

In India, we preserve the national idea through the functioning of democracy. This could be said to suit the democratic temper of our people. Our ancient civilisation has the history of having Sabhas and Samitis where kingdoms and even empires were ruled on the principle of democratic functioning, extending right from the grassroots level in the form of panchayats and councils, which represented the broad as well as specific segments of the populace, to the royal courts where maharajahs took advice from learned and wise elders. This tradition is important to recall since it confirms that both majority as well as minority opinion were given due importance in the formulation of public policy. This was no mean achievement in a nation and society as diverse and heterogeneous as India, with its innumerable groups and socio-religious identities. The law has the responsibility to preserve this diversity and allow each individual component to feel secure within it, and yet guide the nation's progressive evolution.

Laws emerge from a political process that is itself reflective of our society. Parliamentarians are in that sense themselves products of civil society. Our democracy, our thriving free media, our contentious civil society forums, our energetic human rights groups, and the repeated spectacle of our remarkable general elections, have all made of India a rare example of the successful management of diversity in the developing world. It adds to India's 'soft power' and influence in the world when its NGOs actively defend human rights, promote environmentalism, fight injustice. It is a vital asset that the Indian press is free, lively, irreverent, disdainful of sacred cows. All of these work together to promote and expand the Idea of India.

But at the same time a new and disturbing tendency has arisen in our times, of the free press intruding upon the prospects of justice by conducting 'trial by media' in a number of sensationalised cases. While I am the last person who would wish to place any restrictions on press freedom, of which I have been a staunch advocate all my life, I am troubled by the large number of recent instances in which the press, in addition to playing the role of witness and observer—which it must—has also appointed itself prosecutor, judge, jury and even executioner! I raise the question not because I have any answers to offer but because I believe all of us must be aware of this new tendency and conscious of its dangers for our democratic and constitutional system.

After all, judges are also members of our society and are exposed to our media—despite their undoubted judicial rectitude, it is difficult to imagine that they are completely uninfluenced by the media they consume daily.

And then, there is the threat we have seen to law and the Idea of India from disturbing developments of recent years—mob rule, vigilantism and lynchings. When these occur they undermine both the sanctity of the law as the ultimate arbiter of justice and also faith in the law as the cement that binds the Idea of India together. It is vital that we reassert the primacy of law by bringing these self-appointed upholders of justice to justice, to teach them the importance of subordinating their self-righteousness to the majesty of the law.

The 'elephant in the room', of course, is the current challenge to the Idea of India from a law, the Citizenship Amendment Act. Since the constitutionality of the law is before the Supreme Court I will not enter into the merits of it here, but it is without question the first law to question a fundamental underpinning of the Idea of India, that religion is not the determinant of our nationhood and therefore, of our citizenship. Anxiety about the implications of this law has already created an increase in tensions and an eruption of violence that has claimed 56 lives in the nation's capital and left hundreds injured. It has also injured the Idea of India as an inclusive state that honours the equality of all and guarantees that the state will not practise religious discrimination.

Let me turn again to a famous speech of Ambedkar, this one on 4 November 1948, on the subject:

> To diehards who have developed a kind of fanaticism against minority protection, I would like to say two things. One is that minorities are an explosive force which, if it erupts, can blow up the whole fabric of the State. The history of Europe bears ample and appalling testimony to this fact. The other is that the minorities in India have agreed to place their existence in the hands of the majority. ... They have loyally accepted the rule of the majority, which is basically a communal majority and not a political majority. It is for the majority to realise its duty not to discriminate against minorities.

Today, India is in the grip of the very majoritarianism that Ambedkar had so presciently warned against. The

Prime Minister's great hero, Sardar Patel, had urged in the Constituent Assembly on 25 May 1949: 'It is for us who happen to be in a majority to think about what the minorities feel, and how we in their position would feel if we are treated in the manner they are treated.' Given the government's oft-expressed admiration for the likes of Dr Ambedkar and Sardar Patel, one can only hope that they will abandon their current approach, which reduces individuals to their religious affiliations and denies them their agency as free citizens of our democratic republic.

Of course, it is for the highest court in the land to rule on whether this legislation honours the letter of the Constitution, but many of us feel strongly that it violates the spirit—the spirit that animates it, the spirit of the very Idea of India.

# 2

# Positioning India in a Shifting Geopolitical Terrain

AMBASSADOR SHYAM SARAN

> France in 1789, Russia in 1917. Europe of 1930s. The pandemic of 2020. They are all junctures where the river of history changes direction.
>
> *Margaret Macmillan*

The river of history was already changing direction before the Covid-19 pandemic hit us. Now the river is in spate, the banks have been broken and it is unclear where the main stream will appear once the flood recedes. The pandemic and its impact will leave a whole new sediment of unfamiliar experience which will compel new ways of living and earning livelihoods. The quality most valuable among nations and societies will be the ability to adapt to changing circumstances, being nimble in avoiding pitfalls and in seeking opportunities. Above all, leadership will count more than at other moments of history. Since this is a global crisis, India is impacted as every other country is. It can retreat into a shell, build walls behind which to hide or it can seek out and occupy the many spaces that are likely to open up in a period of thoroughgoing transformation. Emerging and aspiring powers such as India are constrained when the international order is stable and its rules of the game are set and enforced by established powers. It is when the order is in flux and the power equations are changing that spaces are created for others. But whether a position of advantage can be achieved depends upon the ability to read the nature and scope of changes, calculate one's assets and liabilities, play to one's strengths and repair one's liabilities, seek partners wherever possible and neutralise adversaries when necessary. This essay attempts to outline a framework within which such an exercise may be undertaken with the aim of locating India in the most favourable position to advance its interests in a rapidly changing geopolitical terrain.

One of the first things to recognise is that there were already significant shifts taking place in the geopolitical landscape that were altering power equations. The end of the Cold War in 1991 brought a brief unipolar moment with the USA as the hyper power unmatched in its economic, technological and military prowess. This came to an end in 2007–2008 with the global financial and economic crisis, which erupted at the very epicentre of the US-led capitalist system. Even though the USA remains the world's most formidable military power, its relative economic status and influence have declined even as that of China has increased. But it is not only China which has gained in power and influence. There is a clutch of emerging and expanding powers, particularly in Asia, and this includes India, Japan, Australia, South Korea, Indonesia and Vietnam. Brazil in Latin America and South Africa and Nigeria in Africa are influential actors in their own regions even though they have not lived up to their promise as emerging economies. Even as Europe continues to fragment, Germany is emerging as the most powerful country in the region. Russia remains a relevant power given its size, resources and significant military assets. There is an unmistakable trend towards a more multipolar world and this is anchored in a multipolar Asia as well. What the pandemic has done is to accelerate the trend toward multipolarity and the shift in the centre of gravity of the global economy toward Asia. This is also reflected in the relative success demonstrated by Asian states in managing the pandemic with the prospect of earlier economic recovery than in the USA and Europe.

The secular diffusion of economic and political power, of which Asia has been the chief beneficiary, is associated with another significant phenomenon, the globalisation of the world economy. The growth of global value chains has been a key feature of globalisation. The International Monetary Fund (IMF) has estimated that almost three quarters of the five-fold increase in global trade between 1993 and 2013 were accounted for by the growth of supply chains. China has dominated these supply chains while India has been a marginal player. The pandemic, by its very nature, has exposed the vulnerabilities inherent in such supply chains, particularly in ensuring critical medical and healthcare materials and equipment. There is an inevitable trend toward onshoring of production of critical products and components or relocating more proximate and shorter chains in countries where the trust factor is higher. In this sense, China may be a loser while India could, with an appropriate mix of policies, position itself as a reliable alternative. Globalisation has stalled, and in some cases, even reversed as countries put in place more regulated borders. Countries are attaching greater value to reliability than efficiency and self-reliance is eroding the notion of interdependence on which globalisation has been predicated. Disruptions in international travel can only partially be made up through digital communications. Cross-border movement of cargo is being impacted by renewed border controls. But once the shock of the pandemic wears off and countries begin to once again look for drivers of growth and recovery, globalisation will reassert itself. There is a greater globalisation already taking place in the digital space and technological advances in digital technologies are likely to advance faster than in pre-pandemic times as their acceptance and adoption are hastened in order to fight the pandemic. When conditions become more congenial physical globalisation is likely to resume with renewed vigour. This means that India has been given a second chance to prepare itself to stay ahead of globalisation 2.0 curve. The current period of 'recessed globalisation' should be utilised to put in place world-class infrastructure, modern logistics, and transparent and supportive regulatory and fiscal regimes to attract supply chains to India. This also implies reversing the recent trend toward more autarkic economic policies with an emphasis on import substitution. India cannot aspire to play an expanded external role from the margins of the regional and global economies.

India's destiny as a great power has always been tied to its subcontinental neighbourhood. If Asia becomes the stage for the geopolitical drama of the current millennium, then no region will be more vital for India than the subcontinent. No credible regional or global role for India is possible unless it is able to manage its own periphery. The Indian subcontinent is a single and coherent geopolitical unit with dense economic complementarities. It is also a shared cultural space. It is currently divided into several sovereign and independent states with India as the largest and most powerful entity. Asymmetry is the defining feature of the region. As the largest state of the region, India's security imperatives are subcontinental in scope but rendered difficult because its security perceptions regarding threats to the region are not shared by its neighbours. The latter, in fact, regard the very asymmetry enjoyed by India as their principal security preoccupation. Overcoming this dichotomy remains the key challenge for Indian foreign policy and one which will not change as a result of the pandemic.

Over the past decade, the subcontinental dilemma has become even more fraught as China has used its substantial resources to penetrate more deeply into our neighbourhood. Its long-standing alliance with Pakistan has deepened with the launch of the China–Pakistan Economic Corridor under China's ambitious Belt and Road Initiative (BRI). The prospect of China constraining India within its own neighbourhood is now very real and ominous and demands a countervailing strategy. Recent developments on the India–China border, which are still playing out, have added further complexity to this challenge. India's neighbours have always been acutely sensitive to the shifts in the political equations between India and other great powers, constantly seeking to expand their own room for manoeuvre vis-à-vis India by balancing Indian dominance through outreach to external powers. Nepal's action to pass a constitutional amendment depicting a large part of indisputably Indian territory as belonging to Nepal is evidence of how the growing tensions between India and China may be seen as an opportunity by our smaller neighbours to advance their own perceived interests at India's expense.

However, as the COVID-19 pandemic causes large-scale and sustained damage to the fragile economies of the neighbourhood, India has the opportunity to rethink its neighbourhood strategy. One important part of this strategy will include how India could become the driver of the economic recovery of the entire region. This would entail the improvement of cross-border connectivity through expanded road and rail links, riverine transport and advanced digital connectivity. The hardware of connectivity must be matched by the efficient software of enabling smooth movement of goods, services and peoples across borders. As more limits are placed on trade with non-regional countries, it will pay to compensate for those flows with greater intra-regional trade. It would require India opening up its market to the goods produced by its neighbours without limit and serving as the transit country of choice for their external trade. An announcement that India will offer national treatment to the trade and transportation of its neighbouring countries would be an important initiative. In this context, the asymmetry which India enjoys vis-à-vis its neighbours is an advantage because its own economy is large enough to absorb their exports. The volume of external trade is a fraction of what is carried on through India's transportation network. The objective should be to make India the market of choice and the preferred transit corridor for trade for our neighbours. This may be difficult to execute in respect to Pakistan, but even here the pandemic offers an opportunity to reorient the relationship in a positive direction. It has been estimated in a World Bank study that the potential of South Asian trade could be around US$36 billion, of which a large chunk would be trade between India and Pakistan. Pakistan is the current host of the South Asian Association for Regional Cooperation (SAARC) but has been unable to convene the summit of its leaders due to opposition by India. Perhaps, the pandemic offers a reason for reviving the summit to deal with the COVID-19 emergency. Prime Minister Modi has taken a positive step by convening an online summit, which the Pakistani Prime Minister did not attend. However, if India were to convey its willingness to participate in a summit convened by Pakistan with a focus on economic recovery post COVID-19, the ice may be broken.

If India is successful in attracting some of the global and regional value chains in an altered political and economic environment triggered by the pandemic, it could share some of these with its neighbours. A dense network of subcontinental supply chains, anchored by India, would enhance India's security through regional interdependence. This opportunity must not be lost.

The one country which impinges most directly and significantly on India's strategic calculus is China. The India–China border remains unresolved, the Tibet issue continues to be a source of tension and the China–Pakistan alliance has become an even greater security challenge than it has ever been. In managing these differences, the growing asymmetry of power between India and China has put India at a disadvantage. The more this asymmetry grows the less the room for manoeuvre India will have. This has become glaringly obvious in the wake of the recent Chinese transgressions in Eastern Ladakh, which, for the first time in more than four decades, led to the loss of lives in a serious confrontation between the two sides. It may not be possible to eliminate the asymmetry within the foreseeable future but one can begin to shrink it over a period of time. As the trend reverses, international perceptions will start to change as well. This is what happened in the period 2003–2007 when India's gross domestic product (GDP) was growing at the rate of 8%–9% per annum and accelerating, while the Chinese economy though already much larger than India's, was starting to slow down. There was the prospect of India not only shrinking the gap but even, at some point, overtaking China. It is this perception of India as the next big economic and commercial opportunity as well as a rising military power that significantly expanded India's strategic space. This is what enabled the successful negotiation of the landmark Indo–US nuclear deal.[1] China, too, responded to India's changed position by agreeing, in April 2005, to establish a Strategic and Cooperative Partnership and to formally recognise Sikkim as a constituent state of the Indian Union; it also committed to seek an early solution to the boundary issue. The conclusion of the Political

Parameters and Guiding Principles for the Settlement of the Boundary Question which also took place in April 2005 set forth a consensus on the set of principles to conclude an agreement. Thus, India managed to expand its options both in its relations with the USA and China. This phase came to an end in the wake of the global financial and economic crisis of 2007–2008 which brought India's high growth phase to an end, while China emerged from the crisis with its economic power and confidence enhanced. It should be apparent from that experience that India needs to get back on a high growth trajectory and improve its relative power vis-à-vis China. The pandemic has created a relatively level playing field on which India can attempt to shrink the economic distance with China. The economic strategy to achieve this has already been indicated in this essay.

Parallel to this economic strategy, India will need to order its relations with major powers in a manner that reduces its vulnerabilities and maximises its foreign-policy options. While US–China relations were already becoming confrontational before the pandemic, this confrontation is becoming sharper in the aftermath of the pandemic. For India, China–US collusion, such as the brief prospect of a G-2 in 2009, is as unwelcome as an all out, across the board confrontation. Both ends of the spectrum constrict India's strategic space.

The USA will be a preferred partner not only because of its military capabilities but also as a source of both capital and advanced technology which India needs for its development. But a military alliance with the USA would turn India into a willing participant in the US policy of containment of China and therefore, provoke a level of hostility which India may be unable to cope with. On the other hand, even if India strengthens its relations with the USA but stops short of an alliance, there could be a Chinese incentive to do enough to prevent that denouement from coming to pass. This is what transpired in the 2003–2007 period. Stronger India–USA relation makes China more sensitive to Indian interests, but an alliance could dilute that incentive.

Will this argument change if the pandemic further erodes and diminishes the narrow edge that the USA has over China in economic and military terms? While China has been damaged by the pandemic, it has been successful in containing the spread of the virus through the imposition of drastic measures. It appears that its economy is on the road to recovery faster than any other major economy. The USA and several European countries have not only seen a much larger scale of infections but the damage to their economies has been deep and substantial. Economic recovery is likely to be slow and painful for them. One cannot rule out the prospect of China emerging from the pandemic as a more powerful state, its economy even larger and more dynamic than that of the USA. While its military capabilities would still be dwarfed by the USA, China could be closing this capability gap faster than before. It may also be argued that if the post-pandemic world is likely to be more reliant on digital technologies and services then China is already well placed with its impressive advances in these areas. This scenario of Chinese ascendancy neglects the reality of Asia being a crowded geopolitical space with several powers in overt or covert contestation. China's efforts to create a hierarchical Asian order led by it are unlikely to succeed. Furthermore, China's prosperity is a creature of a highly globalised economy and being part of complex global supply chains. To the extent that these will be in retreat post COVID-19, China may confront an adverse international economic environment. Its rate of growth may fall to historical lows. Therefore, the assumption that the strategic space for India vis-à-vis China may shrink even further post the pandemic, and thus necessitate consideration of an overt alliance with the USA may not be realistic.

The same argument holds true for India's relations with Japan and Australia, two major regional powers which are also military allies of the USA. While India has strong security arrangements with the USA, Japan and Australia bilaterally, it has refrained from multilateralising these arrangements. In the present and emerging security landscape this appears to be the optimum choice. India should have no hesitation in being part of a coalition to constrain China but avoid becoming part of a US-led containment ring.

In managing the China challenge, India has to recognise that it is in essence an adversarial relationship with more elements of competition and fewer elements of cooperation. The challenge lies in managing the relationship in a manner that limits tensions and prevents the outbreak of hostilities. It would be fair to say that past successive governments had generally been successful in doing so. China, too, has been keen to keep the relationship on an even keel. Regular summit-level meetings may not have resolved outstanding issues but sent a message to their respective systems that leaders attach value to maintaining a stable if not friendly relationship. This tried-and-tested China policy has been undermined by the latest and negative developments in India–China relations. The adversarial character of the relationship is likely to be more prominent going forward. There is now less incentive to work even on areas of convergence such as maritime security, international terrorism, climate change or cyber security.

Going forward, India will have to rework the assumptions on which its China policy has been based hitherto. One, China sees the current power asymmetry with India as creating an opportunity to advance its long-standing territorial claims against India. One should expect continued activism on this score and this may necessitate a reordering of scarce resources to meet enhanced defence requirements. The preoccupation of other major powers in dealing with the pandemic means a distracted international environment in which aggressive moves against India or in other theatres, such as the South China Sea, are unlikely to encounter serious resistance. The fact that China appears to be emerging more successful from the pandemic adds to its sense of power and hubris. However, China may be over-extended and exaggerating its power, and we already see a strong push back to its unilateral assertion of power. Indian diplomacy can tap into this even while undertaking the difficult governance and economic reforms necessary to put it on a high growth trajectory. It is only through such internal balancing that it would be able to meet the China challenge more effectively.

Since its very debut as an independent and sovereign nation, India has been a strong advocate of multilateralism and multilateral institutions. As a poor and developing country, India saw its interests best safeguarded through a rule-based multilateral system even if great powers were often in breach of those rules. It is not so well known that India was a key architect of the Universal Declaration of Human Rights in the 1950s and an early contributor to the United Nations (UN) peacekeeping forces. Despite the country not being a permanent member of the UN Security Council, India has consistently supported the role of the UN and multilateral institutions such as the World Trade Organization and the Bretton Woods institutions, the IMF and the World Bank. There was an early recognition that the salience of cross-national and global issues was only going to increase in the post–World War II period and therefore, multilateralism and a spirit of internationalism were indispensable to resolve a host of issues that also had a particular bearing on the development of emerging independent countries such as India. This activism on the international stage, despite limited economic and military clout, gave India an influential voice allowing it to take part in the norm-setting taking place in the post-war world. This history is instructive and should guide current foreign policy. We are living in a world where the most significant challenges are global in scope. They are not amenable to national or even regional solutions. Climate change is one such looming challenge. We are already living through another, the COVID-19 pandemic. However, for the past decade and more, the world has been moving toward a more nationalistic, even parochial, approach, in dealing with such challenges. There has been a consistent devaluation of the UN and international institutions of governance. Multilateral institutions, which are still functional, have become platforms for geopolitical contestations rather than as instruments of collaboration. India is not an exception in this global trend toward the prioritising of national objectives over global concerns. However, the COVID-19 pandemic offers India an opportunity to renew its commitment to multilateralism and lead the way to the strengthening of multilateral institutions. It is true that, in its current phase, the pandemic is a major domestic preoccupation with little bandwidth to consider cross-national approaches. But whether it is in the search for an effective vaccine or in coordinating the recovery of the global economy, international coordination and collaboration will be required. There is currently an impasse because of the growing tensions between the USA and China, which, as the two most powerful countries in the world, should together have led international approaches in crisis management and in handling the post-pandemic challenge. This presents India with an opportunity to lead the mobilisation of such an international effort. The history of its activism on the international stage, its ability to harness international public opinion on urgent and overarching causes and its credibility as a successful and vibrant plural democracy are the assets that can be leveraged for such a role. But this will need a conscious and determined effort to reverse some of the negative trends that have diminished the political capital built up in the past 70 years. What has been most attractive about India has been its ability to handle vast diversity, its celebration of open debate and intellectual contestation, the strength of its institutions and respect for its Constitution, and a sense that for India to be great it must stand for something more than itself. It is this legacy which has been fraying at the edges. We must reverse this damaging trend. India cannot be a strong state with poor and disempowered citizens.

India took a historic turn when it embraced economic reforms and liberalisation in the early 1990s, abandoning the failed import-substitution strategy and embracing globalisation. The results were spectacular. India became the fastest-growing large emerging economy in the world. India's political engagement with the world could now be anchored in real economic capabilities. This lesson must not be lost in a mistaken belief encouraged by the Covid-19 crisis that we must return to economic autarky. Globalisation is being intensified in the digital space. It will have to return to the real economy where goods and services are exchanged. The digital is relevant only if it remains tethered to the real economy. There is no such thing as a digital economy delinked from the real economy. Therefore, India must remain an open economy. It must be prepared for the resumption of globalisation of real economy, which will re-emerge though altered in many respects. Staying ahead of the curve will serve the country well.

The pandemic is a severe challenge and India will remain preoccupied dealing with it. Nevertheless, it is prudent to look ahead to the post-Covid-19 world that will emerge sooner than later. There are unique assets and advantages that India possesses, which, if marshalled skilfully, can put the country in pole position when the geopolitical race resumes.

3

# National Security Decision-making Process in India and Its Trajectories

GENERAL V.P. MALIK (RETIRED)

> There are hundreds of qualities that a good leader should possess. But if there is one which stands out, it is decision-making.
>
> *Napoleon Bonaparte*

> The military's isolation from India's political leadership is perhaps its only negative contribution to the Indian democracy.
>
> *Anonymous*

## Introduction

The national security apparatus of any country depends on its strategic culture, awareness of its elite, its strategic environment and the emerging trends in the management of conflict and warfare. The challenge faced by such an apparatus is to achieve national security interests without going to war and, if necessary, to achieve that successfully with utmost economy.

India's defence and security report card for more than the past seven decades has been more positive than negative. Despite a weak strategic culture and reactive strategic policies, ad hoc defence planning, intelligence failures, and strategic and tactical surprises, the Indian armed forces have maintained the country's security and territorial integrity better than the armies of any other democratic, developing nation in the world. But the credit for these successes goes less to strategic foresight or higher direction of war, and more to those responsible for operational planning and its execution on the ground. Many a time, we have failed to convert hard-won operational achievements into long-term politico-strategic successes.

## India's Strategic Culture

Strategic culture may be defined as the capacity of the people and society to have the social will and ability for a full and effective employment of its national power. At the time of Independence, the strategic resource pool of thought, talent and specialists in India was non-existent. The institutions and outlook inherited by Indian successors, including the uneasy relationship between the political and military leadership, were colonial in nature. Realpolitik and strategic thinking—with the exception of integrating more than 600 princely states within the Indian nation and the use of military force in Hyderabad, Junagadh and, after some dithering, Jammu and Kashmir (J&K) for that purpose—was not a part of the matrix of the newly independent nation's immediate concerns. Since then, we have fought many wars on our borders and resolved conflicts within and outside India. Tragically, several successive events resulting from the neglect of national security have not acted as sufficient impetus for India till now to formulate and articulate a national security strategy or policy at the requisite high level of national policy-making agenda.

In India, important strategic decisions are seldom recorded in detail and almost never made public. Unlike most democratic countries, we have not followed the practice of declassification of files by making them public after a stipulated period. When the process of and the rationale behind making such important decisions are not known, it is difficult to analyse the events in the correct perspective or to learn lessons from them for future generations. This also discourages research. At the strategic level, one requires a long memory and longer foresight and vision. When memory is missing, floundering knee-jerk reactions and ad hoc decision-making continues. The problem gets exaggerated for the armed forces. Despite the important national security roles envisaged and expected of them, they are seldom in the loop at the policymaking and planning levels—at least till now. And even when included in this loop, only a handful of senior officers are privy to ministerial interactions and decision-making.

In India, at the level of general public opinion, there is an amorphous emotional consciousness about security imperatives of the nation. However, barring small urban segments of society, there is no broad stream of knowledge or analytical awareness of defence matters, such as the material, logistical, technological, sociological and intellectual inputs required to strengthen our defence capacities. Before a conflict, the public remains unclear about the need for providing continuous support to enable the forces to become an effective instrument of the state. Public awareness of defence matters is a sine qua non, a necessity for national defence and security purposes. For this reason, I have always supported public debates and writings so long as they remain professional and do not become agendas for political promotion.

The weakness in our strategic culture and thinking is a major flaw in our higher defence management. It will be overcome only when our policymakers, particularly our political leaders, have adequate awareness and consciousness about defence and security, and we develop a suitable defence management apparatus.

## India's Security Management Apparatus

Decision-making involves the selection of a course of action from among several possible alternatives in order to arrive at a solution for a given problem. At strategic levels, the decision-making process has to be a consultative effort to ensure the efficient functioning of an organisation, in this case, the Ministry of Defence (MoD). It is a continuous and dynamic activity that requires good knowledge of the subject coupled with skills and experience in addition to mental maturity. A major role of strategic management is to bring together various functional areas of the organisation as well as to ensure that these functional areas harmonise and work well together.

After the Kargil war in 1999, the Group of Ministers (GOM) Committee had observed,

> There is a marked difference in the perception and crisis of confidence among civil and military officials in the MoD and Service HQ regarding their respective roles and functions. There was lack of synchronisation among and between the three departments in the MoD, including the relevant elements of Defence Finance. The concept of 'attached offices' as applicable to Service HQ; problems of inter-se relativities; multiple, duplicated, and complex procedures governing the exercise of administrative and financial powers, and the concept of 'advice' to the Minister; all these had contributed to these problems.[1]

The GOM also observed that the Chiefs of Staff Committee (COSC) had serious weaknesses in its ability to provide single-point military advice to the government and to resolve substantive inter-service doctrinal, planning, policy and operational issues. This institution needed to be restructured to discharge its responsibilities efficiently, including the facilitation of 'jointness' and synergy.

The GOM recommended the appointment of a Chief of Defence Staff (CDS) in the MoD to (a) provide single-point military advice; (b) hold administrative control over, and manage, strategic forces; (c) ensure intra-service and inter-service prioritisation of 10-year and 15-year 'perspective plans', and also the 5-year defence plans; and (d) to bring about improvement in the 'jointness' among various units of the armed forces.

As a follow-up measure, an Integrated Defence Staff was created. But the CDS was not appointed. In the absence of the CDS, the Integrated Defence Staff has not been able to deliver the desired integrated and joint paradigm. Each Service Headquarters continued to perform its independent planning and management of matters relating to its own service. There was little improvement in the coordination of military operations, intelligence and tri-service technologies or in military strategic planning. A former Chief of the Integrated Defence Staff, Lieutenant General Satish Dua, had pointed out,

> The existing structure for cross-service cooperation is weak and efforts for jointmanship in the military are proceeding slowly, resulting in duplication of efforts, wastage of resources and delay in decision-making....The weak structure does not lead to effective decision-making.[2]

More importantly, compartmentalisation of civilian and military authority within the MoD continued.

## National Security Decision-making Process

Based on our post-Independence military history and my personal experiences, I would place our national security decision-making process in three distinct situations—in peacetime, in time of war or war-like situations and in post-war conflict resolution situations. I must add, however, that in all these situations, the decision-making process is also impacted by inter-personal relations and rapport amongst civilian and military executives and their political leaders.

*Peacetime Decision-making*

This is the most important decision-making period for the military. In peacetime, the military requires a clear picture of the ever-dynamic strategic environment, likely conflict situations, national security strategy and planning for defence. Based on this picture, the military has to prepare the structure of forces, acquisition plans and financial budget. Since defence planning has to follow national security and military strategies, the military requires much political guidance, intense, continuous civil–military interactions to prepare for probable conflict situations. Most of the decision-making is institutional. It involves senior leadership at the levels of the Cabinet Committee on Security (CCS) or the National Security Council (NSC), several Defence Minister's committees and the Chiefs of Staff Committee (COSC). Unfortunately, due to a flawed higher defence control structure and the MoD conducting its business as per the rules laid down in the 2nd Schedule of the 'Allocation of Business Rules and Transaction of Business Rules', there is little discourse between political and military leaders on the dynamics of geo-strategy and security-related environment, strategies, or on defence planning and military capabilities. The Service Chiefs are invited by the CCS from time to time to discuss ongoing security issues but never long-term security planning. Geo-strategy and security planning (including defence) remain a grey area as the military is kept outside the decision-making loop.

The major disadvantage that impacts planning and preparedness at this stage is inadequate awareness, even interest, in military affairs among our political elite. In decision-making, they are almost wholly dependent on civil bureaucrats. Difficulties of integrated policy initiatives and discussions without a permanent chairman of the COSC, the very informal level of discussions in the Defence Minister's Morning Meetings—in which no agendas or minutes are issued—and the Service Chiefs not being able to attend CCS meetings, and thus being out of the loop when important security policy issues and defence preparedness are discussed tend to make this decision-making process difficult, unbearably slow and, very often, frustrating.

The disadvantages of such a process and its adverse impact on the nation's defence capabilities, planning and preparedness can be easily imagined. Five-year defence plans are prepared but seldom approved by the CCS. They rarely get implemented on time, or as per given priority, because the financial control and responsibility for conducting negotiations for major procurements rest entirely with non-users. This process also creates unnecessary tension between civil and military bureaucracies within the higher defence control structure.

The lack of strategic guidance on national security and preparedness for conflict situations (including in matters of weapons, ammunition and equipment) has been evident in most of the wars fought by the Indian military. Let me cite some examples of this apathy. After Independence, despite a war with Pakistan in 1947–1948, Jawaharlal Nehru's government in 1957–1958 decided to reduce the strength of the Indian Army from 4,50,000 to 3,00,000. Yet, based on wrong intelligence inputs, it adopted a forward deployment policy against China with disastrous consequences in 1962. Shortage of arms, ammunition and equipment has been felt in all wars, and thus a cautious, defensive military strategy has been adopted, except in 1971 when Sam Manekshaw refused to initiate the war to liberate Bangladesh under inappropriate climatic conditions and without adequate build-up. In 1999, Pakistan Army's infiltration in the Kargil sector came as a strategic surprise. On account of the then existing shortage of weapons and equipment, I was compelled to respond that, 'We shall fight with whatever we have.'

## Decision-making during War

The situation changes completely when a conflict is going on or a crisis situation involving the military is envisaged. At such times, everyone has ears for the Chiefs and their principal staff. There is speed and energy in decision-making, and very few queries are raised. The only problem is that it is not possible to build or enhance the military's capabilities during the conflict period.

Let me narrate my experiences of Operation Pawan (Sri Lanka), Operation Cactus (Maldives) and the way in which the Kargil war was managed.

India signed the Indo–Sri Lanka Accord in 1987 with a view to 'resolving the ethnic problem in Sri Lanka, and the consequent violence, and for the safety, well-being and prosperity of people belonging to all communities in Sri Lanka'.[3] Within hours of its signing on 29 July 1987, President Jayewardene of Sri Lanka sought military assistance from India and it was accepted by India's Prime Minister, Rajiv Gandhi, without any consultation with the Chiefs of the armed forces, who at that time were in New Delhi. Overnight, an Indian Peace Keeping Force was inducted into Sri Lanka.[4] Less than three months later, this force was pitchforked into an alien milieu and against the very Sri Lankan Tamil militants it had trained to fight. The Force Commander, Lieutenant General Depinder Singh, later remarked, 'On October 8, 1987 the LTTE [Liberation Tigers of Tamil Eelam] were to be protected; on October 10 they were the enemy.'[5] A force and its commanders who were physically and mentally oriented for a peacekeeping mission, were pushed into a classic counter-guerilla operation in a foreign country, due to political considerations, without adequate notice or intelligence. India lost 1,155 soldiers during this operation. It happened because the Indo–Sri Lanka Accord of 1987 was a political, diplomatic, intelligence and military miscalculation.

In Operation Cactus, India's armed forces created history and a new politico-military benchmark. Within hours of receiving an appeal for assistance from the

Government of Maldives, Indian troops rescued President Gayoom and foiled a coup d'état attempt by rebel forces. Our forces flew non-stop over 3,000 km, from Agra to Male, and restored the Maldives' government's control over its capital. Prime Minister Rajiv Gandhi held the CCS conference in the Army Headquarters Operation Room with officials from all concerned ministries present. After a review of the situation and continuous monitoring, the political objective was meshed with military capabilities and decisions were taken within hours. The single-most important factor for our success in this operation was the speed at which matters were decided, planned and executed jointly by the armed forces.

During the initial stages of the Kargil war, we had no strategic or tactical intelligence, and thus were totally surprised. I was not in India. The COSC could not agree on the fuller employment of the Indian Air Force, and the CCS declined permission for this measure. The situation changed completely after I returned from abroad, got briefed in Udhampur and Srinagar, discussed military strategy with other Chiefs, and then gave our assessment and recommendations to the CCS on 24 May 1999. Thereafter, everyone was closely enmeshed in the politico-military decision-making process.

The CCS met on an almost daily basis till the second week of July 1999. Besides the Prime Minister and other CCS members, the meetings were attended by the National Security Advisor, the Cabinet Secretary, the three Service Chiefs, the Secretaries of Defence, Home, Finance and External Affairs Ministries, heads of the Intelligence Bureau and Research and Analysis Wing (R&AW), and the Secretary, National Security Council Secretariat. Sometimes, for some specific purposes, special invitees were also called in. The Prime Minister would be flanked by other CCS members, National Security Advisor and the Cabinet Secretary on one side of the table. I would sit opposite the Prime Minister along with my services colleagues, other secretaries and executive heads of departments.

It was a refreshing change in the decision-making process, both at the political level as well as at the armed forces level: open and direct. The political leadership received the views of the Service Chiefs first-hand. After discussions, the concerned executive authorities, including the three Chiefs, received directions from the Prime Minister. The National Security Advisor, who was always accessible, facilitated a smooth decision-making process. All these developments led to an integrated approach to 'war management' with the political, economic, diplomatic, media and military aspects meshed together cogently.

At the level of the armed forces, regular daily military briefings were carried out in the Military Operations Room. Besides the three Chiefs, representatives of the Ministries of Defence, External Affairs, Home and the intelligence agencies attended these briefings. Officers from operational directorates of all three services nominated to brief the media along with the Joint Secretary of the Ministry of External Affairs would also attend sometimes. The daily briefings were followed by an 'in-house' discussion on a 'need-to-know' basis.

## Decision-making during Conflict Resolution

India's armed forces have achieved success in all wars and conflicts with one exception, the 1962 India–China war. But the nation has not been able to convert hard-won operational achievements into long-term politico-strategic successes. A major reason has been that the military, a major stakeholder, has been kept out of the decision-making loop.

In 1947–48, when the army was in a position to capture Muzaffrabad and more in the Pakistan-held Kashmir territory, the government decided to take the issue to the United Nations. General S.M. Srinagesh, then Corps Commander in J&K, wrote in his diary,

> For India, the military situation in Kashmir had been adversely influenced by political considerations. Pakistan had no legal or moral right to operate with its army in Kashmir against the expressed wishes of the people and the ruler of Kashmir, whereas India had. Still India referred the matter to the United Nations, which set up [the] UN Commission on India and Pakistan, before which both parties came to an agreement to refrain from offensive action likely to aggravate the situation.[6]

The returning of the strategically important Haji Pir Pass to Pakistan after the 1965 war; returning 91,000 prisoners without making Pakistan agree to a permanent solution to the J&K issue after the 1971 war; dithering for 24 years between the testing of a nuclear device in 1974 and of nuclear weapons in 1998; mobilisation and deployment of forces for 10 months after the Pakistani terrorist attack on our parliament without a clear political aim—all these events reflect the non-strategic mindset in our decision-making processes.

## Current Strategic Environment and Military Functioning

Andrew Gyorgi has stated, 'Geo-strategy would be unimaginable in any other period of history but ours. It is the characteristic product of turbulent twentieth-century world politics.'[7] In the 21st century, geopolitical turbulence has increased manifold. In the current strategic environment, all out war as an instrument of foreign policy has become unviable due to very high costs, casualties and international pressures. Limited wars, sub-conventional armed conflicts and hybrid wars along with high technological interventions have become more prevalent. There is a greater likelihood of limited conflicts and wars in future than all out conventional or nuclear wars. Conflicts, when they do occur, may no longer be taken to the logical conclusion of military victories as in the past. They would be conducted with the objective of achieving political successes rather than a military victory.

In this strategic environment, the separation between tactical, operational and strategic levels of warfare is blurring. While there was always some degree of overlap between these levels, due to the increasingly pervasive influence of information technology (IT) on warfare, this overlap has increased. Enhanced mobility, long reach in surveillance, accurate targeting, and effective command and control have obscured tactical and strategic boundaries. Minor military actions along disputed borders or terrorist acts in the hinterland, such as in Uri and Pulwama, tend to become issues for consideration and decision-making at the strategic level. It is a situation where a junior military officer is expected to understand political considerations and political leaders need to know the tactical and operational considerations.

Indication of political objective(s), the likely duration of the war or the time available to the armed forces to execute their missions and achieve politico-military goals would be crucial for their planning and conduct of operations. This is something on which there would have to be complete understanding between the political and military leadership. We can also expect fairly rigid political terms of reference as were given during the Kargil war.

In such a war scenario, politico-diplomatic factors will play an important role. Careful and calibrated orchestration of military operations, diplomacy and domestic political environment is essential for its successful outcome.

Continuous control of the 'escalatory ladder' requires much closer political oversight and politico-civil-military interaction. It is, therefore, essential to keep the military leadership in the security and strategic decision-making loop and to institutionalise a direct politico-military interface. Some important challenges that are more likely to be encountered are as follows:

- The political definition of the goals and its translation into military objectives. This is always difficult. Sometimes it is uncertain and indirect. Yet, its success is truly critical for the attainment of political goals. The key military concepts pertaining to the desired end result such as decisive victory and success is fundamentally transformed to reflect a much heavier political emphasis and attributes.
- The successful outcome of such a war hinges on the ability to react rapidly to an evolving crisis, which often erupts with surprise. This is a major challenge for the military, for it is expected to be able to react quickly to the changing circumstances in order to localise/freeze/reverse the situation on the ground and to arrest the deterioration, enhance deterrence and diminish incentives for escalation.
- Mobilising and sustaining domestic and international political support for such military operations in the present age of transparency would depend upon the ability of the military to operate in a manner that conforms to political legitimacy, for example, avoidance of civilian and military casualties on both sides and minimisation of collateral damage.
- Political requirements and military targeting would be heavily reliant on intelligence, surveillance and reconnaissance (ISR) for target selection. Surgical strikes would be a common option. Airpower, precision guided weapons, stand off armaments and information would be the weapons of choice.
- Information operation becomes important due to the growing transparency of the battlefield to the public via media and the internet. Political requirements of

> military operations to achieve and retain moral high ground and deny that to the adversary would need a comprehensive public affairs and information campaign. This has to be fully integrated and synchronised with the planning and execution of the military operations.

In India, the era of high moral, preachy politics and reactive strategic posturing seems to be getting over at last. Greater awareness, realism and robustness in security policies, particularly on Pakistan, have been evident ever since the National Democratic Alliance (NDA) government came into power in 2014. The government has adopted proactive and disruptive approaches on several occasions, for example, striking the National Socialist Council of Nagaland (Khaplang) insurgent group camp in Myanmar in June 2015, the India–China border stand-off at Doklam Plateau in 2017, the 'surgical strike' across the Line of Control in Pakistan Occupied Kashmir in September 2016 and the bombing of the Jaish-e-Mohammad terrorist-training camp at Balakot, deep inside Pakistan in February 2019. During the Doklam crisis in 2017 on the India-China border and in the latest conflict situation in Eastern Ladakh, there are signs of proactive strategic posturing. If India is to continue with such proactive strategic posturing, it must have a fully integrated MoD, wherein military leaders remain in the loop in all external and internal security-related decision-making. Unfortunately, despite the appointment of the CDS in December 2019 (details in the following paragraphs) there are no signs of it so far.

## Chief of Defence Staff

Nearly two decades after the GOM Report 2002, on 15 August 2019, Prime Minister Narendra Modi announced his government's decision to create the post of CDS. The Prime Minister also mentioned the transforming nature of military conflicts, the impact of technology and the need for modernisation, coordination and jointness. India's security apparatus must be professional, seamlessly coordinated, well-equipped and innovative, he said. A committee was set up under the National Security Advisor to look into the issue of civil–military relations and to arrive at an organisational model in keeping with the Prime Minister's vision and futuristic defence management trends. On 24 December 2019, the government announced the creation of the post of CDS in the rank of a four-star General who will head the Department of Military Affairs (DMA) in the MoD, function as its Secretary and deal with the following areas[8]:

- The armed forces of the union, namely the army, the navy and the air force
- Integrated headquarters of the MoD comprising army headquarters, naval headquarters, air headquarters and defence staff headquarters
- The territorial army
- Works relating to the army, the navy and the air force
- Procurement exclusive to the Services, except capital acquisitions, as per prevalent rules and procedures

Apart from these, the mandate of the DMA will include the following areas:

- Promoting jointness in procurement, training and staffing for the Services through joint planning and integration of their requirements
- Facilitation of restructuring of Military Commands for optimal utilisation of resources by bringing about jointness in operations, including through establishment of joint/theatre commands
- Promoting use of indigenous equipment by the Services

The CDS, apart from being the head of the DMA, will also be the Permanent Chairman of the COSC. He will act as the Principal Military Adviser to the Raksha Mantri (RM) on all tri-Services matters. The three Chiefs will continue to advise RM on matters exclusively concerning their respective Services. The CDS will not exercise any military command, including over the three Service Chiefs, so as to be able to provide impartial advice to the political leadership.

As the Permanent Chairman of the COSC, the CDS is expected to perform the following functions:

- Administer tri-Services organisations. All tri-Services agencies/organisations/commands related to cyber and space will be under the command of the CDS.
- Be a member of the Defence Acquisition Council chaired by RM and Defence Planning Committee chaired by the National Security Advisor.

- Function as military adviser to the Nuclear Command Authority.
- Bring about jointness in operation, logistics, transport, training, support services, communications, repairs and maintenance and so on of the three Services, within three years of assuming office.
- Ensure optimal utilisation of infrastructure and its rationalisation through jointness among the services.
- Implement Five-year Defence Capital Acquisition Plan (DCAP), and two-year roll-on Annual Acquisition Plans (AAPs), as a follow-up of Integrated Capability Development Plan (ICDP).
- Assign inter-Services prioritisation to capital acquisition proposals based on the anticipated budget.
- Bring about reforms in the functioning of the three Services aimed at augmenting combat capabilities of the armed forces by reducing wasteful expenditure.

It may be too early to comment on the functioning of the office of the CDS. There is much work, particularly on creating integrated theatre commands, ahead of him. But the manner in which the two civil and military departments have been created, it seems that the compartmentalisation and the frigid civil–military relations in the MoD are unlikely to improve soon. The more important observations are as follows:

- The CDS, in the pay grade of Cabinet Secretary/ Service Chiefs, has been designated as 'Secretary DMA', which is a rung lower. This has set a wrong precedent. It will jeopardise the status of Service Chiefs who are at par with the Cabinet Secretary. Being equal in rank with Service Chiefs, the CDS may also face problems while taking decisions on integrated theatre commands.

- After creating a CDS, it is anomalous to retain the responsibility for 'Defence of India and every part thereof...' with a civilian bureaucrat, that is, the Defence Secretary. In fact, the Defence Secretary has been given greater institutional responsibility of 'defence policy and preparation for defence'. This goes against the very spirit of the reforms. On paper, it keeps the CDS outside the strategic-level decision-making loop. In my view, this all-important responsibility of 'defence of India' should be part of RM's portfolio, with both CDS and Defence Secretary mandated to assist him for this purpose.

## Conclusion

War, as Clausewitz noted aptly, has always been a continuation of politics by other means. Recent wars have involved a much greater level of integration of politics and military planning and execution. Even when diplomacy has run its course and a decision to employ the military is made, the political leadership seldom allows autonomous conduct of war to the military. It also reasserts its authority for final conflict resolution as soon as military operations are over. In practice, there is a continuing erosion of the dividing lines between war and politics.

The higher direction of war in the current strategic environment is too vital a subject to be dealt with inside watertight compartments. It is imperative that we change our mindsets and attitudes and look beyond narrow boundaries defined by 'turf' and parochialism. Keeping in view the fast-changing strategic environment and trends in warfare, there is an urgent requirement to review our higher defence control system. We need changes in the structures, processes and procedures that would make it more efficient, resilient and speedily responsive. It is only then that we can be secure internally and externally, fully prepared to take on the role, that we see for ourselves, as a regional power.

# 4

# India and the Maritime Dimension

ADMIRAL ARUN PRAKASH (RETIRED)

## Introduction

'While to other countries, the Indian Ocean is only one of the important oceanic areas, to India it is the vital sea. Her lifelines are concentrated here ... her future is dependent on the freedom of this vast ocean.'[1] These words of Sardar K.M. Panikkar, visionary diplomat and historian, in his 1945 essay titled 'India and the Indian Ocean' sum up India's critical reliance on the sea lanes—for its security as well as for economic prosperity. Implicit in these words is the message that maritime power and a substantive navy—prime factors in the determination of comprehensive national power—will play an important role in India's destiny.

While strategic culture has been the topic of sporadic debate amongst India's cognoscenti,[2] the Indian Navy's (IN's) leadership has been consistent in reminding its countrymen about the inherited affliction of 'sea blindness', and its adverse historical consequences for the nation. Ironically, it was the decline of India's dominant maritime power during the 10th century CE, and repeated overland invasions from the north-west, which gave rise to a stubborn 'continental mindset' amongst India's rulers and decision-makers. It was their belief that 'the Himalayan bulwark' would protect us, and this led to the prolonged neglect of the maritime domain, rendering India defenceless at sea.

The arrival of Portuguese explorer Vasco da Gama off the port of Kozhikode in 1498 marked the beginning of what historian Paul Kennedy calls, the 'Columbian Era'.[3] This was a defining moment because it marked the beginning of European domination of the eastern seas, and the progressive conquest of Asian empires. During the 14th and 15th centuries, Europe had seen remarkable advances in shipbuilding, navigation and gunnery, which enabled mariners to venture further than ever before and to prevail over all opposition. Thus, when small European nations formed business cartels for overseas trade, it was their maritime power—merchant fleets as well as fighting navies—that enabled these predatory companies to subjugate eastern rulers and undertake the commercial exploitation of their lands.

## The Maritime Blind Spot

The year 2020 had dawned on a promising note for India's strategic community with the long-awaited creation of a Chief of Defence Staff (CDS), mandated by government to implement overdue reform in our higher defence organisation. Elation was, however, rapidly overtaken by alarm and despondency as the COVID-19 pandemic, originating in China, suddenly emerged to pose a grave national threat. As it spread, slowly but inexorably, across an unwary and ill-prepared world, including in India, this pandemic showed itself to be far more virulent than anything seen before.

Even as India's resources and energies remain focused on the grim struggle against COVID-19, there have been grave developments on the India–China border. Over a period of a few weeks, commencing April/May 2020, troops of the Chinese People's Liberation Army (PLA) were seen transgressing the undefined Sino–Indian border, termed 'Line of Actual Control' or LAC, at various locations in Ladakh. While negotiations were on between the two armies, a skirmish took place in which 20 Indian Army personnel and an unknown number of PLA soldiers were killed.

At the time of writing, military and diplomatic parleys are underway, but it appears unlikely that, given their track record of intransigent stands and shifting goalposts, the PLA will either pull back from their exaggerated claims or agree to a settlement. This being the case, Sino–Indian tensions are likely to persist, and if an all out conflict is to be avoided, India's national security elite needs to urgently craft a long-term strategy and enter into serious negotiations.

Here, a major factor that India needs to exploit is its maritime influence; a factor that does not, currently, receive due importance in our security calculus, but could add weight to India's negotiating position vis-à-vis China. But in a related context, India's new CDS, soon after assuming his appointment, had triggered a brief discussion in the media, when he publicly rejected the IN's long-standing requirement of a third aircraft carrier, with the remark, 'Anything on the surface can be picked up by satellites and knocked off by missiles. I think the navy needs more submarines than aircraft-carriers, which require their own individual armadas for protection.'[4]

Interestingly, a few weeks later, the CDS went on to declare, 'We are not expeditionary forces that have to deploy around the globe. We have to guard and fight only along our borders and of course dominate the Indian Ocean Region.'[5] There has also been some 'loud thinking' in the media about the Department of Military Affairs (DMA) contemplating the constitution of Theatre Commands, including an 'Air Defence Command' and a 'Peninsular Maritime Command'. Space does not permit an extended discussion of these issues, except to say that issues of such gravity deserve an exhaustive debate at the level of Service Chiefs and Commanders-in-Chief before decisions are arrived at. While such pronouncements may seem to indicate a continental mindset and persistence of 'sea blindness' in India, the situation is not all that bleak, and there has been a 'maritime awakening' of sorts.

## India's Maritime Awakening

According to British economist Angus Maddison,[6] in the mid-18th century, India generated almost a quarter of the global industrial output and had a similar share in the world economy. Just 150 years later, British mercantilism and the industrial revolution had pushed India's share of products down to 2 per cent of the world total. At the same time, Britain's fortunes rose sharply and it became a thriving industrial and economic power. The wheel has come full circle, and today, Asia has more than half of the world's population and delivers more than half of the world's products.

Current predictions are that the 21st century will witness the restoration of Asia to its historical position of economic dominance, and India will be a key factor in this phenomenon. Given the synergistic linkage between national economies and international trade, and the utter dependence of the latter on seaborne traffic, India's rise is going to be inextricably linked to its maritime domain.

The beginning of Independence did little to diminish India's inherited affliction of 'sea blindness'. The fledgling IN remained a 'Cinderella' service, growing at a snail's pace and surviving from one shoestring budget to the next. The IN's repeated reminders that India's security as well as prosperity were dependent on the oceans went largely unheard in land-locked New Delhi. But the following decades were to bring change.

The 1971 Indo–Pakistan war saw the IN being bloodied in action, and the Service contributed significantly to the well-planned and swiftly executed campaign that resulted in the creation of Bangladesh. The IN deployed the full spectrum of its capabilities: carrier-borne air power, missile warfare, submarine and anti-submarine warfare, amphibious warfare and special operations. This war brought home to India's people as well as the decision-makers the critical role that maritime power could play in furthering national interests.[7]

The 1980s, consequently, saw a noteworthy paradigm shift in policy, wherein Indian maritime power was, for the first time, deployed in neighbouring countries such as Sri Lanka and the Maldives. This decade was also witness to a long-delayed upswing in the fortunes of the IN; with a second aircraft carrier, a nuclear submarine, a squadron of reconnaissance aircraft and new submarines and missile destroyers joining the navy in quick succession.

The great Indian Ocean tsunami of 2004 marked another defining moment which established the navy as a credible regional force. Units of the IN (ships, aircraft and helicopters) were despatched overnight and rendered assistance not just to our own citizens but also to our Sri Lankan, Maldivian and Indonesian neighbours in distress. This left a deep impression on international observers. In subsequent years, the navy has responded to many calls for humanitarian assistance from countries as far apart as Mauritius, Myanmar, Lebanon, Libya, Mozambique and Yemen. Four years after the tsunami, came the Wall Street crash of 2008, the impact of which was felt around the globe. Realisation also dawned that globalisation is driven by trade that is carried, overwhelmingly, by sea. Therefore, it became quite clear that the heavy dependence of economies, including India's, on trade and energy had rendered the safety of the Indian Ocean sea lanes of utmost importance.

Then came the upsurge of piracy and hijacking off Somalia. It demonstrated that merchant shipping was as susceptible to the menace of piracy as it had been a couple of centuries ago. The difference was that today's globalised world, being far more dependent on seaborne commerce, could not tolerate any interruption to the free movement of goods and energy without intense pain. The catastrophic threat of COVID-19 that hangs over mankind now offers the clearest proof of global interdependence, for better and for worse.

The anti-piracy campaign had also served as a 'coming out' party for the Chinese PLA Navy (PLAN), which demonstrated, for the first time, its impressive capability as well as resolve to undertake sustained 'blue water' deployments in national interest. Closer home, the Mumbai terrorist strikes of November 2008 provided a grim reminder to India that its long coastline and busy territorial waters—the maritime domain—constitute a huge vulnerability.

Admiral Mahan, writing in 1902, had said, 'War has ceased to be the natural, or even normal, condition of nations, and military considerations are subordinate to the other great interests they serve; economics and commerce.'[8] He insisted that since the true path to national prosperity and greatness lay in peacetime trade, ensuring access to sources of economic well-being, that is, foreign trade, commerce and natural resources were of paramount importance; sea power being only a means to this end.

## India's Maritime Interests

India's central position in the Indian Ocean Region (IOR), astride major shipping lanes, accords it both advantages and responsibilities.[9] Jutting a thousand kilometres into the ocean named after it, the Indian peninsula has a 7,500 km long coastline, containing 200 major and minor ports, with an exclusive economic zone of over 2 million square km, rich in food and mineral resources. India has 1,200 islands, on both seaboards, which are located astride vital shipping lanes that run from the Persian Gulf to the Malacca Straits. The Laccadive group of islands lying across the Arabian Sea shipping lanes and the Andaman and the Nicobar group guarding the mouth of the Malacca Straits constitute strategic maritime outposts.

The waters of the Indian Ocean see over 1,00,000 merchantmen in transit annually, carrying cargo worth a trillion dollars. Both east-bound and west-bound ships pass areas where they are vulnerable to interdiction or interference by states as well as non-state entities such as pirates and terrorists. Amongst these are 1,400 vessels of about 20 million tons flying the Indian flag and almost 2,00,000 Indian sailors serving on board foreign ships. Therefore, the maintenance of 'good order' at sea is not just an international commitment but also essential in India's own interest.

While, the strategic importance of the Indian Ocean is self-evident, less well-known are India's rapidly growing interests in the Pacific. Almost, 55 per cent of India's trade with the greater Asia Pacific area transits through the South China Sea. ONGC Videsh Ltd (OVL) ships transport crude oil extracted from its Russian Far East concessions to the refineries back home. It has also been awarded offshore drilling rights in Vietnam's exclusive economic zone (EEZ) in the

South China Sea, but work has been suspended due to a maritime dispute with China.

In the 1990s, India had launched a vigorous 'Look East' policy in its quest for economic access to the member states of Association of Southeast Asian Nations (ASEAN). Upgraded to an 'Act East' policy, it has seen India establishing close rapport with Pacific nations such as Japan, Australia, Vietnam and Indonesia. Today, India's trading links, investments and large diaspora span an arc extending from Siberia in the east to Africa and Central Asia in the west. Any attempts by other countries to dominate the waters of the Indian or Pacific Ocean would represent a grave threat to India's vital interests.

## The Indo-Pacific Concept

The term 'Asia–Pacific' was coined post-World War II, presumably to create economic and military linkages between the USA and nations of the Pacific region.[10] With the USA focusing mainly on China as well as treaty partners such as Japan, the Philippines, South Korea and Taiwan, the 'Asia–Pacific' concept appeared to leave out everything west of the Malacca Straits, including India and other countries of the IOR. Certain developments in the past few decades have seen the geo-strategic focus shifting away from Asia–Pacific and creating a need for a new and more inclusive paradigm to embrace a broader geographic scope. Salient amongst these factors were the following:

- The near simultaneous rise of China in the Pacific and India in the IOR; both countries have overlapping interests in safety of trade and energy traffic in the Indian and Pacific Oceans.
- China's dramatic technological and military growth, which caught the USA by surprise. This was followed by its show of belligerence in South and East China Seas.
- The attempted 'pivot' or 'rebalance' to Asia; which put a huge strain on US resources and led to a quest to find regional partners.
- A sense of vulnerability felt by countries such as Japan and Australia on account of trade and energy sea lanes running over 10,000 km to the Persian Gulf.

The USA's Indo-Pacific strategy is characterised by a commitment to uphold the principles of 'freedom of navigation' and 'the rule of law'; the aim being to maintain access for US forces and contain China's rise as a regional hegemon. Given these factors, the hyphenation of the Indian and Pacific Oceans to create the 'Indo-Pacific' paradigm was a logical step in the US strategy to balance (or contain) China, because it drew India and others into the same geo-political arena. The military underpinning of this change was conveyed to the world by renaming of the 'Pacific Command' as the 'Indo-Pacific Command' in 2018.

For India, already in a strategic partnership with ASEAN and a member of the East Asia Summit, the Indo-Pacific formulation is in consonance with its 'Look East' policy and should ensure that it will no longer be excluded from economic and security initiatives in that region. The Indo-Pacific also provides a handy umbrella under which India can strike new partnerships across the Malacca Straits with countries such as Japan and Australia—as was attempted in the 'Quadrilateral Security Dialogue' or 'Quad'.

The Quad traces its origins to the post-2004 Indian Ocean tsunami context, in which navies of the USA, India, Australia and Japan came together for coordination of rescue and relief operations. However, when these navies assembled for a joint exercise in 2007, China issued a strong political statement to all four capitals, demanding the rationale behind this joint exercise. This caused alarm amongst the Quad members and this embryo organisation went into hibernation for a decade.

Revived in 2017, the Quad continues to be viewed by China with deep suspicion, and this has, again, led to loss of motivation on the part of its members. While senior Indian and US navy officers have expressed doubts about the continuing utility of the Quad, the first Quad Foreign Ministers' meeting was convened in New York in end-2019.

China's expression of severe displeasure at the concepts of the Indo-Pacific as well the Quad arises from the suspicion that these are signs of its incipient 'containment'. The consequent equivocation on the part of Quad members is manifest in Prime Minister Modi's speech at the Shangri La Dialogue in 2018. He stated: 'India does not see the Indo-Pacific as a strategy or a club of limited members, nor as a grouping that seeks to dominate, and by no means do we consider it as directed against any country....' Without mentioning the Quad, Modi went on to say: 'It is normal to have partnerships on the basis of shared values and interests. India, too, has many in the region and beyond. We will work with them, individually or in formats of three or more, for a stable and peaceful region.'[11]

In order to lend perspective to India's posture in the Indo-Pacific, we need to focus on China's intentions and capabilities.

## A Focus on China

Given its past record, growing economic and military strength, revisionist outlook and recent declarations, China can be expected to push its influence in the region. A manifestation of China's belligerence is the campaign of 'cartographic expansion' that it has mounted through the 'nine-dash line' in the South China Sea[12] and repudiation of the 1914 McMahon line on the India–China border. Other examples of Chinese intransigence are the illegal creation and militarisation of artificial islands in the South China Sea and its contemptuous dismissal of United Nations arbitration on these sovereignty issues. It plans to rewrite the rules of international conduct to suit its own interests and plans for territorial acquisition.

While China's dominant military position on the Tibetan plateau poses a severe challenge to India on land, the establishment of maritime footholds in the Indian Ocean, including military bases in Djibouti and Gwadar, are meant to provide it with a network of port facilities that can support long-range maritime operations. As Indians contemplate these developments, we must remember that China's grand strategic aim is to reshape the geopolitical fundamentals of global power. This would be in conformity with geographer Halford Mackinder's 1904 thesis,[13] in which he had argued that the future of global power lay in controlling the vast landmass of Eurasia, then dominated by the Russian Empire.

Today, it is China rather than Russia which dominates the Eurasian 'world island' through its ambitious Belt and Road Initiative (BRI). One component of the BRI, the 15,000 km Silk Road Economic Belt, connecting Central China to Europe, is creating a transcontinental infrastructure for the economic integration of the world island from within, by developing an internal network of high-speed railways, fibre-optic cables and energy pipelines. At the same time, the ambitious Maritime Silk Road involving 65 countries and expenditure of trillions of dollars promises to transform the economy and geopolitics of the Indo-Pacific.

Ever since Xi Jinping designated the maritime domain as an essential building block of his 'China Dream',[14] there has been a systematic build-up in each element of national maritime power. Today, China is the world leader in shipbuilding, and its 5,000-ship strong merchant marine ranks No.1 in the world. It also owns the largest number of coastguard vessels that protect the world's biggest fishing fleet. Chinese shipyards are rapidly adding to the country's fleet of modern destroyers, frigates and submarines, both nuclear and diesel. In a few years, the PLAN will overtake the US Navy in numbers, but may lag behind in capability.

Given that the Sino–Indian territorial dispute has been festering since the late 1950s, it is difficult to avoid the conclusion that the current lack of clarity amongst our decision-makers is rooted in incomprehension of the long-term strategic aims and objectives that underpin China's belligerent conduct. It would seem that from Jawaharlal Nehru's naïve hopes, encapsulated in the 'Hindi–Chini bhai bhai' (India and China are brothers) mantra to Prime Minister Modi's prolonged courtship of Xi Jinping, India has been groping in the dark while grossly misreading China's real intent. As we watch Beijing's sinister border strategy unfold, the absence of a matching counter on India's part becomes painfully obvious.

Choices, for India, in the face of Chinese hegemony are stark. The constraints of India's political system render it unlikely that it can bridge the economic and military gap vis-à-vis China within a reasonable timeframe, and thus other options need to be sought.

## India's Options

Clearly, the Indo-Pacific concept has roots in the new challenges that Asia and the USA are faced with and tries to address the limitations of the Asia–Pacific construct: mainly its exclusivity. Given India's economic and military rise and the growth of its international stature, the time was ripe for its integration into the Asia–Pacific political and security matrix through the Indo-Pacific concept. This concept, however, received a mixed reception in New Delhi, perhaps, due to a lack of strategic clarity.

The 2015 edition of the Indian Maritime Security Strategy[15] identifies India's 'primary areas of maritime interest' as, essentially, the North and South West Indian Ocean and all its entry, exit and choke points. It then defines the 'secondary areas of maritime interest' that encompass the South East Indian Ocean, Western Pacific Ocean, South and East China Seas, the Mediterranean Sea, west coast of Africa and other areas based on Indian diaspora, overseas investment or other interests. If you conjoin the two, there is a significant conformity with the Indo-Pacific construct.

In our primary area of interest, the main source of concern is the increasing presence of the PLAN. Starting with anti-piracy patrols in the Gulf of Aden in 2008, the PLAN has steadily gained experience and confidence in operations distant from home. The year 2014 saw the first PLAN submarine deployments in the IOR. With the availability of bases in Gwadar and Djibouti and friendly ports in Myanmar, Bangladesh and Sri Lanka, PLAN units can be expected to deploy in our waters with greater frequency. In countering threats posed by PLAN in the Indian Ocean, an asymmetric, 'anti-access, area denial' approach on the part of the IN would be more realistic and effective than trying to match this adversary 'force-on-force' or by threatening China in the Western Pacific.

Fortunately, India is blessed with a favourable maritime geography and the Indian peninsula dominates both the Bay of Bengal and the Arabian Sea.

This geographical disposition highlights the advantages of our 'interior lines of communication' as compared to 8,000 km–10,000 km long 'exterior lines' separating Chinese naval bases from the Bay of Bengal. Moreover, the Andaman and Nicobar Island chain across the exit from the Malacca Straits could be a formidable barrier—provided we fortify them suitably. Surveillance would, however, need to be mounted over the Indonesian straits offering alternate exits from the South China Sea.

## Provision of Net Security

In the past, ASEAN members have sought increased Indian naval presence in their waters as a counter to a rising China. While India had, so far, declined direct involvement in affairs of the Western Pacific and especially in US–China power politics, it has now succumbed to persuasion by the USA and assumed the role of the regional 'net security provider'.

While we frequently express concerns about China's 'String of Pearls' and the BRI, the challenge lies in crafting creative, dynamic and long-term maritime alternatives, and employing the IN as an instrument of policy, as it should be. Countries in India's immediate neighbourhood, many of them island nations, seek maritime security; sometimes through direct naval presence, but more often through urgent requests for material aid, training assistance and advice. Responding to such requests in a reasonable timeframe is very important.

The 2008 Indian Ocean Naval Symposium (IONS) was an initiative to reach out to our maritime neighbourhood and promote a multilateral approach to regional security cooperation in all its dimensions. Mooted by the IN, this 12-year-old initiative has received only lukewarm support from the Ministry of External Affairs (MEA). A tripartite India–Sri Lanka–Maldives agreement on Maritime Domain Awareness (MDA) concluded in 2016 appears to have better chances of success. After its sterling performance during the 2004 Indian Ocean tsunami, India's neighbours expect prompt assistance from the IN in times of natural calamity. The Service has prepared and equipped itself to render prompt humanitarian assistance and disaster relief (HADR) and the current COVID-19 crisis could test its capabilities.

While the 2015 Maritime Strategy[16] speaks of 'areas of interest' and not 'areas of responsibility', it does seek to create a 'favourable and positive maritime environment' in which threats can be regularly monitored and countered through maritime cooperation amongst stakeholders. The promotion of a favourable maritime environment, according to the strategy, 'would also contribute towards providing net security' in the area.

Acknowledging the importance of sustained naval presence and rapid response in maritime areas of interest, the IN has already implemented a new policy of 'mission-based deployments', envisaging sustained warship and aircraft patrols in a number of focal areas. Such deployments can serve the purpose of meeting one or more of the requirements of net security.

## India's Maritime Blueprint

Let me now provide an insight into the IN's plans for capability accretion over the next couple of decades or so. As our decision-makers began to acknowledge the navy's role in state policy, a clear-cut road map became necessary to synergise our national maritime endeavours. Such a road map is available in the navy's Maritime Doctrine and Strategy as well as in the Maritime Capabilities Perspective Plan that is updated periodically.

Despite the 'maritime awakening' mentioned earlier, the navy's share of the defence budget has traditionally remained well behind its sister services. In the 1980s it crept up, slowly, from 6 per cent to 12 per cent and reached an all-time high of 18 per cent in 2012. But in 2019, it fell once again to 13 per cent and India's slowing economy does not give much hope for an increase in the near future. Due to this, the navy's earlier plan to reach the 200-ship mark by 2030 has reportedly been scaled back.

While fiscal stringency demands a cautious approach, the approvals already accorded by the government will enable the navy to add 50 ships in the next decade or so. By the mid-2030s, the IN should have a fleet of about 175 ships, which will still place it amongst the top ranks of modern navies worldwide. Discussed in the succeeding paragraghs are a few details of the navy's plans.

### *Warship Building Capability*

One of the most significant decisions taken by the navy's leadership, way back in the 1960s, was to initiate indigenous warship design and construction. Today, the navy's stature as well as operational capability owes much to the fact that its ships are largely designed and built at home. Four shipyards, belonging to the Ministry of Defence, one each in Mumbai, Kolkata, Goa and Vishakhapatnam, are dedicated to warship construction. They have, over the past five decades, built over 100 modern warships, including destroyers, frigates, submarines, corvettes, landing ships, tankers and patrol vessels. A fifth shipyard, in Kochi, belonging to the Ministry of Shipping has been engaged in building India's first aircraft carrier. In addition to all these, a special facility has been created in Vishakhapatnam for building nuclear submarines.

### *Conventional Submarines*

In the case of submarine construction, India has lagged well behind China as well as Pakistan, and the 2019 force-level of just 13 diesel submarines is woefully inadequate when compared to China's 70 and Pakistan's 15 subs. In the 1980s, India had signed a contract for the acquisition of six submarines of German design, two to be constructed in Germany and the other four in India. Sadly, after construction of just two boats, the programme was killed in 1990 on account of a corruption scandal. After a lapse of 15 years, another project to undertake construction of six Scorpene-class French submarines was started in Mumbai. The first two of these submarines have been delivered and the others will follow. The IN needs to create a force of at least 30 submarines to meet its operational commitments, and the government must address this lacuna with a sense of urgency.

## *Aircraft Carriers*

Since the acquisition of *INS Vikrant* in 1961, the aircraft carrier has formed the centrepiece of IN doctrine and strategy. After *Vikrant* we acquired the *Viraat* from Britain, and since 2013 we have been operating *INS Vikramaditya*, a former Soviet/Russian carrier. The construction of an indigenous aircraft carrier, or IAC-1, commenced in 2009 in Cochin shipyard, and it may be ready for delivery by 2022. For many years, the navy has been contemplating plans for the construction of a larger carrier, but its fate hangs in balance for want of a political decision and funding support.

## *Naval Aviation*

Intense maritime activity in the Indian Ocean and the huge area that has to be kept under surveillance requires substantial maritime reconnaissance and anti-submarine warfare capabilities. The IN has evolved a multilayered surveillance system with a mix of long- and medium-range aircraft as well as unmanned aerial vehicles. New squadrons of the Boeing P-8 (I) anti-submarine and patrol aircraft, armed with anti-submarine as well as anti-ship weapons, have provided a major capability boost. The navy's current carrier-borne fighter is the Russian Mig-29(K), which operates from the *Vikramaditya* and may also fly from its next carrier. Today, every sizeable warship is equipped with one or more helicopters, and is prepared for anti-submarine warfare and other roles.

## India's Nuclear Submarines

Strategic nuclear deterrence is an important mission of the IN. A nuclear-propelled submarine, armed with nuclear-tipped ballistic missiles, once it dives underwater, is invisible and hence, almost invulnerable. Such submarines—termed SSBNs—provide a far greater assurance of retaliation after an enemy nuclear strike as compared to land-based missiles and aircraft. That is the reason why India has sought to create the underwater leg of its 'nuclear triad'.

INS *Arihant*, India's first homebuilt nuclear submarine, undertook its first 'deterrent patrol' in 2018. While this was a significant step in enhancing the credibility of India's nuclear deterrent, the ballistic missile currently carried by the *Arihant* has a relatively limited range. Construction is underway for two more SSBNs which will carry missiles of intercontinental range, and this will provide India with a full-fledged underwater nuclear deterrent.

A second type of nuclear-powered submarine, which carries torpedoes and anti-ship missiles, is called an 'attack submarine' or SSN. A Russian submarine of this type was taken on lease in 2012 and renamed *INS Chakra*. Its roles include protecting carrier battle groups and hunting enemy submarines interdicting enemy shipping. There are also plans to build several SSNs in Vishakhapatnam in the near future.

Initiatives such as China's determined outreach into the Pacific and Indian Oceans, extending well into the African continent, have the potential to threaten India's maritime security and call for a cohesive diplomatic strategy to counter them.

## Conclusion

Even as our statesmen and diplomats approach the Indo-Pacific paradigm with a degree of wariness and deny any suggestions about an Indian 'Monroe Doctrine', it is indisputable that India's security is intimately linked with this oceanic expanse. Moreover, as a leading IOR power, it is natural for India to perceive the overt show of maritime clout by an extra-regional power such as China as undesirable and even provocative. China, on the other hand, refuses to accord India the status of a regional power and views the Indo-Pacific paradigm as a hyphenation of convenience for the US State Department.

In the current scenario, given Chinese intransigence and our misreading of their imperialist–expansionist intent, Sino–Indian tensions are likely to persist. For China, it is advantageous to keep bilateral tensions confined to the Himalayan arena because a continental focus also helps to keep India contained in a 'South Asia box'. To the advocates of maritime power, this seems all the more reason for India to try and shift the confrontation to the 'sea level', where the asymmetry is in its favour.

Notwithstanding its handicaps, India, as a democracy, a nuclear weapon state and a significant economic and military power, must stand firm as a bulwark against regional hegemony. History shows that neither appeasement nor empty bluster works with hegemonic powers. If India is not to cede ground to China, physically or diplomatically, it must muster all elements of its 'comprehensive national power', focusing especially on the maritime dimension.

5

# Facing China's Challenges Robustly

PROFESSOR SRIKANTH KONDAPALLI

Even though the recent official publications of the Indian government have downplayed the threat perceptions emanating from China,[1] the reality is that there are many challenges India is facing from its northern neighbour. These range from traditional to non-traditional security challenges. In the traditional sphere are unresolved territorial disputes, China–Pakistan collaboration in weapons of mass destruction and conventional weapons transfers to South Asian countries as well as military modernisation in Tibet and Xinjiang, bordering India, China's forays into the Indian Ocean, and India's cyber and space domains. In the non-traditional security challenges are competition for resources abroad—specifically in the fields of energy and commodities—control of Tibetan waters and glacier meltdown due to deforestation and infrastructure development, migration, spread of pandemics and responses to terrorism. Another set of challenges is from the Belt and Road Initiative (BRI) that China launched in 2013 and that has been utilised to make forays into South Asia with the intention of physical connectivity in short terms but to become a force to reckon with in the region in the medium to long term. These are discussed in the following pages. It is argued in this chapter that given the comprehensive nature of the challenges that India is facing, it has upgraded its threat perceptions vis-à-vis China from the previous low-level to medium-level threat at the conventional level. At the nuclear level, the previous 'deterring Pakistan, dissuading China' configuration has been changing, with the 'no first use' doctrine becoming conditional and with the deployment of long-range missile systems. In addition, since the last decade, India is preparing for scenarios under nuclear threshold with both Pakistan and China configured. At the diplomatic, economic and other levels, the engagement policy with China is evolving with 'informal summit' meetings becoming more frequent.

## Traditional Security Challenges

Traditional security challenges are mainly related to 'high politics' where the state exhibits substantial interest in addressing such issues. One of the main aspects of such challenges is the defining, delimiting and demarcation of the borders between any two states in order to fix the sovereignty limits. As protection of sovereignty and territorial integrity of a country is left mainly to the armed forces of that country, the territorial issues are considered to be significant in traditional security challenges.[2] In the case of India and China, they have witnessed border clashes in 1962 and frequently exhibit tensions due to border transgressions. While India considers this issue as significant because it lost the 1962 war, for China, border issues with India have not been a main challenge to its security, focused as it were on Taiwan, the South China Sea, Senkaku Islands and other fronts.

*Territorial Dispute*

Even though India and China became independent in the late 1940s, they are yet to configure their respective territorial limits—an anomaly that is continuing despite over three decades of discussions on the issue between the officials of the two countries. The dispute is located in the eastern, middle and western sectors of the border with the border being, from an Indian point of view, about 3,488 km, while China suggests that the length of the border is about 2,000 km. Around 14 pockets are being discussed in the border talks and these have been elevated to the Special Representative level. While both countries made efforts to resolve the disputes through talks and other measures, they had led to border clashes in 1962 as well as frequent tensions during border transgressions. The incidents at Jelep La in 1967, Samdurong Chu in 1986, Daulat Beg Oldi in 2000, Depsang Plains in 2013, Chumar in 2014, Dokhlam in 2017 and Eastern Ladakh in 2020 have been serious with the paramilitaries and the militaries pitching in. The 15 June 2020 incident at Galwan had resulted in the death of 20 Indian soldiers; casualties caused for the first time after the Tulung La incident in the eastern sector in 1975. Hence, we can see that the unresolved territorial disputes have serious implications for bilateral relations as it could trigger military confrontation. The 2020 June incident took place at Galwan despite initiating confidence-building measures (CBMs) since the late 1970s but more intensely in 1993 (Peace and Tranquillity Agreement), 1996 (CBMs in the military field), 2013 (Border Defence Cooperation Agreement) and since the Wuhan and Chennai meetings between Prime Minister Narendra Modi and President Xi Jinping in 2018 and 2019. A new set of CBMs are in work with the implementation of hotlines, proportional withdrawal of troops from the borders, no-fly zones, no military exercises with Line of Actual Control as their strategic direction and the like. These CBMs have contributed in preventing conflict between the two armed forces, with the exceptions of the 1962 clashes, the 1967 Cho La and Jelep La incidents, then 1975 Tulung la incident, and the 2020 Galwan incident.

### *Tibet Military*

A related aspect of the territorial dispute is the fast pace of military modernisation that China attempted in the Tibet Military Command, which comes under the 2015 reorganised Western Theatre of China's People's Liberation Army (PLA) and borders India. The PLA intends to carry out integrated joint operations to secure its borders, which have implications for the India–China border as well.

A number of steps were taken by China in Tibet that have a critical bearing on the Indian security.[3] First, while all provincial military commands were integrated with the National Defence Mobilisation Department of the PLA's Central Military Commission, the Tibet Military Command was brought under the jurisdiction of the PLA. Instead of focusing on militia, reserves and conscription work, this elevation in rank for Tibet-based forces meant acquiring combat roles and preparing for any conflicts with India. More resources are pouring in for this command as a result of this new elevated status and this is also reflected in the stepping up of the border transgressions with India.

Second, China began deploying laser-guided and satellite-guided PLC-181 vehicle mounted howitzers with a 50 km range in Tibet opposite Sikkim and other areas. There are other weapon systems to be deployed at Tibet, according to the Chinese press. These include plans to deploy the 32 tonne, 105 mm gun, T-15 light tank that can be easily transported and a new LW-30 laser defence weapon system that can detect and strike low, slow and small targets including unmanned aerial vehicles (UAVs).

In the light of India acquiring UAVs from the USA, China appears to be already putting countermeasures in place. For more offensive missions, for patrols on Indian borders and for counterterrorism missions, the Chengdu-based units are developing GJ-2 medium-to-high altitude armed unmanned reconnaissance aerial vehicles, with 370 kmph, 20-hour endurance, synthetic aperture radar and an electro-optical pod, carrying 12 small missiles.

Other equipment details are significant as well. China unveiled a 10 tonne Z-20 medium-lift helicopter to be deployed at Tibet. The Y-9 transports are deployed at the frontier areas for early warning, surveillance and transport duties. More spectacular is the information that Y-20 strategic transport aircraft (with maximum payload capacity of 66 tonnes and a range of 3,700 km) were commissioned in 2016 while the stealth fighter J-20 was commissioned in 2017 after testing in the Tibetan high altitude. More alarming was the 10 January 2019 report of China Central TV that the DF-26 manoeuvrable re-entry missile system had been deployed at the north-west of the country for training purposes.[4] Its 4,000 km range is meant for attacking US aircraft carriers in the Taiwan Straits or the South China Sea but is hypothetically applicable to Indian aircraft carriers as well. This is in addition to the DF-21 medium-range missiles deployed at Da Qaidam, Xiao Qaidam and Delingha. China's *People's Daily* had reported that these missiles are rail-mobile in Tibet.[5]

Third, rapid deployment of military equipment needs airfields, roads and railways. Tibet has several airfields, four highways and one railway. China is ramping up the construction for further integration and plans to project its power into South Asia. China had constructed 96,000 km of roads in Tibet by 2018, with over 4,000 km of highways added a year since 2012.

The 409 km Lhasa–Nyingchi Highway (north of Arunachal Pradesh), built at a cost of US$5.8 billion, was commissioned in 2017. A 135 km Yaán-Kangding expressway was constructed at a cost of US$3.3 billion, making it the second expressway to connect Sichuan to Tibet after National Highway 318, which links up with Lhasa. In addition, apart from the Gormud to Lhasa railway line commissioned in 2006, China began construction of the 435 km Lhasa–Nyingchi railway line, to be completed by 2021. In 2019, China plans to launch a 1,700 km Sichuan to Tibet railway line at a cost of US$36 billion, connecting through areas bordering Arunachal Pradesh, and to be completed by 2026. Beidou navigation system is now available all across Tibet both for the civilians and the military.[6] Also, the Ngari Space Observatory, neighbouring Ladakh, was inaugurated in 2010. It now has eight astronomical telescopes of high diameters. Quantum experiments are being conducted here. Apart from the 30 million tourists in 2018 who had utilised these newly developed infrastructure in Tibet—resulting in revenue earnings of over US$7 billion—the PLA is one of the main beneficiaries of the construction work on the 'roof of the world'. The massive construction work has its own flip side. According to the Chinese Academy of Sciences, Tibetan glaciers have shrunk by over 15 per cent in the past five decades.[7]

Fourth, to enhance capabilities for the combat missions that the Tibet Military Command has been tasked with, training and military exercises have been increasing in the region recently. President Xi himself ordered the PLA to enhance training missions in his recent new year message. On an average, the Western Theatre Command in Chengdu conducts over 15 small-, medium- and large-scale exercises a year. The recent ones have become more intensive and India-focused. In December 2018, armed police conducted a counterterrorism campaign in Tibet in 'intensive warlike confrontations'.

Fifth, there are about 15 airfields in and around Tibet—in the western sector: Kashgar, Yarkhand and Khotan; central sector: Hoping, Gonga Dzong,

Donshoon and Nagchuka; and eastern sector: Gormo, Jeykundo, Chengdu, Kantzu, Bangda, Kunming, Paoshan and Mangshi.[8] These airfields can accommodate up to a maximum of 15 fighter squadrons and 12 bomber squadrons. China is deploying third-plus generation fighter aircraft such as Su-27 (J-11), J-10, and even carrying out trials of J-20 aircraft. These are long-range combat aircraft and cover most of the Indian territory.

Such modernisation efforts in Tibet have alerted India, which has now been making preparations to raise a Mountain Strike Corps, construct 44 strategic roads in the border areas, revamp its advanced landing zones, prepare three new airbases at Hashimara, Chabua and Tezpur, and operationalise the Agni series of ballistic missiles and BrahMos cruise missiles.

The events in Eastern Ladakh–Xinjiang/Tibet borders since 5 May 2020 suggest that the PLA deployments in Tibet have the purposes of deterring India and nibbling away at territories that are perceived to be 'no man's land' on the Line of Actual Control. The mobilisation of nearly four divisions by China at Galwan, Pangong Tso, Hot Springs, Depsang Plains and other areas in the region suggested of the backup they received over a period of time from preparations in Tibet, which have a direct bearing on Indian security.

### *Sino–Pakistan Military Collaboration*

While huge asymmetries exist between India and Pakistan in favour of the former in terms of land, population, location, resources, economy and military strength, China's support of Pakistan, specifically in acquiring weapons of mass destruction, has led to concerns in New Delhi. Also, cumulative conventional arms transfers to other South Asian countries—although not yet a current and present danger for India—is a security concern. Such arms transfers to Pakistan and other South Asian countries from China has been increasing in the recent times.

China has had good relations with Pakistan since the 1950s, but the relationship acquired more strategic dimensions after the India–China border skirmishes in 1962.[9] Relations between the two flowered in all respects, with Pakistan receiving the maximum aid from Beijing among all South Asian countries. Arms sales to Islamabad is also the maximum compared to other South Asian states, including nuclear and ballistic missiles or related technologies. China has become a larger player in the global arms industry in recent years and exports have been shifting from low-end weapons to increasingly advanced ones. Chinese arms sales have surged in the past five years.

Pakistan continues to receive advanced weapons systems from China, including army, navy, airforce, and nuclear and ballistic missile equipment or systems or components. The Stockholm International Peace Research Institute databases cited later point to such stepped up cooperation. The *Al-Khalid* Main Battle Tank is being manufactured in Taxila with Chinese technical cooperation. Developed under Project 711, which began in the 1980s, these tanks are considered to be modern. Naval vessel transfers include Romeo-class conventional submarines, Jiangwei frigates, Hainan-class, Huangfen-class, Hegu-class and Huzhuan-class

FACs and ship-to-ship missiles and systems. The Pakistan navy has also acquired four advanced F-22P frigates under an agreement signed with China in early 2003 at a cost of US$600 million.[10] Pakistan's navy has also been planning to buy eight submarines from China. Fighter aircraft transfers include F-6, F-7M, F-7MG, F-7P, FT-7P, proposed transfers of FC-1, JF-17, A-5, Y-12 transports, AEW, K-8 trainers and Z-9C helicopters.

Several reports indicated China's cooperation with Pakistan in strategic weapons programmes.[11] These include not only the supply of about 5,000 ring magnets but also designs of nuclear weapons, missiles and missile technologies. With Pakistan's inveterate animosity towards India, the transfers of these weapons of mass destruction by the PLA appear to be well thought out. Chinese assistance to Pakistan include supply of ballistic missiles and launchers of 34 M-11/DF-11 missiles (to Pakistan's PAF Base Mushaf in Sargodha near Lahore), delivered in November 1992; M-11 transporter-erector-launchers (1991); HY-1 and 2, FL-1 and 2 Cruise missiles; and possible assistance to indigenous Pakistani missile programmes of Hatf-1 and 2 series of ballistic missiles and Anza surface-to-air missile. China has also transferred 10 tonnes of ammonium percholate rocket fuel; missile guidance systems including gyroscopes, accelerometers and on-board computers, and has assisted Pakistan in the missile production factory at Fatehgarh (Fatehgunj) near Islamabad.[12] Chinese assistance has also been traced behind the Pakistani testing of cruise missiles. In addition, it has also transferred M9 missiles to Syria, reportedly by a circuitous route through Pakistan and Iraq. When news of Pakistani nuclear scientist A.Q. Khan's clandestine transfers to Iran, Libya and North Korea surfaced linking China to such transfers, China expressed 'serious concern'. Chinese-supplied designs to Pakistan were reportedly found in Libya.[13] China has declared its intent to intensify nuclear cooperation with Pakistan and has promised investments worth several billion dollars in expanding the Chashma project in Pakistan.[14]

China's arms transfers to other South Asian countries have also seen an upsurge. While it was mentioned that these need to be seen mainly in commercial terms, strategic considerations of balancing India are clear nevertheless. Conventional weapon transfers from China to Bangladesh further cemented bilateral diplomatic ties between the two countries. Such transfers to Bangladesh, mainly made on 'very easy financial terms', credit purchases and 'spread out' payments to the Chinese, give certain political mileage in the bilateral relations. Also, given the high cost of such weapons in the Western or Russian arms bazaars, 'cheap' Chinese products are an attractive proposition for the Bangladeshi government.[15] China State Shipbuilding Corporation had transferred three Shadhinota-class C13B corvettes for the Bangladeshi navy till 2018. Bangladesh is also cooperating with China for submarine transfers. By 2019, Bangladesh had also received two Chinese Type-053H3 frigates, *Jiaxing* and *Lianyungang*. For expanding cooperation, China and Bangladesh are also pursuing mutual high-level military contacts. Sino–Sri Lankan military cooperation is reflected partly in the arms transfers to the latter to fight its insurgency problems relating to the Liberation Tigers of Tamil Eelam (LTTE). Apart from Israel and other countries, China was one such principal supplier of the weapon systems for Sri Lanka. The China North Industries Corporation carried out most of these transactions though even in this sphere, they are not without controversies related to corruption and suchlike. Now, since the Hambantota port has been leased by China, after the inability of Sri Lanka to pay back debts, China's role in the intelligence set-up of the country is increasing, specifically after the terror attacks on a church recently. In the case of Nepal, procurement of US$200 million worth of arms from China in the late 1980s had riled New Delhi, which blockaded the borders of Nepal. Similarly in the 2000s, such transfers from China to Nepal have created further differences with India. While these arms transfers to South Asian countries are not huge in volume, they tend to create frictions in India's relations with other South Asian countries.

### *China's Forays in the Indian Ocean*

Although China has attempted to enter the Indian Ocean region since the 1960s at a political level and through the 'Indian Ocean Zone of Peace' proposal, given its lack of naval power, this objective did not fructify. However, recently, with double-digit growth in the defence budget since the 1990s, and with power projection forces like the navy promoted, China has now been making a concerted effort to be a power in the region. Three objectives drive China in the Indian

Ocean: to secure its energy resource imports from the region, to become a global and regional hegemon, and to follow the 'two ocean strategy' in the Indian and Pacific Oceans and to counter India's geographical advantages in the region. Since 1993, China became a net importer of energy resources, mainly from West Asia and Africa. Today, it imports more than 400 million tonnes of oil. China's energy deals with these regions have also increased substantially. Citing such energy dependence, President Hu Jintao coined the term 'Malacca dilemma' and suggested naval expansion, build-up of infrastructure projects such as the China–Myanmar Economic Corridor of energy pipelines and dual use maritime facilities, and construction of ports such as Gwadhar and Hambantotoa. The Djibouti naval base, which China has control over since 2015, could also come in handy for the country in this drive. In order to also secure its energy interests, China has been despatching regular naval contingents since 2008 for counter-piracy operations and so that it can gain important experience in the naval domain through these operations. By 2020, China has conducted 36 such naval operations, some involving amphibious operations and air defence objectives, in addition to evacuation of Chinese nationals from trouble-torn Libya, Egypt, Yemen and other places. Such evacuation operations provided China with rich experience in dual-use deployment of air and naval forces abroad. Citing the Malabar exercises of India and the USA (and Japan, since 2015), China has been strengthening its presence in the Indian Ocean. The Indian navy in this context reported that China has been sending submarines to the region in addition to conducting 'research' activities regularly with the ostensible purpose of first knowing the terrain and then making naval operations regular. At the moment, excepting Djibouti, China is constrained by power projection in the region and is without any air bases. However, China is expected to acquire such capabilities in the medium term. The US Defence Department's extensive report of 1 September 2020 on the PLA suggested that China has surpassed the USA in the number of naval ships it has, even as it is making inroads in Sri Lanka, Bangladesh and Myanmar, besides Pakistan.

### *China's Cyber and Space Challenges*

Since the last few years, China has been making major efforts not only to consolidate its domestic cyber capabilities in what the Oracle team recently mentioned as a secure and exclusive 'intranet' for the whole country but also in the regulatory framework issues and expanding overseas through the 5G networks and others in what is billed as occupying the 'centre stage' of global policies as directed by the 19th Communist Party Congress in 2017. China's cyber capabilities have enhanced in the domain of technology, specifically in the areas of Artificial Intelligence (AI), ICT, telecommunications, supercomputing, space, aviation and cryptography. China, today, is at the forefront of the 5G network, which is going to provide a quantum jump in internet speed. Its telecommunication and e-commerce giants such as Huawei, ZTE, Alibaba, Tencent and others have established themselves as global players. Huawei and ZTE (Zhongxing) are also bidding for 5G projects across the globe, including in India. However, even though India had allowed Huawei to participate in trials, it is concerned about the cyberattacks emanating from China. Many cyberattacks in India, such as cyber espionage and cybercrimes, have been traced to China. A number of computers in the Indian security establishments and nuclear establishments have come under attack with the origins of these in China. In the light of the 15 June 2020 killing of Indian soldiers, India retaliated by banning nearly 200 IT applications originating in China citing cybersecurity concerns. The measures also included restricting investments from China in infrastructure projects and curbing illegal financial flows.

Another security challenge that India is facing from China in the 'global domain' is in the outer space programme. In 2007, China conducted an anti-satellite test. While this appears to be a signal for the USA, India is also concerned given its dependence on very few military satellites. To counter this, India recently conducted an anti-satellite test of its own and carried out measures to strengthen GPS coverage of the Indian Ocean.

## Non-traditional Security Challenges

In comparison to the traditional security challenges where the state and its apparatus take a proactive role, in the 'low politics' of non-traditional security challenges, the state's role has not been decisive—though the state did intervene in the India–China dynamics—with commercial, societal or other lobbies playing a certain role in mitigating these issues. Again, while the military has played a vital role in addressing traditional security challenges, the armed forces have less of a role in mitigating the non-traditional security challenges. Nevertheless, in the recent times, the challenges posed by non-traditional security challenges have been considerable across the world, including in China and India.

*Environment*

As much of the industrialisation in China is in its north-east and south-east coastal regions, acid rain is a problem that plagues other East Asian countries; but regions in South and South-east Asia also suffer from a major environmental challenge arising from China in the forms of river-water flow.[16] Tibet is home to the major rivers of Asia with their sources in the region's glaciers. However, China has begun river-diversion projects including the three South–North River Diversion Projects; the last one, the Great Western River Diversion Project to be completed by 2050, presents major challenges for the lower riparian states in South and South-east Asia. China has started to divert the Yangtze River and the Yarlung Zangpo toward the north, which has so far transferred 10 billion cubic metres of water from the south to the draught-prone north. Water pumped from the Yangtze River has gone to Beijing, Tianjin and the provinces of Henan and Hebei along the middle route of the water diversion project. This route of the project carries water through canals and pipes from Danjiangkou reservoir in central China's Hubei Province. It came into operation in late 2014. China is also planning to build over 20 hydroelectric projects on the Yarlung Zangpo at the Great Bend where it joins the Brahmaputra river in India. The Indian Parliament has discussed the challenges posed by such projects. Two memoranda of understanding have been signed for sharing hydrological data on this river although during the Dokhlam crisis in 2017, such data sharing was put on hold. The Indus river also poses concerns for India in its upper reaches as China has started constructing barrages in Tibet. This has led to washing away of apple orchards in Kinnaur and Lahaul Spiti due to dam bursts.

Another non-traditional security challenge India is facing vis-à-vis China relates to the Tibetan migration since the late 1950s with estimates of over 1,60,000 Tibetan refugees shifting to India citing lack of religious, cultural and educational autonomy in Tibet. In 1962, China had obliquely cited this aspect as one of the reasons for entering into armed conflict. Although there is stability in bilateral relations on the Tibet issue, this was made possible with Indian concessions on not allowing Tibetans to 'play a political role' and without any reciprocal gestures from China on Kashmir.

Energy security can be termed as a challenge for India as China has begun competing for global energy resources. The then External Affairs Minister Pranab Mukherjee, speaking to the National Defence College, stated as much when he said that competition for resources with a rising China is a major challenge for India.[17] Today, China is the second largest and India the fourth largest importers of energy resources, mainly from West Asia. Due to the focus on the state-owned enterprises, China has been able to leverage its might in bagging oil contracts in many regions of the world, some at the cost of Indian companies.

More significantly, the spread of pandemics is becoming a major non-traditional security challenge for many countries, including India. In recent times, China has become the centre from where these pandemics spread including SARS, bird flu and COVID-19. While a few memoranda of understanding have been signed with China to share information and medical practices, such pandemics are taking a heavy toll on India. The first COVID-19 cases in India were reported by students returning from Wuhan, which was the epicentre from where the virus spread. While India took measures such as stopping flights to and from China, cancellation of visas and others to contain the spread of infections, still it has been increasing taking a heavy toll on Indian lives and economy.

### *Belt and Road Initiative*

China launched the BRI in 2013 which includes a continental connect with the Eurasian region and a maritime connect with the Indian Ocean Region. In 2014, China signed an agreement with Pakistan and termed the China–Pakistan Economic Corridor (CPEC) as the 'flagship' programme of the BRI. It made an initial allocation of US$42 billion for this purpose but increased it to US$62 billion. While India does not object to the CPEC per se, India did object to the BRI since it is to pass through Kashmir. At the geo-political level, the BRI intends to connect Asia with Europe and Africa, with connectivity in the continental and maritime domains. While India has not expressed interest in the continental domains, the proposed Maritime Silk Road passing through the South China Sea and Indian Ocean has an obvious impact on India. Indeed, China's major interest in approaching India in the BRI project is mainly in the Indian Ocean Region although the latter has not shown any interest in this domain. A former Ambassador of China to India, Le Yucheng, had suggested that India's Project Mausam[18] be merged with the Maritime Silk Road of China.[19] This proposal was not accepted by India.

Another area of focus for China in the BRI has been the Bangladesh–China–India–Myanmar (BCIM) initiative which was proposed in 1999. Discussions from track-two level have been upgraded to track-one level although progress on any project implementation is tardy. India officially accepted the BCIM in May 2013 during Premier Li Keqiang's visit to India (and thus preceding the September 2013 speech on the BRI by President Xi Jinping).[20] The 22 May 2015 meeting between Prime Minister Modi and Premier Li Keqiang led to an understanding on the BCIM Economic Corridor. However, New Delhi was concerned about the continuing small arms transfers by China to rebels in India's north-east and the opening up of the politically fragile north-east to China's influence. For this reason, even though three high-level official meetings took place on the BCIM, no progress was made except on tourism and transportation networks. China on the other hand, while having included the BCIM Economic Corridor as one of the six corridors of the BRI, has in late 2018 began emphasising a new China–Myanmar Economic Corridor, much akin to the China–Pakistan Economic Corridor, both of which intend to provide maritime access to China through the Bay of Bengal and Arabian Sea to the Indian Ocean. In this background, India–China equations in the maritime domain have become complex.[21]

Differences are emerging between China and India on the BRI. First, while both India and China are fast-rising countries in Asia, they are still careful in protecting their minimalist foreign policy goals. Both have expressed concern over a period of time on any violation by any country on aspects of their sovereignty and territorial integrity. China has bound many a country with its 'one China' policy, such as recognising Taiwan and Tibet as a part of China. China had utilised its veto power at the United Nations Security Council to stall those seen as violating its 'one China' policy. In the case of India, many of China's leaders have expressed sensitivity on the issue of Kashmir (Jammu and Kashmir and now Jammu and Kashmir and Ladakh Union Territories), which joined the Indian Union in 1947. However, despite Indian sensitivities, China termed the CPEC, which passes through Kashmir, as its 'flagship' programme of the BRI in 2014.[22] This has become a contentious issue for India, which had earlier accepted the 'one China' policy. Indeed, India's Prime Minister Narendra Modi has been categorical in stating that no infrastructure of a connectivity project can ignore sovereignty claims of other countries, but to no avail so far from China.[23] Likewise, India's Ministry of External Affairs spokesman stated that India objects to the BRI for violating the sovereignty principle, as there are issues such as its lack of transparency, unilateralism, debt financing and environmental concerns.[24] While former foreign minister Sushma Swaraj, during her visit to Beijing in January 2015, stated that India is willing to consider 'synergy-based' cooperation[25]—such as in the Asian Infrastructure Investment Bank or other areas—the sovereignty aspect remained central to Indian concerns.[26] It was reported that when the Indian side summoned China's Ambassador to New Delhi to explain China's position on sovereignty issues in the region, the latter brushed aside Indian reservations by suggesting that the Silk Road initiative projects in Pakistan are of 'commercial' value. Yet, some Indian analysts suggest that China's investments in the disputed territories in the northern areas of Kashmir violate one of the key principles of the 28 March 2015 document on the BRI, which upholds 'mutual respect for each other's sovereignty and territorial integrity'.[27]

## Conclusion

The analyses in this chapter suggest that the nature of challenges emanating from China are becoming more comprehensive in the traditional and non-traditional security domains and also in the international space. Such challenges are taking different forms and dimensions and increasing in intensity and periodicity. In the face of such challenges, India has tried to address these through diplomatic, defence, strategic and other means. First, as one of the challenges come from shrinking space in the international and regional arenas, in addition to conducting dialogues with China, India enunciated a 'neighbourhood first' policy and Act East policy, and had also joined the Indo-Pacific configuration. In the last few years, India has realised that China's rise has led to stress in Asian leadership and that this needs to be addressed in a more comprehensive manner. This also explains India's refusal to join the China–dominated Regional Comprehensive Economic Partnership agreement. Second, India began a proactive policy of acquiring 'leading' positions and began preparations for such events as Uri surgical strikes, Dokhlam stand-off and Balakot strikes. In the aftermath of the Galwan incident in June 2020, India has also mobilised forces in that region and on 29 August took control of Helmet Top and Black Top in the southern bank of the Pangong Tso. Through these, India has been drawing a no-tolerance zone in its neighbourhood and regarding its territorial disputes. Third, India has been making military preparations both in the conventional and strategic spheres to reinforce its neighbourhood first policy. Fourth, China's BRI has triggered other initiatives such as North–South Transit Corridors initiated by Russia and other Central Asian Republics, the Turkmenistan–Afghanistan–Pakistan–India (TAPI) pipeline, India's Project Mausam and the recent investments in Chabahar port in Iran and Sabang in Indonesia as well as the Asia–Africa Growth Corridor (AAGC). The AAGC is an initiative led by think tanks of India, Japan and Indonesia. A Vision Document was prepared at a meeting of the Africa Development Bank in Ahmedabad in May 2017 although this was earlier mentioned in the joint statement of Prime Ministers of India and Japan in November 2016. According to the document, four components are important, that is, development and cooperation projects, quality infrastructure and institutional connectivity, enhancing capacities and skills, and people-to-people partnership. The European Union has also begun 'sustainable connectivity' and the US Secretary of State Mike Pompeo has raised a US$60 billion fund for infrastructure development in the Indo-Pacific region. These initiatives are bound to impact the progress of the BRI in the coming years.[28] These measures are expected to pose robust responses to the challenges emanating from China in the coming years.

6

# India's Economic Challenges and Countering China

MOHAN GURUSWAMY

The COVID-19 shock has hit all world economies and has caused a serious contraction in all of them. Ironically, it exposed the intrinsic strengths in the advanced economies, such as the USA, the UK, Japan and others, with highly evolved social security systems that were, by and large, able to absorb the labour displacement and were, able to quickly put together a fiscal fightback plan. Even China has been able to quickly recover its pole position as the world's leading exporter and industrial production centre.[1] In India, COVID-19 has exposed our comorbidities and has further opened up the traditional fault lines, with the large unorganised labour cohort bearing the brunt of the costs. At the last count, the Centre for Monitoring Indian Economy (CMIE) estimated that over 130 million daily wagers in the urban centres were rendered jobless and homeless.[2] India's economy, which has been in distress for most of the last decade, in now seriously stricken.

When India's economic history is written in the future, and when a serious examination is done of when India lost its way to its 'tryst with destiny', the decade of 2010–2020 will be highlighted. The facts speak for themselves. India's real gross domestic product (GDP) growth was at its peak in March 2010 when it scaled 13.3 per cent. The nominal GDP at that point was over 16.1 per cent. The nominal GDP in September 2019 was at 6.3 per cent, its lowest in the decade. Since then, the downward trend is evident and we are now scraping the bottom at about a real GDP growth rate of 4.5 per cent, this too with the push of an arguably inflationary methodology. Our previous Chief Economic Advisor (CEA), Arvind Subramaniam, estimated that India's GDP growth is overestimated by at least 2.5 per cent. Subramaniam Swamy, a Member of Parliament from the Bharatiya Janata Party (BJP) and economist, was even more pessimistic. He estimated it to be 1.5 per cent.

The decline in the growth promise of the country is amply evident from the change in the make-up of the economy during this decade. In 2010, agriculture contributed 17.5 per cent of GDP, while industry contributed 30.2 per cent and services 45.4 per cent. In 2019, that has become 15.6 per cent, 26.5 per cent and 48.5 per cent respectively. The share of industry has been sliding. This is the typical profile of a post-industrial economy. The irony of India becoming post-industrial without having been industrialised must not be missed.

The most significant cause for the decline of growth is the decline in capital investment. It was 39.8 per cent of GDP in 2010 and is now a good 10 per cent lower.[3] Clearly, without an increase of capital investment one cannot hope for more industrialisation, and hence higher growth. What we have seen in this decade is a huge increase in services, which now mostly means an increase in public administration and informal service providers such as pakora sellers.

The turn of the century, when China's GDP began its great leap forward (from about US$1.2 trillion in 2010 to US$14.2 trillion in 2019), was also a heady moment for India whose GDP of US$470 billion began a break free from the sub 5 per cent level of most of the 1990s to the rates we became familiar with in the recent past (to hit a peak stride of 10.7 per cent in 2010). At that pace, if growth rates kept creeping up, we could have conceivably gone past US$30 trillion by 2050.[4] But for that the growth rate was required to be consistently above 7 per cent. It seemed so feasible then; in 2010, it seemed we were well on track. But now we are struggling to get past US$3 trillion, and the US$5 trillion rendezvous that Prime Minister Modi promised by 2024 will have to wait longer.

To be fair to Narendra Modi and the National Democratic Alliance (NDA), the decline began early in the second term of the United Progressive Alliance (UPA) government, when capital expenditure growth had begun tapering off. Dr Manmohan Singh is too canny an economist to have missed that. But UPA2 also coincided with the increasing assertion of populist tendencies encouraged by the Congress president and her extra-Constitutional National Advisory Council. The decline in the share of capital expenditure was accompanied by a huge expansion in subsidies, most of them unmerited. Instead of increased expenditure in education and healthcare, we saw a huge expansion in subsidies, such as on liquefied petroleum gas (LPG) and motor fuels, to the middle and upper classes. Even fertiliser subsidies, which mainly flow to middle and large farmers with irrigated farmlands, saw a great upward leap. Clearly, the money for this came from the reduction in capital expenditure. Modi's fault in the years since 2014 has been that he did nothing to reverse the trend and only inflicted more hardship through his foolish demonetisation policy and ill-conceived goods and services tax (GST) roll-out.

The realities are indeed stark. The savings/GDP ratio has been in a declining trend since 2011 and Modi has been unable to reverse it. Consequently, the tax/GDP ratio and the investment/GDP ratio have also been declining.[5] The rate of economic growth has been suspect and all objective indicators point to it being padded up. The drivers of economic growth such as capital expenditure are dismal. Projects funded by banks have declined by over half since 2014 to less than ₹600 billion in 2018–2019. Projects funded by the market have dropped to rock bottom. Subsequently, the manufacturing/GDP ratio is now at 15 per cent. Corporate profits/GDP ratio is now at a 15-year-old low of about 2.7 per cent. You cannot have adequate job creation if these ratios are dipping. Declining rural labour wage indices testify to this.

Between October 2007 and October 2013, rural wages in the agricultural and non-agricultural sectors grew at 17 per cent and 15 per cent respectively. Since November 2014, however, agricultural and non-agricultural sector wages grew at only 5.6 per cent and 6.5 per cent respectively. In 2019, average rural wage growth further fell to 3.1 per cent.[6]

It is very clear now that the urban areas have been moving well in India. Indeed, so well that an Oxfam study revealed that as much as 73 per cent of the growth during the last five years accrued to just 1 per cent of the population.[7] This does not mean that it is just the tycoons of Mumbai and Delhi who are cornering the gains. The government now employs close to 25 million persons, and they have now become part of a high-income enclave. The number of persons in the private and organised sector is about another 10 million. In all this, the high-income enclave numbers not more than 175–200 million (using the rule of thumb of five members per family). Much of the consumption we tend to laud is restricted to just these.

Agriculture is still the mainstay of employment. Way back in 1880, the Indian Famine Commission 'had observed that India had too many people cultivating too little land'. This about encapsulates the current situation also. While as a percentage the numbers of farmers and farmworkers have reduced as a part of the workforce, in absolute terms their numbers have almost tripled since 1947. This has not only led to a permanent depression in comparative wages but has also led to a decline in per farmer production due to fragmentation of holdings. The average farm size is now less than an acre and it keeps further fragmenting every generation.[8] The beggaring of the farming community is inevitable. The only solution to this is the massive redirecting of the workforce into less skilled vocations such as construction.

The simple fact that the share of agriculture is now about 15.6 per cent of GDP and falling while still being the source of sustenance for almost 60 per cent of the population reveals the stark reality. A vast section of India is being left behind even as India races to become a major global economy.

As the decade ends, the Bharat and India divide has never been more vivid. Our social scientists are still unable to get a grip on this because the class, cultural and ethnic divides still elude a neat theoretical construct. Yet, there can be little disagreement that there are two broad parts to this gigantic country and one part is being left behind in the path of progress. The distance between the two only increased from 2010 to 2020. This is indeed the lost decade. Recovering from this will take a long time and will be painful. If we take too long, we might use up a good bit of the 'demographic dividend' and the demographic window of opportunity. The ageing of India will be upon us by 2050.[9]

In the recent months, the onslaught of COVID-19-induced lockdown has been quite relentless. From 2004 to 2014, India's GDP grew at an average of 7.8 per cent. At its peak, it went past 10 per cent in 2010–2011. Then it started slowing down. The new government was unable to return to the old growth rates because it didn't care to learn from the experiences of the previous regime, which began to spend more on giveaways, misguidedly thinking it was welfare economics, and took the accelerator off capital expenditure. Even though capital expenditure is driven in India by government spending, this sort of government spending is very different from subsidies and giveaways. Subsidies generally tend to be misdirected with the already well-off garnering most of it. Minimum support prices (MSPs) are a huge annual subsidy[10] and 90 per cent of it accrues to the states of Punjab, Haryana and the coastal region of Andhra Pradesh. Fertiliser subsidies tend to accumulate to the advantage of large and medium farmers or to about a quarter of all landholdings. Ditto for free power. The only welfare expenditure to benefit farmers is investment in irrigation, rural infrastructure and social welfare such as education and health. Unfortunately, this has been on the decline. This has exacerbated disparities, both local and regional. With capital expenditures declining, job creation has suffered and the inevitable slowdown of GDP growth has taken place. As we started diving, the government inflicted the so-called demonetisation adding to our woes. Just as things began to look up, the COVID-19 pandemic overtook us.

Now the only dispute on national income is how much will be the contraction. The Finance Ministry hopes that there will not be any. The International Monetary Fund has officially said it will be 4.5 per cent. The rating agencies predict a contraction of 6.8 per cent, while many more are suggesting something closer to 10 per cent. How do we deal with it now? The Government of India has tended to be 'conservative' in its outlook and has made no serious suggestion about economic stimulus. What it calls a stimulus is actually not that. The problem is more philosophical.

The divide between the Keynesians and the Chicago school of economists is as intense and often antagonistic as the Sunni–Shia, Catholic–Protestant or Thelakarai–Vadakarai Iyengar divides.

Keynesian economics is a theory that says that the government should increase demand to boost growth.

Keynesians believe consumer demand is the primary driving force in an economy. As a result, the theory supports expansionary fiscal policy. The Chicago school is a neoclassical economic school of thought that originated at the University of Chicago in the 1930s. The main tenets of the Chicago school are that free markets best allocate resources in an economy and that minimal or zero government intervention is best for economic prosperity. They abhor fiscal deficits.

The only reason why the actual stimulus package announced by the government recently is only ₹6.3 trillion is because of the obsession with fiscal deficits of Chicago economists such as Raghuram Rajan and his former student, the hapless Krishnamurthy Subramaniam, our present CEA. They are true disciples of the Washington Consensus to judge countries such as India by their fiscal deficit size. The instruments used to beat countries such as India into submission are ratings agencies such as Moody's, which just downgraded India. We should not lose too much sleep over it. India is hardly a borrower abroad and is more of a lender, holding US$538 billion as reserves.[11]

That is why the CEA, when asked about a big stimulus said, 'There are no free lunches!' That is exactly what Milton Friedman said. But they quite happily ignore the fact that the biggest deficit-financed economy in the world is the USA. Raghuram Rajan told Rahul Gandhi on his videoconference with him that a stimulus of ₹6.3 trillion would suffice in the present situation.[12] The Nobel Laureate Abhijit Banerjee and former CEA Arvind Subramaniam suggest a stimulus package such as the USA's or Japan's.[13] The USA has just announced a stimulus of over US$3.5 trillion or over 15 per cent of GDP. Modi's stimulus is a mere 0.3 per cent of GDP.

What is a 'fiscal deficit'? A fiscal deficit occurs when a government's total expenditure exceed the revenue that it generates, excluding money from borrowings. Deficit differs from debt, which is an accumulation of yearly deficits.

Many economists regard fiscal deficits as a positive economic event. For instance, the great John Maynard Keynes believed that deficits help countries climb out of economic recession. On the other hand, fiscal conservatives feel that governments should avoid deficits in favour of balanced budgets.

The fastest-growing economies in the world, and now its biggest—the USA, China, Japan and most of Western Europe—have the highest debt/GDP ratios. Japan's debt/GDP was over 253 per cent before the announcement of the latest stimulus of 20 per cent of GDP. China's debt is now over 180 per cent of its GDP. The USA's debt/GDP is close to 105 per cent, yet it is raising US$3 trillion as debt to get it out of the COVID-19 quagmire. India's debt/GDP ratio is by contrast a modest 62 per cent and yet it intends to pump in a mere 0.3 per cent of GDP as stimulus.

Pump priming the economy by borrowing is not bad per se. It is not putting the debt to good use that is bad. Nations prosper when they use debt for worthwhile capital expenditure with assured returns and social cost benefits. But we in India have borrowed to give it away as subsidies and to hide the high cost of government. To give an analogy, if a family has to make a choice of borrowing money to fund children's education or to support the man's drinking habit, the rational choice is obvious. The children's education will have a long-term payback, while the booze gives instant gratification. But unfortunately, our governments have always made the wrong choices.

If borrowed money is used productively and creates growth and prosperity, it must be welcomed. We do not want to hear from the government about fiscal deficit targets, but about economic growth, value addition, employment and investment targets. Our governments have hopelessly been missing all these targets.

So what can Modi do now to get us out of this quagmire? If the regime abhors a stimulus financed by deficit financing there are other options that can be exercised. But he is hamstrung with a weak economic management team with novices as the two key players, the Finance Minister and the Reserve Bank of India (RBI) governor.

India has over US$538 billion nesting abroad earning ridiculously low interest. Even if a tenth of this is monetised for injection into the national economy, it will mean more than ₹3.5 trillion. At last count, the RBI had about ₹9.6 trillion as reserves. This is money to be used in a financial emergency. We are now in an emergency like we have never encountered before or foreseen. Even a third of this or about ₹3.2 trillion is about five times the present plan.

There are other sources of funds too, but tapping these will entail political courage and sacrifices. Our cumulative government wages and pension bills amount to about 11.4 per cent of GDP. After exempting the military and paramilitary, which is mostly under active deployment, we can target raising worth 1 per cent of GDP just by cancelling annual leave and leave travel concession (LTC), and rolling back a few dearness allowance (DA) increases.

The government can also sequester a fixed percentage from bank deposits, say 5 per cent of deposits between ₹1–₹10 million and 15–20 per cent from bigger deposits for tax-free interest-bearing bonds in exchange. The 10 big private companies alone have cash reserves of over ₹10 trillion.[14]

There is money in the trees, and all it needs is a good shake-up to pick the fruits. The pain of the lockdown must not be borne by the poor alone. The government can easily target raising 5 per cent of GDP or about ₹10 trillion for the recovery fund as an immediately achievable goal.

This money can be used to immediately begin the following: a Universal Basic Income scheme by transferring a sum of ₹5,000 per month into the Jan Dhan accounts for the duration of the financial emergency; fund GST concessions to move the auto and engineering sectors in particular; begin emergency rural reconstruction projects to generate millions of new jobs; and get our core infrastructure sectors such as steel, cement and transportation moving again.

Generating money to move India again is not a huge problem. What comes in between are the philosophical blinkers. Call it Chicago School of Economics or the Gujarati mindset.

# 7

# Revisiting India's Nuclear Doctrine

BHARAT KARNAD, EMERITUS PROFESSOR

The second decade of the 21st century has highlighted the importance of nuclear weapons for relatively weak states to fend off powerful adversaries. North Korea has shown how rhetorically matching the bluster of US President Donald J. Trump, and simultaneously testing nuclear weapons and test-firing missiles to show intent, compelled Washington to back down. Pakistan, a frequent nuclear sabre rattler, has likewise capped, even prevented, hostilities. It deterred India from retaliating after the terrorist attacks on the Parliament (13 December 1999) and in Mumbai (26 November 2008). And the 1998 Kargil conflict was only a longish, high-intensity, border skirmish that the Atal Bihari Vajpayee regime avoided escalating by barring Indian Air Force combat aircraft from violating Pakistani airspace.

The disruptive but peace-enforcing potential of nuclear weapons, their effect, in particular, of forcing a conventionally superior adversary to rethink its offensive plans is not, however, a lesson that India seems to have learned. Consequently, an expansionist China extended its claim line on the disputed border in May–June 2020, annexed Indian territory in Eastern

Ladakh and restricted India's approaches to the Karakorum Pass. This brazen land grab should have occasioned swift Indian military action to recover the lost territory but did not, owing, perhaps, to the Indian government's fear of sizeable Chinese forces in that sector. But restoration of the status quo ante that External Affairs Minister S. Jaishankar declared on 19 June 2020 to be India's goal is unlikely to be realised without a limited war backed by Indian threats of nuclear first use. After all, any armed conflict involving nuclear weapon states automatically brings nuclear weapons into play. This chapter will advocate India adopting a proactive nuclear strategy to keep China from exploiting its comprehensive military prowess. The international milieu, it turns out, is conducive to India taking this step.

The 1968 Non-Proliferation Treaty (NPT) regime is dead and proliferation will, hereafter, be less bridled with North Korea withdrawing from the treaty in 2003 and the USA—until recently the main prop of the global non-proliferation order—disavowing the Joint Comprehensive Plan of Action for Iran.[1] Further, the Trump administration has ditched the Intermediate Nuclear Forces Treaty in Europe and stalled the Strategic Arms Reduction Talks with Russia. The USA, Russia and China have all but renounced the Article VI obligations under the NPT with their ongoing nuclear force upsizing and modernisation programmes. Moreover, as if to motivate more countries to go nuclear, Trump weakened the North Atlantic Treaty Organization (NATO), complained about 'free riding' by traditional Asian allies and did not dilute the advice he offered them in 2016 as a presidential candidate that they should secure *their* own nukes.[2] But, strategically dense as ever, India has still to come to grips with the radical changes underfoot. A habitual free rider, it relied on the erstwhile Soviet Union during the Cold War for its ultimate security and in the new millennium is banking on dubious US security promises.[3]

In a fraught international landscape where big states are driven by strategic goals, India, other than showing a pumped up tactical-level resolve to take on a lowly Pakistan, does not seem inclined to address the more onerous threat from China. It suggests confusion or inability on the Indian government's part to sift the strategically significant from the tactically valuable and revealing, in the process, an alarming level of unfamiliarity about the multifarious uses that nuclear weapons can be put to. Thus, the country displays simpleton-ish nuclear instincts, stays stuck at the minimalist end of 'minimum deterrence' and swears by obsolete concepts such as 'massive retaliation'. This when minimum deterrence, in practice, necessitates a large force of nuclear missiles and other nuclear weapon delivery systems to guarantee even a 'modest' retaliatory capability because, as the pioneering nuclear strategist Bernard Brodie noted, deterrence is 'a relative thing' varying with the adversary's 'degree of motivation' and, in case of deterrence failure or breakdown, the capacity to wage 'total war effectively'.[4] Owing to its ample stock of fissile material India is in a position to speedily build up its inventory of nuclear bombs and nuclear-warheaded ballistic missiles of medium, intermediate and longer ranges, but lags behind even Pakistan in the size of its arsenal.[5]

## Pakistan Fixation

The Indian government by minimalising deterrence has reduced nuclear weapons to dissuading the lesser, fairly inconsequential foe, Pakistan, rather than gearing up strategically to take on the primary and sole threat India faces, namely China.[6] Delhi apparently finds it hard to handle the Pakistani tactics of alerting its nuclear forces, threatening first use, and alarming the United Nations (UN), the USA and the West into interceding on its behalf whenever it finds itself in a military crisis with India (1987 Brasstacks, 1999 Kargil).[7] Invariably, Delhi rises reflexively to Islamabad's bait and is induced into making similar noises, taking similar steps, thereby strengthening the Western perceptions of parity and justifying their hyphenated South Asia policies.[8] In reality, however, the professional Pakistan Army has proved that it takes risks (1947 Kashmir raiders, 1965 Operation Gibraltar, Kargil) but is pragmatic, not foolhardy, and regarding nuclear weapons is very careful. There are two reasons for this: the 'nuclear taboo' and a skewed 'exchange ratio'—the loss of two Indian cities for Pakistan ceasing to exist as a social organism.[9] It is Pakistan's version of Israel's mutual-suicide strategy—the 'Samson Option' from an earlier time—which Islamabad cannot reasonably implement even if it mustered the will to do so.[10]

India is constrained to fight wars with Pakistan that the late Major General D.K. Palit said resembled 'communal riots with tanks', involving short duration, geographically contained, counter-force engagements. The reasons are (a) partitioned Muslim communities retaining strong cross-border kith and kinship links, (b) shared language, culture, religion and social values organically tying the two countries in an albeit prickly embrace, (c) the swing vote in tightly contested elections wielded by Indian Muslims that no political party can disregard and, assuming Partition is reversed, (d) a likely twofold-plus increase in the Muslim population of India that will be a recipe for perennial civil conflict. Hence, a war of annihilation of Pakistan has always been deemed politically infeasible by the Indian leadership, making small, short duration wars of manoeuvre the norm since Partition.[11]

There is one situation, however, where India's restraint might disappear. Pakistan's first use of tactical weapons on its own territory against advancing Indian armoured units—the option the Pakistan Army's Strategic Plans Division, Chaklala, envisages—could result in the nuclear debris seeding clouds. Winds blowing west to east in the winter 'campaign season' will carry these clouds across the border where the ensuing rain would precipitate radioactivity on border villages, towns and cities. Even if inadvertent, it will be tantamount, as I have contended, to a nuclear strike on India because 70 per cent of deaths and casualties in any nuclear attack are caused by radioactivity. Pakistan's tactical first-use decision could thus become a prod for strategic-level, city-busting, Indian retaliation.[12]

## Nuclear First-Use Policy against China

China is India's only credible security threat, economic peer competitor and ideological rival in Asia. But bilateral relations are bedevilled by the unresolved territorial dispute periodically flared by the People's Liberation Army's (PLA's) attempts to make the Line of Actual Control (LAC) conform to its 'perceptions' of the disputed border and, by the by, flex its military muscle. Also, India, by not reacting to China's nuclear missile arming Pakistan by equipping states on the Chinese periphery in Southeast Asia with similar strategic armaments and imposing like costs on Beijing, has rewarded it with permanent geostrategic advantage.[13] The Indian government's adhering, moreover, to the nuclear no first use (NFU) principle is, in the circumstances, egregious even though it is a hollow and wholly impracticable idea.[14] It is, moreover, an operational liability because it will require India to absorb a nuclear hit before responding when the fact is that the Indian state cannot even deal with the first monsoon strike! Then, there's no knowing what will happen in the aftermath of a nuclear attack, what parts of the Indian command and control grid and decision-making system will survive, enabling what level of retaliatory strikes.[15] So sticking unconditionally to nuclear retaliation only policy is, on the face of it, an absurd strategy considering what India is facing.

The extraordinary pace the PLA has set to transform itself into a 21st-century military force nonpareil—with cutting-edge cyber warfare, artificial intelligence (AI) and quantum computing capabilities consolidated into a separate PLA 'Support Forces Command'—is a matter of wonder and worry.[16] Comparing the phenomenal rise of the Chinese military with the still placidly industrial-age Indian armed services is, at one level, to acknowledge the futility of playing catch-up. So how can India neutralise China? The answer is: borrow from the early Chinese playbook.

In the 1950s, a rifle and rice bowl–equipped PLA faced the first world American armed forces in Korea, fought them to a standstill and refused to be intimidated by nuclear threats held out by US President Dwight D. Eisenhower. Later, it faced down the US Secretary of State John Foster Dulles in the 1958 Quemoy–Matsu crisis, who talked of using the Bomb, which Maozedong dismissed as a 'paper tiger'. His regime, however, fast-tracked with Soviet help programmes for thermonuclear weapons and long range delivery systems.[17] Having speedily secured the megaton hydrogen bomb in 1967, just three years after exploding a fission device, China used its nuclear clout thereafter to ward off the US and Russian conventional military pressure, and as cover for its policies to extend its global influence in the developing world. A not dissimilar strategy was used by the United Kingdom and France against the Soviet Union in the Cold War.[18] Not surprisingly, an outgunned Pakistan and North Korea, borrowing from the experience of their Chinese patron, are wedded to first-use precepts to thwart India and South Korea, USA and Japan respectively. It is a successful strategy for weak nuclear weapon states to keep militarily stronger countries at bay, and it is time India too followed it. Diplomacy, as India's recent sad and futile experience of negotiating a peaceful Chinese withdrawal from Indian Ladakh shows, is not a viable alternative.[19]

### *A War Scenario with China*

A nuclear first-use strategy recommends itself because India cannot in the next 50-odd years, at least realistically, hope to close the economic and conventional military gap with China, especially if cyber, AI, robotics and quantum computing domains are tacked on. It is a mismatch too glaring to gloss over.[20] In this context, consider a scenario. Per China's 'comprehensive war strategy', PLA initiates a war by pre-emptively shutting down forward area Indian battlefield communications and various land- and space-based sensors, throwing the Indian Army and Air Force into disarray. It would then not matter very much whether or not the troop numbers or deployed hardware match up locally and in-theatre, considering the outcome would be predetermined.[21] Assume further that a local affray were escalated by the PLA to major action to teach India 'a lesson'; how exactly would the Indian military react to a wide-area onslaught on multiple axes using its superiority in the cyber, AI and quantum computing realms?[22] Suppose further that the PLA combines its vast and variegated capabilities, for which India has no meaningful counters, with 'strategic surprise'—the Chinese military's forte. Won't the game pretty much be over before it has begun?[23]

India readily provides Beijing with both the incentive and the opportunity for such a denouement.[24] The incentive is in the form of plainly inadequate Indian land and air forces minus the kind of extensive border infrastructure and secure communications set-up, and easy access to the LAC from their staging areas on the Tibetan Plateau available to the PLA; and the opportunity is in terms of showing up India as a terminally timid, 'creeper vine' of a country seeking US support to rise, and one, moreover, that is 'all talk and no show' and cannot protect itself leave alone be a credible 'security provider' to smaller states in its vicinity.[25] An India without the stomach for a fight and with military services dependent on imported armaments and, therefore, unable to fight long-duration wars is an attractive target for China to diminish in the eyes of the former's potential strategic partners in the Indian Ocean, Southeast Asia and even the USA, France, Australia and Japan. In this context, a short war to show up India as militarily infirm may appear to Beijing to be worth risking.[26] Who is to say China's annexationist initiatives in 2020 in Ladakh were not intended to test resolve—a test India failed—and are not a prelude to more sustained hostilities in the future?

The issue is this: How to utilise the Indian nuclear wherewithal and weapons it can quickly put together—such as the relatively easy to configure atomic demolition munitions (ADMs)—to prevent China from believing it can easily muscle India into submission? As first steps in this direction, India needs to jettison the NFU and accelerate the canisterisaton of all Agni missiles, in particular the 700 km nuclear Agni-1 and for the Strategic Forces Command (SFC) to plan and prepare expressly for nuclear warfighting. It is the only way to convince China that India means business. If the Chinese Second Artillery Strategic Forces Command (SASFC) sees the SFC making such preparations, conducting nuclear wargames involving ADMs and tactical use Agni-1s, and espies high levels of readiness of the Indian strategic and air forces, the message will hit home.[27] China will become more wary and cautious about offering conventional military provocations. These measures, however, run smack into the dogma Indian security managers have been weighed down by since the 1998 Shakti tests about nuclear weapons being exclusively for 'deterrence', not 'warfighting'. It is a position that ensures India is able to neither deter nor fight a nuclear war.[28] Hence, a warfighting mindset and an appropriately sized and equipped force is essential for the nuclear first-use solution to work against China.

*The Failsafe Line, Nuclear Tripwires*

Strategic Forces Command activity has to become more visibly China-centric. For a start the government, in consultation with SFC, has to draw a secret failsafe line on the map as the nuclear tripwire for the Indian armed services, and to let Beijing know that there is this red line. As Henry Kissinger repeatedly advised, communicating clearly to the enemy one's intention to use nuclear weapons if he crosses a certain line is central to making deterrence effective.[29] This will have to be done in lockstep with stockpiling dozens of 1–3 kiloton yield ADMs for placement in undisclosed locations on the failsafe line in mountain passes in the central and eastern sectors of the LAC. The ADMs will afford India the ability to bring down mountainsides on PLA group armies after they have swept past this line in strength. The collapsing mountains will bury the second bulk echelon of the aggressor force and the resulting radioactivity—heaps of soil/earth being the most effective absorbent of gamma rays.[30] The large PLA force trapped on the Indian side can then be destroyed in detail, or taken prisoners of war. The ADMs manifest the nuclear first-use principle in a revised nuclear doctrine that should not be made public, as the original one unwisely was. It will maximise ambiguity and uncertainty in the minds of the Chinese Central Military Commission (CMC) and the SASFC, and positively affect PLA's behaviour. It also helps politically that ADMs are environment friendly and match the Indian government's traditionally passive defensive-reactive mindset.

The ADMs, however, will have to be meshed with the pre-emptive and retaliatory capabilities, requiring specifically the air vectors to be aligned to the single most valuable Chinese target within the reach of manned aircraft—the Three Gorges Dam. Pilots in SFC-designated Mirage 2000/Su-30MKI/Rafale squadrons for nuclear strike missions will have to be intensively trained in terrains and weather conditions similar to those found around this gigantic 1.4 km long, 607 feet high dam on the Yangtze River. The dam annually produces 84.7 billion kilowatts of electricity, which if nuclear bombed, will devastate the Chinese industrial and agricultural economy by flooding the land down to Nanjing.[31] Should China escalate to a fuller exchange, the other premier targets would be the nuclear weapons complex at Lop Nor in northwest Xinjiang and, besides Beijing, the extended Shanghai metropolitan area on the eastern seaboard—the country's economic and wealth-producing core. The Shanghai region, responsible for 3.5 per cent (or US$487 billion) of China's US$14.2 trillion 2019 GDP, is central to its export trade.[32]

All strategic-missioned strike assets are controlled by the SFC but, in time of war, conventional strikes by Indian Air Force aircraft may be used for shots 'across the bow'. Precursors to conventional strikes on secondary targets around the Three Gorges Dam, such as the Gezhouba Dam and the railway bridge over the Zhi River would, post-ADM use, constitute warnings to Beijing that the main Three Gorges Dam is in Indian crosshairs and to cease and desist from escalating the conflict. The K-4/K-5 submarine launched ballistic missiles (SLBMs) of 3,000 km–5,000 km range and the intercontinental range K-6 SLBM once it is ready for deployment—launched from Arihant-class submersible ballistic, nuclear SSBN submarines, and the Agni-5 intermediate range ballistic missiles (IRBMs) capable of taking out Beijing and totalling the Lop Nor complex and the extended Shanghai coastal belt—can be held in reserve for contingent use. While Agni-1 medium-range ballistic missiles (MRBMs) can be assigned to the dam, possible nuclear attacks by aircraft will inject flexibility into India's response calculi in the early stages of a nuclear engagement and for strategic messaging. Facing an imminent attack, the Chinese authorities can rapidly empty the vast catchment area of the Three Gorges Dam. Except, their doing so at the first hint of an incoming aerial or missile strike will have the same horrendous effect as actually bombing the dam—downstream inundation and economic ruin. Because of its consequences, merely hinting at an imminent strike may get Beijing to back down.[33] Should matters nevertheless spiral out of control, Agni-5 IRBMs can target the Lop Nor nuclear weapons complex and the Shanghai metropolitan area, underlining India's goal to cripple China economically and to equalise the exchange ratio somewhat, no effort or resources spared. The SLBMs could be set aside for a final set of disembowelling strikes.

In the escalation ladder, the use of conventional bombs–laden fighter bomber aircraft are on the lowest rung, the ADMs and Agni-1 MRBMs for tactical use would be on the second higher rung, manned platforms conveying nuclear bombs on the third rung, nuclear warheaded cruise missiles for precision strikes will be on one higher rung, with Agni-3/Agni-4/Agni-5 IRBMs, and K-4/K-5 SLBMs at the highest rung in an all-out war.

ADMs as tripwire are, however, better suited for use in the mountain passes in the central and eastern sectors of the LAC. The high-altitude desert in the northern and north-western sectors in Ladakh, as also the northern Sikkim plains in the east, pose a different problem. The Ladakh terrain, for example, has wide plains separated by mountain ranges, like in the Depsang area, that merge with the Tibetan Plateau. This landscape permits large land forces to traverse it. This is where the canisterised part of the Agni force, because of its launch-on-warning

(LOW) and launch-on-launch (LOL) attributes, is usable and will constitute the proverbial 'joker in the pack' with elastic end-use possibilities to keep the Chinese CMC and SASFC guessing. Moreover, as ready-to-fire mobile weapons positioned behind the LAC, they would be the right weapons to retaliate with if the SASFC fires any of its short-and medium-range missiles concentrated in Tibet, which will trip the nuclear wire. Why? Because in the absence of technology to distinguish conventional and nuclear warheads, any missile(s) launched from Tibet in southerly or westerly direction will have to be assumed to be nuclear, and the canisterised Agni batteries on LOL and LOW readiness states will be activated. Of greater significance is the fact that these forward-deployed Agni-1s will provide strategic cover to the Indian Army for actions it might undertake against the PLA to recover territory, remove blockades (such as at the Y-junction in the Depsang Plains) and otherwise to take the fight to the Chinese. These missiles will, in essence, restore to the army its freedom to mount conventional operations at will. The canisterised Agni-1 batteries will, however, need to be singly and safely stored for instant use in small, secure, mountain tunnel complexes (that will need to be built).[34] It is imperative that Beijing be made aware of the ADMs on the failsafe line in the north and the north-east, the canisterised Agni-1s in Ladakh and the precursor Chinese PLA actions that would trigger them.

The former National Security Advisor, Shivshankar Menon, has wondered why India's threat of nuclear first use would be credible to China, but Pakistan's first-use policy against India is discountable.[35] Unlike Pakistan, with whom India shares much, China is the unknown, inscrutable other with little in common, and generates hostile feelings laced with the ineradicable memories of military humiliation in 1962. Familiarity may breed mutual contempt where India and Pakistan are concerned, but the organic links between the two societies are natural inhibitors of the use of weapons of mass destruction whence, as already noted, India engages Pakistan in mainly counter-force actions with extremely limited objectives. No such factor intervenes as regards China. Shared culture and ethnicity, or their absence, matter in wartime decisions. It explains why, for instance, US President Franklin D. Roosevelt interned Japanese-Americans in camps during World War II but spared Americans of German origin similar treatment, and why his successor, Harry Truman, dropped atom bombs on Japan, not Germany.[36] In any case, as territorially large countries, exchange ratios will impact India and China only in a full-blown nuclear conflagration.

What will make the Indian threat of nuclear first use universally acceptable is that it will be strictly in response to Chinese actions crossing well-publicised red lines. This threat will be credible precisely because of the potential for the nuclear situation to get out of hand, resulting in the definite destruction of prized Chinese economic and military assets, gutting China's efforts to attain super power status, and imperilling 'President for life' Xi Jinping's reign and the Tianxia system of world order he hopes to realise.[37] In contrast, India has less to lose. It is still a poor, maladministered country with an inefficient and corrupt apparatus of government and an underperforming and over-regulated economy that, while failing to generate growth rates to put India on the map, denies China nuclear targeting leverage of the kind India has vis-à-vis the Three Gorges Dam and the core Shanghai region. Ironically, the more the gap with China widens the greater will be India's leverage.

## Conclusion

A passive, minimum deterrence strategy based on nuclear NFU has opened up India to Chinese bullying and expropriation of its territory, and reinforced its image as a timid, soft-headed state. For a traditionally risk-averse India to ignore the ways in which even its limited nuclear means can stop China in its tracks, and to wilfully disregard the compounded utility of nuclear weapons to permanently discomfit, dissuade and deter China, is to ill-serve the national interest. The nuclear means include operationalising the first-use concept, transferring strategic ballistic and cruise missiles to Southeast Asian states (as payback for Beijing's policy of nuclear missile arming Pakistan), and realigning the SFC and Indian nuclear strategy mainly against China. The strategy should involve ADMs deployed at secret and changeable sites on the failsafe line in mountain passes behind the LAC in the central and eastern Himalayas to defeat possible conventional military thrusts by the PLA, and canisterised Agni missiles, occasionally in mobile mode, employed as tripwire in Ladakh. Between the ADMs and the Agni-1s, the Indian armed forces will enjoy the nuclear overhang under which to safely undertake decisive actions to vacate any Chinese aggression.

India's adopting a proactive nuclear stance will preclude China's becoming militarily assertive on the 4,056 km long disputed border, and may even incentivise Beijing to quickly agree on a formal boundary. The Indian government and the armed services, alas, lack the great power vision, an understanding of the many politico-military uses of nuclear weapons, the requisite strategic nerve and imagination, and, principally, the iron political will to implement such nuclear first-use strategy.

# 8

# India–Pakistan: The Way Forward

AMBASSADOR SHARAT SABHARWAL

A clichéd argument flung at me by my Pakistani interlocutors during my stints as Deputy High Commissioner and High Commissioner of India was that India could not realise its ambition to be a great power without resolving the Kashmir issue and building peace with Pakistan. It was evidently the fall back posture of the weaker country, which, after having failed to realise its unrealistic aspiration to be the equal of India and militarily impose its will on India, was content to be a drag on India's march toward its due place in the comity of nations. My answer was that Pakistan's relentless hostility over the years had failed to halt India's progress. I also counselled them to focus on moving Pakistan up rather than pulling India down.

Pakistan obviously does not have a veto over India's rise as a great power, but is certainly a distraction from single-minded pursuit of that goal. We have had to expend considerable resources and diplomatic capital to thwart Pakistan's designs against us and enlist the support of international partners to that end. Other countries have exploited the India–Pakistan rivalry to promote their own interests in the region.

Repeated attempts by India to normalise relations with Pakistan and build ties of mutually beneficial cooperation have been rebuffed with aggression and, in more recent years, cross-border terrorism. We have tried to promote people-to-people bonhomie drawing upon the shared heritage of the two countries, taken recourse to military means, when forced to do so by Pakistani aggression, reposed faith in dialogue to resolve mutual differences and address Pakistan's concerns and offered lucrative linkages with our larger economy. However, all these have failed to put an end to Pakistan's animosity.

It is clearly in our interest to persuade or compel Pakistan to give up its relentless hostility against us and, failing that, to contain its potential to harm and distract us.

## Normalising Relations with an Abnormal State

India's fraught relationship with Pakistan is the result of the aberrant nature of the Pakistani state and therefore, cannot be normalised unless Pakistan becomes a normal state.

Carved artificially out of India on the basis of the two-nation theory, Pakistan faced an identity problem, more so because a large number of Muslims chose to stay on in India. The Pakistani leadership resolved it by giving a negative identity to the newly created state—defining it as Pakistan because it was not India.

The creation of Bangladesh delivered a fatal blow to the two-nation theory, accentuating the identity problem and continued reliance on negative identity.

The negative identity necessitated an adversarial posture toward India. Two natural consequences of this stance toward a much bigger and potentially much more powerful neighbour were a sense of paranoia and Pakistan coming to regard itself as a security state, where the defence of borders against the 'external adversary' would get primacy over all other elements of national security. This, in turn, led to the Pakistan Army projecting itself as the guardian of Pakistan's physical and ideological frontiers and acquiring a prime position in the polity. It has ruled the country directly for around 33 years, and even when it has not been in charge directly, it has continued to exercise considerable influence over governance, particularly in the areas of defence and foreign affairs.

Pakistan is not a monolith in terms of its attitude toward India. Its hostility has been driven essentially by the institutional interest of the army to sustain the 'India bogey' for justifying its pre-eminent position in the Pakistani polity and its stranglehold over the state. Despite claims to the contrary by apologists of the Pakistan Army, it has shown no sign of revising its world view. Its posture toward India is supported by its terror proxies and political protégés. However, a large body of opinion in Pakistan favours a stable relationship with India. It includes political leaders capable of winning power through electoral politics, who regard improved relations with India as a way of undermining the army's salience (this, more than his business interests, has been the reason for Nawaz Sharif's advocacy of better relations with India), and large sections of business and industry lured by economic opportunities in India. The focus of people at large, like people everywhere else, is on bread and butter issues. It is only periods of heightened tension, such as the ongoing phase, that see consolidation of support for the perspective of the army, seen as the saviour.

Each time the Pakistan Army has suffered a setback, most notably after Pakistan was cut in half in 1971, it has managed to bounce back in ever-ingenious ways. The last such phase followed Musharraf's ouster from power, when the army found itself discredited after nine years of direct rule and its reputation suffered further because of rampant terror, including an attack on the General Headquarters in Rawalpindi, perpetrated by its own proxies turned rogue. Transition of power through elections from one civilian government to another in 2013 brought hope of democratic consolidation. However, the army systematically undermined the third-time Prime Minister, Nawaz Sharif, eventually getting rid of him in July 2017 through a selective accountability process and pliant judiciary. It tilted the field significantly against Nawaz's party, Pakistan Muslim League (Nawaz) or PML(N), in the 2018 election to ensure the victory of Pakistan Tehreek-e-Insaf (PTI). Imran Khan has so far complied with its wishes. However, should he ever try to break loose from its influence, he would see the army promoting another collaborator to take his place.

The experience of the last few years confirms yet again that Pakistan's internal dynamics, notably dominance of the army and the resulting dysfunctionality of the state, are not about to change anytime soon. Consequently, our policies cannot be premised on Pakistan becoming a normal state and putting an end to its hostility in the foreseeable future.

## Engaging with the Army?

Dealing with Pakistan has constantly thrown up the question, 'Who do we deal with?' Frustration with repeated spiking of our peace moves with civilian governments by the army has led to the suggestion in our strategic discourse to engage with the army, 'the real power centre'. However, it needs to be seen in the context of the absence of any change in the army's outlook toward India. Unable to challenge us militarily, it aims to retain the capacity of using terror while denying us the possibility of employing our superior conventional military power to inflict intolerable damage on it. It has, therefore, been expanding Pakistan's nuclear arsenal at a feverish pitch and has threatened use of tactical nuclear weapons and lowering of the nuclear threshold. Reduction of terror activity against us, whenever it has taken place, has been a tactical move to turn down the terror tap, while leaving the terror fuel intact. What I heard from my military interlocutors during my tenure as High Commissioner (2009–2013)—a time when Pakistan was traumatised by widespread terror, had a raging insurgency in Baluchistan, highly volatile conditions on its western border and, above all, a bumpy relationship with the USA—was that while the army leadership saw the need to mend the relationship, the army as an institution would be slow to change. Hardly reassuring, to say the least.

In view of the foregoing, while it would be useful to maintain such contacts with the Pakistan Army as are possible in the interest of managing the relationship and reducing levels of violence, it would be unrealistic to expect such contacts to change the fundamentals of the relationship in the absence of a change in the army's world view.

## Jammu and Kashmir and Other 'Outstanding Issues'

Pakistan does not care for Kashmiris, and for a long time has had no hope of making any territorial gains against us. Differences over Kashmir that arose immediately after the Partition have, over the years, become an instrument in the hands of the Pakistan Army to keep alive the 'India bogey' and bleed India by keeping the valley on the boil.

Pakistan's dubious case on Kashmir no longer garners much international sympathy and even within Pakistan does not resonate with the people as it used to in the past. This is what Rustam Shah Mohmand, former Chief Secretary of the erstwhile North Western Frontier Province (NWFP) and former Ambassador of Pakistan to Afghanistan had to say on the subject:

> ...there have been no studies or surveys to show whether the people of Pakistan have any deep attachment to the cause of Kashmiris and whether

> the dispute has any resonance for the broad majority of the country. What is not realized or is overlooked is that amidst the teeming millions of Pakistan, in Sindh, rural Punjab, Khyber-Pakhtunkhwa and Balochistan, there is no urgent wish to see Kashmir become integrated with Pakistan. The people in all regions of Pakistan are more fixated on issues like poverty, education, jobs, health care, electricity, police excesses, water supply, irrigation, roads, sanitation, corruption in government departments and social injustice. Never in the last many decades have people—the rank and file Pakistanis—ever agitated over the issue of denial of rights to Kashmiris.[1]

All attempts, so far, to resolve the Kashmir issue have failed. Changing the territorial status quo would involve a devastating war involving China, which is now deeply invested in the so-called 'Gilgit-Baltistan' because of its strategic investment in the China–Pakistan Economic Corridor (CPEC). At least twice in the last 50 years, a solution involving freezing of the territorial status quo has been attempted. In his book *Indira Gandhi, the 'Emergency' and Indian Democracy*, Mrs Gandhi's senior aide P.N. Dhar, who was present at the discussions leading to the Simla Agreement in 1972, speaks of an understanding between Indira Gandhi and Zulfiqar Ali Bhutto that the Line of Control (LoC) resulting from the agreement would be gradually endowed with the 'characteristics of an international border'.[2] Bhutto, as we know, did not honour the understanding. Serious discussions on Jammu and Kashmir (J&K) also took place in 2004–2007 in back-channel dialogue. In a statement[3] made in his personal capacity at a seminar at the University of Kashmir on 13 May 2014, S.K. Lambah, the then Special Envoy of the Prime Minister and our interlocutor in the back channel, made, inter alia, the following suggestions of a possible outline of a solution:

- Any agreement must ensure that the LoC is like a border between any two normal states.
- It is imperative that people of J&K on either side of the LoC should be able to move freely from one side to the other.
- There is meaningful trade in specified locally produced goods between the two sides of the LoC.
- There has to be an end to hostility, violence and terrorism.
- Once this happens, it would be important that military forces on both sides of the LoC are kept to the minimum, particularly in populated areas.
- It would be important to ensure self-governance for internal management in all areas on the same basis on both sides of the LoC.
- Cooperative, consultative mechanisms between the two parts of J&K should be put into place to look into socio-economic issues such as tourism, travel, pilgrimage to shrines, trade, health, education and culture.

This is the closest that we can get to the elements that may have formed part of the understandings arrived at in the back channel. The progress made in the back channel during the Musharraf era could not be carried forward, primarily because the Pakistan People's Party (PPP) government (2008–2013) neither had the political capital nor the backing of the army under Ashfaq Parvez Kayani, Musharraf's successor as the army chief, to take the process forward.

Given the civil–military dynamics in Pakistan and the unchanged outlook of the army, it would be an uphill task for any civilian government to accept a solution involving conversion of the LoC into an international border or de facto acceptance of that situation. On our side too, going against the political consensus—contained in the resolution[4] passed unanimously by our Parliament on 22 February 1994 that 'The State of Jammu and Kashmir has been, is and shall be an integral part of India…' and that 'Pakistan must vacate the areas of the Indian State of Jammu and Kashmir, which they have occupied through aggression'—would not be easy. This is more so today when Pakistan's obduracy and terror over the years have hardened the public sentiment in India. Moreover, withdrawal of the special status of J&K and its split into two union territories has changed the paradigm on Kashmir, which would rule out some of the above-mentioned suggestions, particularly the one concerning 'self-governance for internal management'. In sum, no solution to the Kashmir issue is possible without a pragmatic and forward-looking approach on both sides, more so on the part of Pakistan.

Amongst the other key issues included in the 'composite dialogue' held in the past, adoption of confidence-building measures plateaued over a decade ago because of Pakistan's insistence on proposals seeking to tie us down to bilateral arrangements while ignoring our larger security environment. Finding a solution to Siachen has become increasingly complex because of Pakistan's perfidy in Kargil, the vast trust deficit, China's heightened interest in the so-called 'Gilgit-Baltistan' and the recent Chinese incursions in Eastern Ladakh.

## Can Pakistan Be Coerced into Changing Its Behaviour?

If Pakistan is not amenable to reason and persuasion to change its adversarial posture toward India and give up its terror card, can it be coerced into doing so? Our strategic discourse over the years has thrown up some ideas.

During phases of heightened tension, use of water as an instrument to punish Pakistan has topped the wish list of our strategic community. Suggestions range from reducing water flows to Pakistan to withdrawal from the Indus Waters Treaty. The treaty does not have a sunset clause and can be abrogated only by concluding another treaty for the purpose. Examination of legal implications of a unilateral withdrawal by India is beyond the scope of this essay. As for the practical aspect, a significant reduction of flows to Pakistan would necessitate development of infrastructure through difficult terrain in J&K to divert water from the Indus, Jhelum and Chenab (rivers allotted to Pakistan under the treaty) for our use in the plains. Let alone development of such infrastructure, we have not been exploiting fully our share of water of these rivers under the treaty. Further, because of lack of infrastructure, a part of our water from Sutlej, Beas and Ravi—allotted entirely to us—has also continued to flow to Pakistan over the years. Following the Uri attack in 2016, the government of India expressed the intent to build the necessary infrastructure to fully exploit our share of water and reiterated it after the Pulwama attack in 2019. This work should be completed expeditiously. Stoppage of our share that has been flowing to Pakistan would cause some hurt to them.

India withdrew the most favoured nation (MFN) status granted to Pakistan in 1996 (which had remained unreciprocated) in the wake of the Pulwama attack and increased tariff on imports from Pakistan by 200 per cent. The legal trade between India and Pakistan had hovered in the range of US$2.5 billion per annum—Indian exports in the range of US$2 billion and Pakistan exports ranging from US$300 to US$400 million, which is less than 2 per cent of their average annual exports. Therefore, while the move may have hurt some individual Pakistani exporters, it does not have the potential to change the calculus of their security establishment. It would have also pushed up cost of imported items for Indian consumers. Pakistan suspended bilateral trade in August 2019 following withdrawal of special status of J&K. The decision, while hurting Indian exporters, would hurt Pakistan's economy more by depriving it of cheaper imports from India. The short-sightedness of the Pak move was evident within a month, when it allowed import of life-saving drugs from India despite the trade ban.

## Use of Military Means to Deter/Coerce Pakistan

India has never aggressed against Pakistan, but responded robustly to each Pakistani aggression, giving it a solid blow in 1971 when it lost its eastern wing. Having failed to realise its fanciful ambition of imposing its will militarily on India, Pakistan changed track, resorting to cross-border terrorism in a strategy to bleed India. Barbaric terror acts perpetrated by Pakistan in Kashmir, and elsewhere in India, are etched deep on the psyche of the Indian public. For a long time, India exercised strategic restraint, depending essentially on counterterror measures and mobilising international opinion. However, cross-LoC raids by Indian forces in response to Pak acts of terror were not unknown, though these seem to have remained confined to a single target at a time and were not publicised. In September 2016, India carried out 'surgical strikes' at terror launch pads along the LoC within days of an attack by the Pak-based Jaish-e-Mohammed (JeM) at Uri, resulting in 19 Indian Army personnel losing their lives. The Indian Director General of Military Operations (DGMO) stated that the strikes were meant to prevent the terrorists amassed at the pads from endangering the lives of Indian citizens, and significant casualties were caused. However, punitive element of the action in response to the Uri attack was evident. Unlike the earlier single-target strikes, the above-mentioned strikes were across a broader front (the DGMO spoke of action against 'several' launch pads) and were made public. Pakistan rejected the Indian claim, though acknowledging some casualties in 'cross border fire initiated and conducted by India…'[5] and ramped up terror in the ensuing weeks. The Pulwama terror attack of February 2019 was followed by the Balakot strike involving use of air power to hit a terror target in Pakistan, which represented a notable shift in India's approach. However, Pakistan's retaliation the following day raised the possibility of an escalation with an uncertain trajectory and outcome. In a classic Indo-Pak script, other influential countries got involved and the situation de-escalated.

Both the 'surgical strikes' and the Balakot strike were necessary and fully justified in the face of Pakistan's brazen use of terror, would have caused some uncertainty in the minds of Pakistan's terror planners and raised the cost of their 'low-cost option' by making them adapt and possibly pull back their terror-training facilities deeper inside their territory. The Balakot strike also put an end to our self-imposed restraint of not using air power for punitive action against Pak terror. However, these strikes by themselves were not enough to coerce Pakistan into abandoning its terror card. The impact of our tactical punitive actions in the past has been temporary till Pakistan recovered, adapted and went back to its bad ways.

Putting an end to Pakistani terror militarily would require an all-out war to give it a decisive blow, which would entail a heavy human and economic cost, totally disproportionate to the threat posed by it. Pakistan lags behind us in all walks of life. Its economy is one-ninth ours and the gap continues to grow. Its terror has not halted our progress. It cannot pose an existential threat to us by itself and is at best a terror irritant that has managed to perpetrate large scale terror attacks occasionally. Such events, though highly tragic, should not make us oblivious to our larger challenges of economic transformation and dealing with an increasingly assertive China. Further, the nuclear dimension of a large-scale war cannot be ignored. At the time of Operation Parakram, in February 2002, Lieutenant General Khalid Kidwai, the then head of Pakistan's Strategic Plans Division, outlined the following scenarios that would lead to the use of nuclear weapons by Pakistan:

India

- conquering a large part of Pakistan's territory (including Pakistan occupied Kashmir [PoK]);
- destroying a large part of Pakistan's armed forces;
- pushing Pakistan into political destabilisation; and
- strangling Pakistan economically.[6]

Pakistan has also overplayed India's so-called cold start doctrine to justify the development of tactical/battlefield nuclear weapons and short-range NASR/Hatf IX missiles to deliver them to their targets.

Pakistani nuclear rhetoric apart, post Kargil, no serious Pakistani strategist has proceeded on the assumption that its nuclear capability had put an end to exercise of all military options by India. Pakistan regards its nuclear weapons as a shield against an all-out war by India to give it a decisive blow. There is clearly a good deal of bluff in the red lines mentioned here. 'Large part of Pakistan's territory and armed forces' is a vague expression subject to different interpretations. However, the red lines lie at the higher end of escalation. None of our military actions post-1998, including the Balakot strike, has come close to any of the red lines. Our strategic and military experts have been looking for ways to circumvent Pakistan's nuclear capability and will continue to do so. However, the bitter truth is that while the nuclear dimension may not have ruled out completely the use of conventional military power by us to inflict pain on Pakistan, it has severely constrained our ability to coerce Pakistan into changing its behaviour through military means.

## No Silver Bullet to End Terror

In fact, there is no silver bullet to put an end to Pakistan's terror. It requires action on a broader front. Continuous strengthening of our counterterror capabilities and punitive action, when necessary, have to be combined with continuing efforts to turn greater heat on Pakistan in collaboration with other countries. Thus, Pakistan's inclusion in the grey list of the Financial Action Task Force (FATF) since 2018 has forced it to rein in its terror machine, even if as a tactical move. India has worked closely with other members of the FATF. President Trump's decision at the beginning of 2018 to exert pressure on Pakistan to cooperate in the context of Afghanistan may have moved things in the right direction from our point of view; though the Americans, having reached an agreement with the Taliban to exit Afghanistan with Pakistan's help and needing Pakistan for its implementation, and the interests of some other countries, may prevent Pakistan's shift to the blacklist. Pakistan has reluctantly taken some steps as per recommendations of the FATF, including conviction on terror-financing charges and imprisonment of its terror poster boy Hafiz Saeed. However, since the very state that has been using terror as an instrument of state policy is being called upon to put an end to it, the actions taken by Pakistan so far cannot be relied upon and are reversible, once pressure is off. The noted Pakistani scholar Ayesha Siddiqa opines that the prosecution deliberately secured Hafiz Saeed's conviction on weak grounds to provide him relief later on (during the appeals process). She also notes the Imran Khan government's claim that it does not know the whereabouts of Masood Azhar and states that the likelihood of the Pakistani military in eliminating its terror assets in the short to medium term is minimal.[7] Therefore, we will have to continue our efforts to build international pressure on Pakistan.

## Isolating Pakistan Internationally

Let's be clear that building international pressure to the extent possible is not the same as isolating Pakistan. Other countries know fully well Pakistan's deep links with terror, but act according to their own interests.

The *US* relationship with Pakistan, which was always transactional, has become even more so in recent years. From making it an ally during the Cold War to using it during the Afghan jihad against the former Soviet Union, the 2001 military operation against the Taliban regime in Afghanistan and now to exit from Afghanistan, the Americans do not seem to run out of reasons to court Pakistan. With the advantage of hindsight, President Trump's famous tweet[8] of 1 January 2018 blaming Pakistan for indulging in lies and deceit while taking billions of dollars in aid was more a pressure tactic to enlist its support in talks with the Taliban than a signal to abandon and punish it. The Americans have publicly acknowledged Pakistan's assistance during the negotiations leading to their agreement with the Taliban. The need for Pakistan's help during implementation of the agreement is likely to sustain the current bonhomie between the two sides. Transactional nature of the relationship notwithstanding, the Americans are clearly not about to abandon Pakistan.

It is Pakistan's close and deepening nexus with *China* that should be of greater concern to us. Rooted in their shared animosity against India, the China–Pakistan relationship has deepened and diversified over the years. According to a SIPRI report released in 2018, China accounted for 70 per cent of the total arms imports of Pakistan—its share jumping from 45 per cent in 2008–2012 to 70 per cent in 2013–2017.[9] The Chinese supplies cover all the three arms of Pakistan's armed forces. Pakistan had acquired nuclear capability much before its tests in May 1998, assisted by technological exchanges with China, including the supply of the design of a weapon tested by China in the 1960s. China has overstretched the 'grandfather clause' of the Nuclear Suppliers Group (NSG), which it joined in 2004, to continue providing nuclear power reactors to Pakistan by invoking a

1986 agreement on cooperation in construction and operation of nuclear reactors, which puts no limit on the number of such reactors to be set up by China. Pakistan, therefore, continues to get from China the nuclear technology and material for which we had to get a special dispensation from the NSG and the International Atomic Energy Agency (IAEA). Pakistan's missile programme has benefited from outright supply of M-11 and M-9 Chinese missiles in the 1990s and assistance in development of other delivery systems. Interoperability between the armed forces of the two countries is growing.

Traditionally reluctant to underwrite Pakistan's profligacy by giving outright grants or loans to tide over balance of payment crises, China has of late played that role by providing funds in 2017–2018 to shore up Pakistan's foreign exchange reserves.

China is more deeply invested in Pakistan than ever before with the CPEC. Described as an economic corridor, the considerations underlying it are largely strategic, with the corridor serving as one of the routes for China to bypass the maritime choke points in the east. The Gwadar port could also eventually serve as a strategically located naval facility for the Chinese. Notwithstanding the widespread criticism of the CPEC investment within and outside Pakistan, notably because of its potential to lead Pakistan into a debt trap, Pakistan is not in a position to resist the Chinese designs—reminiscent of its serving the interests of its earlier mentor, the USA, by, inter alia, collaborating in the Afghan jihad, often at the cost of the long-term interests of its people.

Since Pakistan can pose a serious threat to us only in conjunction with China, the primary threat for us to deal with is clearly from China. This fact has been brought home tellingly by China's aggressive moves in Eastern Ladakh. Keen to ensure the safety of its strategic investment in the CPEC, which passes through territory claimed by India, China should be in favour of an Indo–Pak settlement in J&K along the existing ground reality. However, with the fissures in its own relationship with India widening as a result of its recent aggressive behaviour, China may be tempted to encourage Pakistan's ambitions vis-à-vis India, making a rapprochement, even if one were possible despite Pakistan's internal dynamics, that much more difficult.

## Pakistan's Vulnerabilities

While brazenly seeking to exploit vulnerabilities of other countries to perpetrate terror for advancing its agenda, Pakistan has been ignoring its own vulnerabilities. Besides the religious and sectarian fault lines fomented by the short-sighted policies of the state over the years, Pakistan continues to face a high degree of disaffection in Baluchistan and its Pakhtun belt. Baluchistan has witnessed five insurgencies since 1948, all suppressed by the army by unleashing a reign of terror. However, since it remains extremely poor and grossly exploited, and because of dependence of the state exclusively on force to control the situation, Baluchistan will continue to simmer. The Pakhtun fault line, which surfaced immediately after the creation of Pakistan when Afghanistan opposed Pakistan's admission to the United Nations in 1947—because of its opposition to the Durand Line and the demand for the Pakistani Pakhtuns to be given the right to self-determination—is far more serious than the Baluch problem. Pakistan's Pakhtun belt, which saw a high degree of radicalisation during the Afghan jihad, was rocked by the most intense wave of terror following Musharraf's half-hearted U-turn post 9/11. The Pakhtun discontent has in the more recent years manifested itself in the form of the Pakhtun Tahafuz Movement (PTM), headed by a young human rights activist from Waziristan, Manzoor Ahmad Pashteen, which has acquired a large following. It seeks redressal of the injustice meted out to the Pakhtun people and restoration of a life of dignity for them. The Pakhtun fault line will continue to remain a cause for serious concern for Pakistan, more so because of the large Pakhtun presence on the other side of the Durand Line.

High-profile punitive military action, though necessary at times to assuage our public opinion, invariably draws global attention and intervention because of its potential to lead to an escalation. Therefore, punitive military action, when absolutely necessary, needs to be supplemented by discreet, calibrated action in this space.

## Dialogue with Pakistan?

In the recent years, we have consistently stood by the policy 'terror and talks cannot go together'. Our disappointment with dialogue results from the fact that it has failed to change Pakistan's overall posture toward us and put an end to terror. Such an outcome is ruled out by Pakistan's internal dynamics. However, even though incapable by itself of changing Pakistan's behaviour, dialogue and diplomacy do have a role in managing the relationship so as to keep to the minimum its violent swings that distract us from our bigger challenges mentioned earlier. In the past, it has also enabled us to make incremental gains in areas such as trade and people-to-people contacts that are anathema to Pakistan's security establishment. Therefore, we need to adopt a more nuanced approach to dialogue with Pakistan.

## Conclusion

It is axiomatic that our policy toward Pakistan should be based on ground realities, bitter as some of them may be. Acting out of anger can do us more harm than good. For the foreseeable future, there is no alternative to managing this relationship by combining dialogue with discreet and calibrated deterrence/punitive action.

The economic gap between India and Pakistan has widened over the years and will continue to grow. Pakistan's posture toward India necessitates heavy military outlays, more burdensome for its smaller economy than India's. India's international stature has grown, whereas Pakistan's has diminished over the years. The international community has given up India's hyphenation with Pakistan. Even its all-weather friend, China, may be forced to rethink at some stage its pursuit of two contradictory aims of seeking to use Pakistan as a strategic partner and transit route, and exploiting its India obsession, which is the main cause of its economic problems and instability. Therefore, time works in our favour, provided we do not take any missteps out of impatience or frustration and do not bring back a hyphenation of sorts by giving a needlessly high profile to Pakistan in our national discourse.

9

# India and the Two-front War

LIEUTENANT GENERAL D.S. HOODA (RETIRED)

## Introduction

In September 2017, speaking at a seminar in New Delhi, then Army Chief General Bipin Rawat stated that the possibility of a war on two fronts, with China and Pakistan, could not be ruled out.[1] This was not the first instance that the Indian Army (IA) commented on the possibility of a two-front war, but any talk of such a scenario often draws sharp criticism from some defence analysts.

It is argued that despite the historical collusion between China and Pakistan, a two-front threat never emerged in all the wars fought by India since Independence. If it now happens, it would be a massive failure of Indian diplomacy. It is sometimes stated that the bogey of a two-front war was used by the army to bolster its case for additional forces, and that the cost of new formations that were raised to counter this threat have adversely impacted the army's modernisation plan.[2] A senior strategic analyst suggests that India should abandon 'two-front war thinking' and 'seek acquisitions based upon defined threats and stop open-ended capability-building'.[3]

Senior military officers disagree that a two-front threat should be dismissed. General V.P. Malik, Chief of the Army Staff during the Kargil War, writes, 'The dimensions of a China–Pakistan military collusion could vary from; one, collusive support without direct military intervention; to two, activating a second front militarily. The transition from one to the other could also occur seamlessly.'[4]

General Deepak Kapoor, Chief of the Army Staff from 2007 to 2010, has expressed the view:

> Till our boundary differences with both or one of our neighbours get resolved, the possibility of a two-front threat to us would remain. With the growth of stronger ties between China and Pakistan, this threat is likely to get accentuated. The challenge for us is to develop capabilities to enable us to defend ourselves against such a threat. Alternately, we have the option of continuing to keep ignoring reality and glossing over the envisaged threat, hoping that it would go away with passage of time. This ostrich like approach would only make us more vulnerable in the long run.[5]

It is not easy to dismiss either viewpoint. The recent accretions in the IA, primarily to strengthen our military posture along the northern borders, have certainly had an unfavourable impact on the modernisation plans. It is for this reason that the raising of the second division for the Mountain Strike Corps (17 Corps) was stalled and is unlikely to be revived in the near future.[6] However, it would also be a serious error of military planning if the possibility of a collusive threat to India was completely ignored.

The recent Chinese transgressions in Eastern Ladakh have reignited the debate on a two-front war. Many strategic experts have linked the Chinese actions to Indian statements following the abrogation of Article 370 that talked about Indian claims in Pakistan Occupied Kashmir and Aksai Chin. Some media reports had indicated that Pakistan had moved 20,000 troops into Gilgit-Baltistan, matching Chinese deployments in Eastern Ladakh.[7] This could pose a credible two-front threat.

It is, therefore, essential to carry out an analysis of the shape and contours of a two-front threat, the conditions under which such a threat could emerge and a possible Indian strategy and force structure to counter this challenge. However, before such an analysis is attempted, it would be useful to study the individual Indian military strategies vis-à-vis Pakistan and China and see how effective these would be during a two-front war.

## The India–Pakistan–China Military Balance

TABLE 9.1 *Military Balance in China, India and Pakistan*

| *Type of Equipment* | *China* | *India* | *Pakistan* |
|---|---|---|---|
| Total aircraft | 3,210 | 2,123 | 1,372 |
| Combat aircraft | 1,232 | 538 | 356 |
| Transport aircraft | 224 | 250 | 49 |
| Attack helicopter | 281 | 23 | 56 |

| *Type of Equipment* | *China* | *India* | *Pakistan* |
|---|---|---|---|
| Combat tanks | 3,500 | 4,292 | 2,200 |
| SP artillery | 3,800 | 235 | 429 |
| Field artillery | 3,600 | 4,060 | 1,226 |
| Rocket projectors | 2,650 | 266 | 100 |
| Aircraft carrier | 2 | 1 | 0 |
| Submarines | 74 | 16 | 8 |
| Destroyers | 36 | 10 | 0 |
| Frigates | 52 | 13 | 9 |
| Mine warfare | 29 | 3 | 3 |

Source: Global Firepower 2020 Military Strength Ranking[8]

Table 9.1 shows the military balance of the three countries. However, it would be simplistic to draw direct conclusions from the numbers. Pakistan's military is entirely India-centric, while China's threat perceptions include internal separatism, disputes in East and South China Seas, the festering problem of Taiwan's independence, instability in the Korean peninsula and a desire to contest US dominance in the Pacific Ocean.

Although the Chinese military outnumbers the Indians in almost every sphere, it is in the application of these forces that there are significant challenges. The Himalayan watershed is a formidable obstacle, and the IA has deployed a considerable number of acclimatised forces along the northern border. Logistic and terrain difficulties will limit the number of soldiers that can be employed by China's People's Liberation Army (PLA). Operating from high-altitude airfields in Tibet would restrict the payload capabilities of the

PLA Air Force (PLAAF) and constrain sustained high-tempo air operations.

In the maritime domain, India has naval dominance in the Northern Indian Ocean over the Sea Lanes of Communication that carry 80 per cent of China's oil imports. While there is growing concern in India over the increasing presence of the PLA Navy (PLAN) in the Indian Ocean, it is generally accepted that as of now, 'neither China nor Pakistan can seriously threaten India's main axes of maritime approach'.[9] This could, however, change in the future.

With this backdrop, let us look at the Indian military strategies in case of a war with Pakistan and China. In studying these strategies, it is useful to look at both the continental and maritime domains. Air power will play a crucial role, but it will be in support of winning the battle on land and at sea.

## India–Pakistan Conflict

The IA's conventional warfighting strategy has been heavily influenced by the lessons of Operation Parakram, a one-year stand-off between the two armies of India and Pakistan following the terrorist attack on the Indian Parliament in 2001. The IA ordered complete mobilisation of its forces in December, and it took almost three weeks before the 'strike corps', which are primarily responsible for offensive operations into Pakistan, reached their operational locations near the border. By then, the Pakistan Army, with lesser distance to travel to the border, was already fully mobilised.

The delay in mobilisation also gave time to the international community to put pressure on both countries to back off from war. On 12 January 2002, President Musharraf, in a televised address, condemned the Parliament attack and promised that 'no organization will be allowed to indulge in terrorism in the name of Kashmir'. There was again a quiet appeal to India to give Musharraf a chance.

Operation Parakram, called the 'most punishing mistake' by former Navy Chief Admiral Sushil Kumar,[10] led to much introspection within the army. If India had to exploit its conventional superiority, it would have to launch rapid offensives, within 48 to 72 hours, into Pakistan and achieve its objectives in a short, swift war before international pressure forced an end to hostilities. The aim would not be to capture vast swathes of territory but to cause crippling damage to Pakistan's military capability. It is the IA's view that there is space for a conventional India–Pakistan conflict that does not breach the nuclear threshold.

This led to the adoption of the so-called 'Cold Start Doctrine', though there has been no official acceptance of this. Over the next few years, the IA refined its mobilisation schemes, relocated some formations closer to the border, raised a new South Western Command, and carried out several exercises to refine and validate its doctrine.

There has been much analysis and some criticism of the 'Cold Start Doctrine'. Leaked cables from the US Embassy in New Delhi stated,

> The IA's 'Cold Start Doctrine' is a mixture of myth and reality. It has never been and may never be put to

> use on a battlefield because of substantial and serious resource constraints... If the GOI were to implement Cold Start given present Indian military capabilities, it is the collective judgment of the Mission that India would encounter mixed results.[11]

Despite the resource constraints, the 'Cold Start Doctrine' is seen by the IA as the best strategy for achieving military victory over Pakistan. In the execution of this strategy, the Indian Air Force (IAF), with clear superiority over its counterpart, will play a key role.

For many years, the IAF had given priority to winning the air battle by achieving air dominance prior to conducting a joint air–land campaign. This has changed in the recent past with an emphasis on 'parallel warfare', or the simultaneous application of combat power from day one of conflict, and missions such as shaping the battlefield and interdiction of the enemy's combat potential before it can be applied in battle.[12]

At sea, the Indian Navy (IN) has an overwhelming superiority over the Pakistan Navy and will aim to control the Arabian Sea. As brought out in the 'Indian Maritime Security Strategy,'

> Sea control is a central concept around which the Indian Navy will be employed. It is a key component of the strategy for conflict and a prerequisite for most naval operations. The Indian Navy will undertake the range of naval missions and tasks commensurate with the degree and duration of sea control required for execution of the operational plan. These will

> include developing MDA [maritime domain awareness], power projection and force protection, in all dimensions, against the adversary.[13]

The naval strategy may appear a little disconnected from the air–land battle, but its coercive influence is immense. The maritime strategy points out that 'the strategic effect of maritime operations will finally be measured upon land'.[14] Pakistani strategic commentators also understand that 'Pakistan Navy would be no numerical match for India's conventional or strategic inventory' and throw up the usual argument that 'Pakistan has seen its nuclear arsenal as the only and a vital strategy to counter India's huge conventional navy'.[15]

## India–China Conflict

India's strategy against China has been based on a realistic appraisal of China's capability to conduct offensive operations along the forbidding terrain of the northern borders. After the 1962 war, India adopted a dissuasive defensive posture against China by positioning sufficient forces to guard against any surprise attack. In the 1980s, it was also visualised that the PLA would require one summer season to build up adequate forces and logistics in Tibet for launching a large-scale offensive across the Himalayas.

The Wangdung incident of 1986 saw a significant change in the Indian deployment along the Line of Actual Control (LAC), as the disputed northern border is called. Responding to an intrusion by the

PLA south of the LAC in the Tawang sector, the IA airlifted a brigade to Zimithang and, over the next one year, strengthened its forward deployment. The Chinese were reported to have moved eight divisions into Tibet, but the IA stood firm.[16]

One consequence of the Wangdung incident was that it triggered a period of diplomatic rapprochement with the visit of the Indian Prime Minister Rajiv Gandhi to Beijing in 1988, and the signing of the 'Agreement on Maintenance of Peace and Tranquillity along the Line of Actual Control' in 1993. However, this period of calm also had an unintended effect. While the Indian soldiers remained deployed along the LAC, infrastructure development was neglected.

On the other hand, China was carrying out massive infrastructure improvements in Tibet. The Qinghai–Tibet railway, operationalised in 2006, significantly cut down the time for PLA's mobilidation into Tibet. It was in the mid-2000s that India took serious note of the growing mismatch between the two militaries and reworked its strategy. In 2006, a decision was taken to build 73 strategic roads along the LAC,[17] and in 2010, two new divisions were raised to strengthen the deployment in Arunachal Pradesh.[18]

In 2013, the Indian government sanctioned the raising of a Mountain Strike Corps for the northern border.[19] Although the raising of the strike corps has not been completed, and infrastructure development remains tardy, there has been a change in strategic thinking. Two noted Indian experts have pointed out that the new IA strategy has shifted from 'deterrence by denial' to 'deterrence by punishment'.[20]

The basic thought process in the IA is to make it prohibitive for the PLA to achieve major territorial gains across the LAC. The additional reserves and the Mountain Strike Corps have given the IA additional depth in its defences as well as a limited capability to undertake a counteroffensive across the LAC. In addition to raising additional formations, the IA is also procuring the M-777 ultra-light Howitzers, has deployed an armoured brigade in Ladakh,[21] and improved its surveillance capability along the LAC.

The IAF has traditionally held an edge over PLAAF as its airfields are located in the plains, enabling air operations with full payloads. PLAAF, operating from high altitude airfields with rudimentary facilities, would be forced to operate with reduced payloads.[22] However, focus in the past had remained on Pakistan.

In the last decade, the IAF has shifted its attention to the northern borders. Su-30 aircraft were deployed at the Tezpur airbase in 2009, and Hasimara, in West Bengal, is being readied for Rafale aircraft.[23] There has also been a significant increase in strategic airlift capability. The induction of the C-130, the C-17 and the Chinook helicopters has tremendously improved the ability to switch additional forces to a threatened sector. All this has led to a more offensive mindset.

The IN is concerned about the growing presence of PLAN in the Indian Ocean, its military facility in Djibouti, and the control over Hambantota in Sri Lanka and Gwadar in Pakistan. Currently, India has a huge geographical advantage, and in conflict, will seek to block the entry of PLAN through the narrow straits leading from the South China Sea into the Indian

Ocean, and engage in commerce warfare by interdicting Chinese trade.

The IN has good maritime domain awareness capability through its P-8I Poseidons, which are now supplemented by Su-30 aircraft armed with the BrahMos missiles in the newly set up squadron based at Thanjavur in Tamil Nadu.[24] The IN also has an ambitious plan to build three aircraft carriers and six nuclear attack submarines for sea control and sea denial.

It might appear that in an India–China conflict, India could hold its own, particularly in the air and maritime domain. While that may be true today, the edge is also fast eroding. The IAF numbers are dwindling, and the IN's share of the budget reducing. This could have a significant impact during future wars, particularly in a two-front scenario.

## A Two-front War

### *Likely Scenarios*

There are different scenarios under which a two-front conflict could break out. General V.P. Malik has listed three:[25]

- Pakistan-led or China-led conflicts.
- Either state may take advantage of an adverse situation for India brought on by the other.
- It could be part of a grand design between China and Pakistan to bring India down to its knees.

While the 'grand design' scenario would be the worst possible contingency for India, it is also the most unlikely. At least in the near future, there does not appear to be either any compelling reason or the appetite in the three countries to engage in a full-scale all-out war that could transcend into the nuclear dimension.

An India–Pakistan conflict would most probably be triggered by a major act of terrorism in India that has the direct imprint of Pakistan-based groups. While the IA doctrine calls for rapid launch of offensives into Pakistan at the commencement of war, in actual fact, a conflict would probably result from a series of escalatory actions following the Indian military response to the terrorist strike. In such a contingency, the IA would have to modify its 'Cold Start Doctrine' to seek military domination at each step of the escalation ladder with more limited objectives (at least, in the initial stages) than currently envisaged.

In this scenario, India would have the majority of the international opinion on its side, and it is unlikely that China would buck this trend to initiate active military hostilities to bail out Pakistan. However, we could see an increase in LAC intrusions in disputed areas, some induction of ground and air assets in Tibet and increased PLAN presence in the Indian Ocean. This could tie down some Indian military assets from being employed against Pakistan, but it would not have a significant impact on the final outcome of the conflict.

A war between India and China will, in most cases, be initiated by China, and their strategic aim will decide the character of the conflict. If the idea is to teach India a sharp lesson following a border stand-off, the conflict could be geographically limited to a specific sector. If there is a larger geopolitical objective, a more expansive air, land and sea campaign could be launched by the PLA.

Under these circumstances, Pakistan could attempt to take advantage of the Indian military's preoccupation along the northern borders to undertake operations along the disputed Line of Control (LoC) in Jammu and Kashmir (J&K) to improve its positions and put spotlight on the Kashmir dispute. This is the most likely scenario for a two-front war.

### *Contours of a Two-front War*

A two-front war will possibly begin with an India–China conflict. Since the initiative lies with China, the PLA will certainly carry out adequate preparations before launching the operations. Additional forces would be inducted into Tibet by both rail and road. At this stage, there would not be an open declaration of hostilities, and therefore, the mobilisation of forces into Tibet would be uncontested.

In addition to ground forces, the PLAAF would activate its 14 airbases in Tibet with fourth generation aircraft such as the J-10, J-11 and Su-30MKK. An extensive air defence umbrella would be set up, comprising medium-range surface-to-air missiles such as the HQ-12 and HQ-16, and area defence systems such as the S-300 and HQ-9, supplemented by the newly acquired S-400. It is also estimated that the PLA Rocket Force has about 1,200 short-range ballistic missiles in its inventory (DF-11, DF-15 and DF-16), a number of which could be moved into positions from where they could strike Indian strategic targets.[26]

During this period, additional PLAN assets, particularly submarines, would be deployed in the Indian Ocean. Surface vessels could be positioned at Djibouti and Gwadar, and anti-ship ballistic missiles like the DF-21D and DF-26 would be readied.

In response to the PLA's actions, the Indian military would also enhance its operational readiness and mobilise to wartime locations. One dilemma facing the IA could be the decision to move its dual-task formations from the western theatre to the east. A premature deployment would weaken India's offensive potential against Pakistan, but attempting such a move after hostilities have commenced could make the troops and equipment moving by train vulnerable to enemy strikes and delay their arrival.

The IAF would move some additional assets to airfields in the eastern sector, and Su-30s with BrahMos missiles could be deployed to Andaman and Nicobar Islands. The IN will adopt a more offensive posture in the southeast Indian Ocean, while deploying surface vessels and submarines to keep surveillance over the Malacca, Sunda and Lombok Straits. Some assets would also be positioned in the Arabian Sea to keep a watch on Pakistani ports and traffic out of the Persian Gulf.

The Chinese war aims would be to present India with such adverse military conditions that she is forced to sue for peace on Chinese terms. The PLA would not seek large territorial gains, although a defeat of the IA in selected areas is a necessary prerequisite to achieving victory. The Chinese military would exploit its advantages and shield its weaknesses through the use of superior technology.

The war could begin with a barrage of ballistic missile attacks against strategic targets and Indian airfields. In 2015, the RAND Corporation carried out a study that included the Chinese capability to attack US airbases in the western Pacific with ballistic missiles. It was estimated that if the PLA employed 36 ballistic missiles against the Kadena Airbase at Okinawa (12,000 feet, twin runway), it could close the airbase for fighter operations for four days.[27] Indian airbases have shorter runway lengths and very limited capability to defend against attacks by ballistic missiles.

The PLA would extensively use its electronic warfare and cyber capability, combined with psychological operations, to achieve information dominance and degrade India's command and control (C2) networks. A C2 system is seen as 'the heart of information collection, control, and application on the battlefield. It is also the nerve center of the entire battlefield'.[28] The PLA believes that future battles will not be based on the destruction of enemy forces but will be a confrontation between operational systems like C2, intelligence and firepower systems. If these can be degraded, the enemy loses the will to fight.[29]

Ground offensives would be launched to capture key terrain under cover of massive artillery barrages and precision strikes against choke points such as bridges to isolate the battle area and delay the arrival of reinforcements. In my view, a large-scale airborne offensive can be ruled out as the PLAAF will be unable to achieve a favourable air situation that is an essential condition for such an operation.

Though the road infrastructure on the Indian side is still poor in places, the forward defences are in good shape. The soldiers are well-acclimatised, familiar with the terrain, battle-ready, and pre-deployed in sufficient numbers. By this time, the dual-task formations from the west would be in position, and sufficient reserves would be available. Even if roads are cut off, there is adequate helicopter lift capability to move additional troops to threatened sectors. The PLA will find it extremely difficult to achieve a quick breakthrough with soldiers who have been recently inducted from the Chinese mainland and are unfamiliar with the terrain.

The IAF will target airfields, logistic installations, and C2 systems in Tibet. Railway lines and road networks would be struck with air and missile strikes to delay the arrival of additional troops into the theatre of operations.

Depending on the progress of the operations, at some stage, India would consider the employment of the Mountain Strike Corps to take the battle into Chinese territory. The recent decision to reorganise the strike corps into leaner integrated battle groups is an attempt to create forces that can rapidly be launched for an offensive.[30]

The IN will exploit its advantage in maritime domain awareness, primarily employing the P-8I Poseidons to locate the PLAN and use shore-based aircraft armed with BrahMos for strikes from long ranges. Key choke points in the Indian Ocean will be guarded to prevent the transit of PLAN reinforcements.

Based on the progress of the war, and if India appears to be under military pressure, Pakistan could attempt to take advantage by opening up a front along the LoC in J&K. Eleven Corps of Pakistan Army, located in the Khyber-Pakhtunkhwa province, could be moved across J&K and tasked with taking offensives in selected areas. The rest of the Pakistan military would go into a defensive posture.

A corps-level offensive by the Pakistan Army is likely to achieve some initial success, particularly as most of Northern Command's reserves would have got pulled into Ladakh for the battle against the PLA. Facing a two-front war, a critical strategic decision that would have to be taken is whether the IA should restrict its operations on the western front to the J&K theatre or take the war across the international border into Punjab and Sind.

Under normal circumstances, India's 'Cold Start Doctrine' envisages offensive operations all across the border with Pakistan. However, the offensive component of the three 'Strike Corps', which are tasked for the western front, would have been diluted with the move of certain dual-task formations to the eastern front.

The IAF would also have to consider whether it has the capacity to support a full-scale offensive against Pakistan, while also engaged with the PLAAF. Some estimates point out that the IAF would commit 70 per cent of its combat squadrons to the Chinese theatre, leaving only 30 per cent for operations against Pakistan.[31] In 2016, Air Marshal B.S. Dhanoa had admitted, 'Our numbers are not adequate to fully execute an air campaign in a two-front scenario. The probability of a two-front scenario is an appreciation which you need to do. But are the numbers adequate? No. The squadrons are winding down.'[32]

An entirely defensive posture on the western front could encourage Pakistan to continue and, perhaps, strengthen its attacks in J&K. This would force the IA to undertake at least one or two armour-heavy offensives across the international border. India would now be wholly engaged in a two-front war. Under pressure, India would also have to decide whether the Mountain Strike Corps should be applied against China or Pakistan.

The IN is perhaps best placed to fight a two-front war because of its geographical advantages. Apart from direct naval engagements, it is in a position to interdict Chinese trade through the Indian Ocean. However, as time goes by and if the PLAN is successful in marshalling greater resources into the Indian Ocean, the IN's advantage could rapidly diminish.

Attempting to hazard a guess about the outcome of a two-front war is fraught with risks, and no such attempt is being made in this essay. However, what is apparent is that the Indian military will be under tremendous pressure, and our individual strategies for dealing with the Chinese and Pakistani threats will have to undergo major changes.

A simple answer would be to state that more resources are required. Some experts estimate that the IAF needs 60 combat squadrons to deal with a serious two-front threat.[33] The IN's perspective plan call for a 200-ship navy by 2027, and the IA needs a massive infusion of capital to modernise its vintage equipment.[34] However, the reality is that the budget to support these ambitious plans will not be forthcoming.

*Force Development*

The Indian military will have to take a hard look at how it wishes to develop a force structure that is capable of dealing with a future scenario that involves China as the primary theatre of operations and with Pakistan exploiting this situation to open up a secondary front.

Our excessive reliance on manpower and the number of major platforms will need to be replaced by capabilities that maximise our geographical advantage and neutralise PLA superiority in specific areas. Some recommendations that include restructuring of the forces and capability development are as follows:

- Create two theatre commands for the northern borders. There have been some suggestions to have a single theatre command to deal with China, but in my view, the exercising of control over the entire northern border by one command is not a practical proposition.
- Integrate the Eastern Naval Command (ENC) and the Andaman and Nicobar Command (ANC) into one. The current arrangement of the ENC under the Navy Chief and the ANC administered by the Chief of Defence Staff will adversely impact integrated operations in the southeast Indian Ocean.
- Improve capabilities to enhance maritime domain awareness in the Indian Ocean, coupled with long-range precision strike capability by air and naval assets. The IN will also have to decide whether it

wants to invest more in an undersea fleet rather than surface vessels.

- The IAF should acquire greater capability for stand-off attacks against strategic targets in Tibet through both manned and unmanned aerial systems. It must also enhance its ground air defence capability to protect its airfields from ballistic and cruise missiles.
- Strategic and tactical lift capability must further improve. The ability to quickly move troops to threatened sectors will lessen the requirement to ab initio deploy a large number of soldiers on the ground and could ultimately lead to an overall reduction of manpower in the IA.
- There has to be greater investment in electronic warfare, cyber and space as these are the realms in which future wars will be fought. If we are unable to neutralise China's advantages in these areas, the battle would be lost.

## Conclusion

A two-front war is a worst-case scenario for the Indian military, but it would be strategically imprudent to ignore it on the grounds that it is out of the realms of possibility. India has an implacably hostile foe in Pakistan and a strategic competitor in China, with which it has a long and unsettled border. Sino–Pakistan collusion is also a reality.

It is often stated that military plans should be based on capabilities of the adversaries and not the intent because the latter can always change. Looking at the capabilities and strategies of our adversaries, it is apparent that India will be extremely hard-pressed to engage in a two-front war successfully. This should force an introspection on our future doctrine and force development.

10

# India's Relations with West Asia and Energy Security

AMBASSADOR K.C. SINGH

Independent India and the Islamic world have a relationship with roots in the freedom struggle, starting with the 1920 pact between the Indian National Congress (INC) and the leaders of the Khilafat Movement, protesting to preserve the status of the Turkish Sultan as the Caliph. Turkey, having aligned with Germany during World War I, came under increasing pressure after the war. The Ottoman empire was eventually dismembered in 1920 under the Treaty of Sevres. For the INC, this support was to ensure communal unity in opposing the British colonial regime.

This arrangement ended when a Turkish secular-nationalist Kemal Ataturk overthrew the old order, thus anyway ending the Caliphate. However, the principle had been enunciated that the Muslim community in India was a part of the undivided umma stretching beyond Indian shores. Therefore, developments affecting that community in India or abroad linked domestic politics to international geopolitics. This assumed urgency post-1948 to keep the Islamic nations from aligning behind Pakistan on the Kashmir issue.

The Islamic world was fixated on the birth of Israel in 1948 and the dispossession of Arab Palestinians of land occupied and owned by them for centuries. The status of Jerusalem was also important as in it, on the Temple mount, was located Al Aqsa Mosque, the third-holiest mosque for followers of Islam. These considerations informed the Indian decision to recognise Israel but not establish diplomatic relations at that stage.

From 1961, when the Non-Aligned Movement (NAM) was formed at Belgrade, the Palestinian issue became intertwined with Cold War as the erstwhile Soviet Union was seen as more supportive of the Palestinian cause while the USA invariably backed Israel. But for India, it became a geostrategic trap as India's seminal thinking regarding justice for Palestinians as a precondition for normal relations with Israel restricted India's diplomatic space. This persisted from 1947 to 1991. India steadfastly backed Palestinians even after Egypt under President Anwar Sadat accepted peace with Israel and signed the Camp David Accords with Israeli Prime Minister Menachem Begin in 1978. Even though India quietly kept a channel open with Israel, she preferred clandestine engagement to diplomatic relations. But at the multilateral level India's strong advocacy of the Palestinian cause enabled India to stymie Pakistan as secular Arab nations such as Iraq, Syria, Egypt and others remained lukewarm, if not dismissive, towards Pakistan's pleadings over Kashmir.

Although Arab unity gradually dissolved once Egypt had accepted the existence of Israel and opted for peaceful coexistence, India stuck to its original stand. It took the collapse of the Soviet Union and end of the

Cold War in 1991, as indeed the accidental selection of Prime Minister P.V. Narasimha Rao following the unfortunate assassination of former Prime Minister and Congress leader Rajiv Gandhi, to bring fresh pragmatism to Indian foreign policy. Retaining the External Affairs Ministry and, from December 1991, with a dynamic new Foreign Secretary J.N. Dixit, Rao rapidly adjusted India to the post-Cold War reality. He was compelled alongside to fix a shattered Indian economy, critical for which was the goodwill of the USA. Linked to this outreach was a need to calibrate relations with Israel, and thus indirectly with the Jewish lobby in the USA. Palestinians also began adjusting to a perceived unipolar world by examining new proposals for peace with Israel.

The Madrid Peace Conference commenced in October 1991. Palestinians were beginning to engage Israelis but India was out of the loop despite its vociferous past support to the Palestinian cause. The USA conveyed to the South Block that no nation could be invited, even as an observer, to planned meetings of subgroups unless it had diplomatic ties with both Israel and Palestinians. Through some quick diplomatic moves, with Prime Minister Rao going through the motions of taking Palestinian leader Yasser Arafat into confidence, India established diplomatic ties with Israel in January 1992. Conventional wisdom that this would upset Indian Muslims was not borne out as they were smart enough to separate Indian national interests from the historical baggage of support for Palestinians. After all, India did not publicly dilute its stand on the issue as relations with Israel developed. That is why no

Indian Prime Minister visited Israel till Prime Minister Narendra Modi in July 2017, two decades and a half after opening diplomatic doors.

The peace process between Israel and Palestine acquired its own momentum, but also faced setbacks such as the assassination of Israeli Prime Minister Yitzhak Rabin in 1995. This process finally wound down with the failure of the last-ditch effort at comprehensive peace by US President Bill Clinton during the dying days of his presidency in 2000. But the salutary side of this process was that post the 1995 Oslo Accords II, a notional Palestine state came into existence, diminishing pressure on India to vociferously support the Palestinian cause at multilateral fora. At the United Nations, India's affirmative voting on resolutions berating Israeli actions continued, as in the past. The first change began to be noticed under the Modi government.

However, geopolitics is never static and as this issue was losing currency, following the Soviet withdrawal from Afghanistan in 1988–1989, a new and more disruptive force was taking shape. The Soviets exited Afghanistan after military exhaustion at the hands of a new hybrid entity created by the marriage of Saudi funds and Wahhabi tenets of Islam, with provisions of Pakistani foot soldiers formed of illiterate or Madrasa-educated youngsters ready for jihad and US arms and intelligence. The USA withdrew from the region declaring its mission accomplished but soon got involved with Saddam Hussein's invasion of Kuwait. But the hybrid monster of jihadis left behind first waged civil war to capture power in Afghanistan and simultaneously fuelled militancy in Jammu and Kashmir (J&K) from the early 1990s. The new warriors sought to achieve Caliphate on earth or reward in heaven if martyred. In reality, they fulfilled Pakistan's aim of gaining strategic depth in Afghanistan and trying to wrest Kashmir from India by blatant use of non-state actors.

Concomitantly, the Bharatiya Janata Party (BJP) was bringing its agitation to build the Ram Mandir at Ayodhya to a peak at this time. On 6 December 1992, the Babri Masjid was pulled down by a mob in the presence of senior leaders of the party. It remains unclear whether the then prime minister P.V. Narasimha Rao naively believed the assurances of BJP leaders or dithered ordering the paramilitary forces to enforce the law and disperse illegal assembly. Following the destruction, Muslim protests mushroomed but were put down by force. Earlier, the BJP had won elections and formed governments in Himachal Pradesh, Rajasthan, Madhya Pradesh and, most significantly, Uttar Pradesh. Gujarat and Maharashtra led the states with the most loss of life, numbering 246 and 259 respectively. Uttar Pradesh was not far behind with 201 dead.

India's secular credentials were tested based on its treatment of its largest minority. Naturally, it became an international issue. The Congress-led union government dismissed the four BJP state governments mentioned earlier and unleashed a diplomatic offensive to contain the damage. Pakistan, and to a lesser extent Bangladesh, allowed mobs to attack Hindu minorities and their places of worship. Iranian Supreme Leader Ali Khamenei called it a 'crime against Muslim holy places'. He instructed his Foreign Minister Ali Akbar Velayati to convey to India that Iran would not tolerate such attacks and Muslims of Iran and elsewhere 'supported the Muslims of India'.[1]

The Gulf Coordination Council (GCC), the six-nation grouping of Gulf Arab nations, also reacted at its 13th summit in Abu Dhabi. Although Saudi Arabia was the most vehement in its criticism, the final communique took India by surprise. A separate resolution titled 'Aggression Against the Babri Mosque' called the destruction 'sacrilege and unpardonable act'. Even more significantly, the normally moderate and friendly United Arab Emirates (UAE) was also publicly critical. The Indian Ministry of External Affairs reacted by calling the resolution unhelpful when the Indian government was wrestling with 'the challenge posed by communal elements'. It was an interesting defence, which shared with the Islamic world the domestic challenge faced by the rise of right-wing, majoritarian forces. Perhaps understanding this dilemma, Saudi Arabia, within days, agreed to receive Minister of State for External Affairs R.L. Bhatia. India moved its then ambassador to Iran, Hamid Ansari, as Permanent Representative to the United Nations at New York to ensure that an urbane and nationalistic Muslim face defended India's syncretic culture, despite the one act of indefensible Islamophobia.

Interestingly, in the aftermath of the Babri Masjid destruction a visit by Israeli foreign minister Shimon Peres was not postponed. India was emerging from old unproven dictums that the Indian Muslim minority would resent an outreach to Israel. The community now had more immediate concerns, principal amongst which was the rise of a more openly religion-spouting BJP with a specific majoritarian agenda. As yet these forces were restrained by a more egalitarian and statesmanlike A.B. Vajpayee. The Islamic world too paid little attention to the rightward lurch in Indian domestic politics as Iraqi President Saddam Hussein marched into Kuwait in August 1990. Seven months later, he was ejected by a force led by the USA but it began the presence of US forces in the Gulf, eventually leading to the 2003 overthrow of Saddam Hussein.

The world had seemingly entered a unipolar phase. In 1989, China stumbled in with its handling of the student agitation culminating in brutal use of force at Tiananmen Square. But adroit Chinese leader Deng Xiaoping steered the nation back to rapid growth. India contended with Pakistan's non-conventional war in J&K using non-state actors. But the world, specifically the Islamic world, had no time for Indian complaints. A proxy battle between India and Pakistan commenced in Afghanistan as the Taliban was born and found a ready ally in the Pakistani military and state. In 1996, Kabul fell to them but the Northern Alliance, consisting of non-Pashtun groups, led by the redoubtable Ahmad Shah Masood, continued to resist, albeit at one point reduced to just controlling Panjshir valley. During this period, 1996–2003, strategic convergence between India and Iran became close as both opposed the Taliban. Domestically, the period 1996–1998 saw political drift as a third-front government, supported by the Congress, filled the gap with a change of leaders in-between.

A number of new developments laid the foundation of the 21st-century India. A BJP-led government was formed under Prime Minister A.B. Vajpayee in 1998. India tested nuclear devices in May, followed a fortnight later by Pakistan, setting off an international crisis as the USA and its allies—besides China, but with the exception of France and to some extent, Russia—declared different levels of sanctions against India. But three months later, on 7 August, massive bombs exploded outside US embassies in Nairobi and Dar es Salaam. Al-Qaeda, with their umbilical link to the Taliban regime in Kabul, emerged as the perpetrators and announced their arrival as the world's principal terror syndicate. US President Bill Clinton on 20 August ordered cruise missile strikes against Osama bin Laden's suspected training camps in Afghanistan. Global, and particularly, US attention began to focus on the emerging threat of international terrorism, which now had found refuge in a state run by those who shared their vision of an Islamic Caliphate as indeed their loathing of the USA. Although Indo–US dialogue had commenced between Indian External Affairs Minister Jaswant Singh and President Bill Clinton's university friend and US Deputy Secretary of State Strobe Talbot, the strategic interests now began converging between the two democracies after endless on–off flirtation during the Cold War. The BJP, in any case, did not carry the ideological anti-US baggage of the earlier era as it had never held power, except as part of the Janta Party in 1977–1979.

As Indian foreign policy veered toward closer engagement with the USA it was natural that Islamic nations that were de facto US allies began to assess strategic relations with India. This involved the commencement of them rebalancing their relations with Pakistan. Two examples are the UAE and Saudi Arabia. When I arrived as Indian envoy in the UAE in April 1999, only three nations recognised the extremely regressive Taliban regime in Kabul, that is, Pakistan, Saudi Arabia and the UAE. But the UAE was already beginning to look at India as more than a supplier of good expatriate labour. However, they were still unwilling to recalibrate their strategic perspective being unsure of BJP's world view.

The limited conflict in the summer of 1999 as India hit back to eject Pakistani intruders in the Kargil region of Kashmir was watched by the Islamic world with studied neutrality. It helped as Pakistan was claiming innocence and lack of complicity. But Chinese unwillingness to be drawn into the imbroglio and President Bill Clinton telling a rattled Pakistani Prime Minister to fully vacate any Indian territory held by its intruders across the Line of Control began to shift thinking of the ruling families in the Gulf. When the Bamiyan Buddhas were blown up by the Taliban in March 2001, despite Pakistani and Saudi entreaties to Taliban Supremo Mullah Omar, it was clear that the puppet was now out of their control.

The 9/11 terror attacks on US brought all these nascent trends to a boiling-point. It brought into direct conflict Pakistan's old ally, the USA, which had for decades been its sponsor, arms supplier and financial crutch, and the Taliban, their new protégé and strategic ally in Kabul. The latter alliance had become critical for Pakistan as it gave it a perceived strategic depth in Afghanistan besides keeping its anti-India terror machine oiled and supplied with committed jihadis for sustaining decade-old terrorism in J&K. US intervention to eject the Taliban from Afghanistan and eliminate Al-Qaeda required Pakistan's active assistance for a number of factors. First, it was necessary to have Pakistan deny shelter and support to fleeing cadres of both organisations. Once President Pervez Musharraf threw in his lot with the USA, he was asked to seal the border with Afghanistan to catch particularly Al-Qaeda leadership in a pincer move as the USA and its allies drove them from within Afghanistan. Pakistan did so half-heartedly and selectively. The Taliban's top leadership was permitted, if not enabled, to relocate to Quetta. Al-Qaeda leaders were also selectively betrayed to keep the US satisfied, although as the USA would complain later that this was always piecemeal. This became manifest a decade later in 2011 when the USA launched a raid, without telling Pakistan, to grab Osama bin Laden ensconced in an estate a stone's throw from Pakistani military establishments at Abbottabad.

In fact, Pakistan's Inter-Services Intelligence (ISI) then commenced a double game of ratcheting up terror against India while becoming poster boys of the US war on terror. The terror attack on the Indian Parliament in December 2001, with potential to kill, injure or abduct Members of Parliament or even ministers heralded the new game. The audacity of this attack had complex reasoning driving it. It sent a signal to the anti-India jihadi network that alliance with the USA did not preclude support to them on the eastern front. In addition, they calculated that by provoking an Indian military response they could justify not moving their troops in large enough numbers to seal their western frontier, as demanded by the USA. This became for the next two decades the template for US–Pakistan cooperation, despite the USA even characterising Pakistan as a non-NATO ally. The USA pleaded with India to engage Pakistan in the hope that it could wean away Pakistan from its addiction to using terror to pressurise India. They hoped that as the dialogue process gathered momentum this would be possible. Prime Ministers A.B. Vajpayee and his successor Manmohan Singh repeatedly tried this gambit but were stymied each time by revived terror attacks, each one deadlier than the one before.

But despite this saga and internet-facilitated advocacy of and recruitment for jihad, the nearly 2 billion Indian Muslim population did not see any meaningful radicalisation of youth. Pakistan failed to create a communal divide. Even the 2002 riots at Godhra in Gujarat, when now Prime Minister Narendra Modi was the Chief Minister of that state, did not trigger a wider all-India conflagration. Prime Minister Vajpayee's stature and ability to reassure minorities and his public critique of Chief Minister Modi defused the issue. Although Chief Minister Modi retained his job, internationally he became a pariah. Visas were denied to him by the USA and many Western nations. But the world too had changed post 9/11. There was greater empathy for multicultural democracies and their challenges in insulating domestic opinion from the global war on terror which caused loss of innocent civilian lives and collateral damage as the USA and

NATO operations expanded from Afghanistan to Iraq and West Asia.

Henry Kissinger notes that India has managed to insulate itself from the threat of radical Islam by 'enlightened treatment of its minorities and a fostering of common Indian domestic principles—including democracy and nationalism...'. But he also warns that 'this outcome is not foreordained, and maintaining it will require concerted efforts'.[2] But India, its Islamic neighbourhood in the Gulf and West Asia, and the world have changed dramatically since Kissinger's 2014 book. First, Narendra Modi-led BJP to electoral success and power in 2014 using a new majoritarian idiom that Vajpayee never adopted, or perhaps would not have even approved. Donald Trump followed him by winning the US presidential election in 2016, again decrying globalisation, free trade (his party's core belief) and danger from immigrants. In the United Kingdom, Boris Johnson similarly tapped pro-Brexit and anti–European Union and xenophobic instincts of the working-class white majority to catapult the Tories back into retaining power with an even larger majority. In Brazil, Jair Bolsonaro became President with a similar combination of neo-fascist formulae for tackling crime and economic decline.

Francis Fukuyama explains this phenomenon in his book *Identity* (2018) as a 'broader trend in international politics'. 'Populist leaders', he adds, 'seek to use the legitimacy conferred by democratic elections to consolidate power.'[3] If the challenge in the first decade of the 21st century came from radicalised Islam and jihad, in the second decade it has been complicated by, first, the Arab Spring in 2011, rising from Tunisia and through popular protests overthrowing autocratic rulers in Libya, Egypt and Tunisia. Additionally, it set off civil war in Yemen and Syria. In Bahrain, it drove the nation deeper under Saudi tutelage and then created divisions in the six-nation GCC. It also saw the sudden rise of the Islamic State of Iraq and Syria (ISIS, now officially the Islamic State [IS]), overrunning in months much of northern Syria and Iraq and creating a post-Taliban Islamic Caliphate. But unlike the Taliban, this state bridged parts of two existing nations, had access to oil and resources, and created a refugee problem that spilt Europe and prepared fertile ground for rise of extreme right-wing populists and parties.

President Barak Obama, committed to withdrawing US forces from wars in the Islamic world, realised that other than recommitting US forces to combat ISIS the only alternative was to unshackle Iran from US and UN sanctions, imposed after discovery of its clandestine nuclear programme in 2003. He approved the P-5 plus German nuclear deal that began the lifting of a complex web of trade and financial sanctions against Iran. The Joint Comprehensive Programme of Action (JCPOA), as the deal was called, was signed in 2015. By 2017, the tide had turned as Mosul and Raqa were liberated. In 2019, ISIS leader Abu Bakr al-Baghdadi was killed and most of the territory it occupied vacated. Iranian success was due to Shia militias created by Iranian Major General Qassem Soleimani—killed in a US drone strike in 2020—combining with Hezbollah fighters from Lebanon, the Syrian Army and Syrian

Kurds. Air support was mainly given by Russia and, in the Kurdish zone, by the USA.

This success naturally led to an increase in Iranian influence and power in what began being called the Shia crescent, running from Iran to the Mediterranean. It was also naturally resented by Sunni powers Turkey and Saudi Arabia, along with the United Arab Emirates (UAE), boxing above its weight despite its limited population. President Donald Trump assumed presidency voicing rejection of the JCPOA with Iran. He went on his first visit abroad to Saudi Arabia to attend a gathering of Sunni nations and vociferously began his campaign against Iran. The USA withdrew from the nuclear deal, imposed stiffer sanctions and created new fissures in the Islamic world by not only engendering a Shia–Sunni divide but even letting Saudis and Emiratis confront Qatar, thus dividing GCC.

A further destabilising move, unveiled on 28 January 2020 is the Trump Peace Plan for the settlement of the Palestinian dispute, titled Peace to Prosperity. The Arab League on 13 April warned of serious repercussions if the totally pro-Israel proposal was implemented. Even US Jewish supporters are warning the Israeli government that unilateral annexations would be unacceptable. Annexation of the Jordan valley will likely force Jordanian King Abdullah to abandon peace agreement with Israel.

While all this has been brewing, two additional developments have further complicated the scenario. Just as the USA and the Taliban agreed on withdrawal of US troops from Afghanistan, coronavirus began ravaging the region. Moreover, at this time when the world needs unity and cooperation, the United Nations Security Council could not even approve a French proposal seeking suspension of all conflicts due to US–China differences. Iran has been the source of the COVID-19 spread in the region as it was late in barring religious congregations at Qom and flights from China, among other factors. Turkey has adopted a disjointed approach, further hampered by the past purging of 1,50,000 civil servants after the unsuccessful coup. Those include 15,000 health professionals. In Egypt, hundreds stormed the public health facilities for COVID-19 tests.

This is the complex and emerging scenario in the Gulf and West Asia. The implication for Indian foreign policy is self-evident due to Indian dependence on this region for trade and energy, besides the 6–7 million Indian diaspora living and working there. Can Indian domestic politics be insulated from this is a relevant question. The BJP will have to reassess its use of communal fault lines to distract from economic malaise and rally electoral support. This is so as it must now contend with the COVID-19 pandemic and its economic consequences. Logic dictates that following the twin challenges posed by the pandemic and the aggressive Chinese posture at the Line of Actual Control since April 2020, the government should have been seeking national political consensus and solidarity with the opposition. Foiled attempts to dislodge the Congress government in Rajasthan showed that the ruling party BJP's domestic agenda was not going to be modified or delayed. In keeping with this pursuit of its majoritarian agenda, Prime Minister Narendra Modi participated in the highly choreographed foundation stone–laying ceremony of the Ram Mandir at Ayodhya.

Two further developments cast a shadow over the geopolitics of the Gulf and West Asia. China announced a 25-year strategic partnership with Iran, promising US$400 million investment in the latter. China would now not only have free access to Chabahar, which India treated as its counter to Chinese development of the Pakistani port at Gwadar, but will develop the more strategically located port at Jask, literally at the mouth of the Strait of Hormuz. Thus, in effect, China literally gets total maritime dominance of the northern coast of the Arabian Sea. This negates the US attempt to isolate Iran by 'maximum pressure', with which India has been quietly compliant.

The second development is the sudden announcement of normalisation of relations between the UAE and Israel under the approving gaze of US President Donald Trump. As a notional concession Israel agreed to 'suspend' annexation of settlements in the West Bank. It gave Trump much needed distraction from daily bad news on pandemic deaths and the struggling US economy less than 90 days from the forthcoming presidential election. But Iranian reaction was immediate as Iranian Revolutionary Guards Corps (IRGC) threatened retaliation against the UAE, which was gambling on Iran desisting as the UAE is Iran's vital financial and import conduit. It, nevertheless, has sharpened the emerging groupings of nations with clashing interests and world views. On the one side are China, Russia and Iran, opposed by the USA and its allies Saudi Arabia, the UAE and Israel, the last two being now in open dalliance. Turkey, Malaysia and Indonesia would be balancing powers in this new schism. Pakistan will find its space constricted as it becomes more difficult to play all sides. Whether Trump is re-elected or not the sharpened divisions between Shia and Sunni, and intra-Sunni fault lines, with rival global powers backing either or even both sides, will persist. India has welcomed the UAE–Israel handshake but by doing so put itself more in one corner than at diplomatic equidistance.

Now, if ever, is the time for all nations to rise above geopolitics and face collectively the twin challenges of pandemic and economic dislocation. Chinese belligerence all around its periphery negates this approach as crass opportunism—to gain territorial or strategic edge when others are distracted—is driving Xi Jinping's vision of Chinese dominance. Hong Kong has been literally annexed, destroying China's own doctrine of one-nation, two-systems. Globally, despite the danger of the COVID-19 pandemic spreading due to popular protests, mass protests have been held in Beirut and earlier in Iraq.

But in J&K a sullen calm persists, leading to Pakistani frustration over Islamic nations not echoing its slogans over Indian handling of the issue. But the new reality is that China is now militarily positioned to work with Pakistan in the Ladakh–northern Kashmir theatre in a pincer move. Thus, while India has been able to wean away Saudis and Emiratis from Pakistan on the Kashmir issue, it cannot ignore the recent diplomatic fallout of its Kashmir policy and protests against the Citizenship Amendment Act (CAA). There was a strident reaction from Iran, Turkey, Malaysia and Indonesia on the CAA.

This may have been a reason why the union government earlier allowed Tabligi Jamaat members from Malaysia and Indonesia to attend the Delhi meeting, despite danger of the pandemic spreading, as an outreach to neutralise their governments. Thus, we find that Indian domestic politics and diplomacy get intertwined when India has a right-wing BJP government with an agenda derived from its majoritarian beliefs.

What a post-COVID-19 global order looks like will depend on the November US presidential election and Chinese reassessment of their current aggressive stance. Unless some miracle repurposed drug or vaccine is discovered in the next few months, the re-election of President Trump seems an uphill task. Historically, the kind of economic dislocation underway can be fatal for an incumbent's re-election. Pandemics, wrote Arab historian Ibn Khaldun having survived a great plague, in the past have caused the rise and fall of empires. Global rethink is inevitable on national security, merits of globalisation, centrality of health and ecology, rejigging of supply chains and so on. China's aggressive rise and role in the global order is now factored into global thinking on peace, security and stable trade. For instance, no system can be sustainable if China, the creator of the current global crisis, is the source of 90 per cent of US antibiotics and 70 per cent of ingredients for drugs.

Francis Fukuyama's notes, 'Our present world is simultaneously moving toward the opposing dystopias of hyper-centralisation and endless fragmentation.'[4] In a peculiar way, the epidemic reflects this: it requires the world to unite to fight it, but also requires social distancing to block its spread. But as the world passes through this nightmarish dystopia, all political leaders, democratically elected or autocrats, will get tested. Some such as President Moon Jae-in, leader of South Korea's Democratic Party, will emerge stronger after an election win due to stellar performance in containing the epidemic. Others such as Hungarian leader Viktor Orbán will subvert democratic institutions on the pretext of combating it. In the Gulf and West Asia, existing schisms will get accentuated due to the USA's unpredictable leadership and current strategic deficit. India can only fill that gap if its domestic politics reverts to the inclusive, egalitarian path laid by the founding fathers of the union. Otherwise, a balanced foreign policy will become unsustainable as India is seen by the world as choosing opportunism over morality, or conflicted between, as late US strategic thinker and former National Security Adviser titled his book, power and principle.[5]

11

# The Shifting Borders of Conflict[1]

DR AJAI SAHNI

The absence of a 'strategic culture' and of an institutional infrastructure for long-term policy planning by the Government of India has long been lamented, particularly within the security community. Current crises and conflicts consume national capacities; there are enduring deficits across all institutions of governance and entrenched disincentives—particularly within the security hierarchy—for all but the high-profile executive positions (and the perks and privileges that go with these). Moreover, a failure to integrate any academic or research institutions into the tasks and apparatus of policy projection and formulation is endemic across the institutions of governance throughout India.[2] There is, consequently, limited awareness of the dramatic transformations that envelop the world today, radically altering the very nature of national boundaries, the fundamental character of national sovereignty, and the augmenting and complex threats emerging from an increasingly tenuous world order.

In the early 1970s, environmentalist Lester Brown's *World without Borders*[3] was making tremendous ripples internationally. At the height of the Cold War, at a time when more than half the globe was still struggling with state formation and consolidation, and where the state and its democratic administration were thought to be the highest aspirations of mankind, Brown proposed that the state could be abolished and that impartial internationalism was not only a possibility but increasingly a necessity for mankind. He argued, broadly, that the traditional international system based on competition and conflict was no longer a viable model, and that the nation state and balance of power were dated concepts. Such a proposition was difficult to accept at that time and—despite a global pandemic and a rising environmental crisis nudging humankind to think of its common future rather than competitive interests of state—still seems untenable in the real world.

At the present stage of human development, the state remains the most powerful instrument of human transformation, for better or for worse. Competition, conflict and the balance of power remain as urgent today and have become infinitely more complex in an age of unprecedented and rapid change. Indeed, while the human technological profile has become immeasurably more sophisticated, we see a social and political regression to primitive tribalisms, to irrational ideologies of religious extremism, of ultra-nationalism, of ethnic sub-nationalism and a rising spectre of conflict everywhere. As Hannah Arendt observed, 'It is much easier to change the world than our ways of thinking.'[4] If anything, states have become more assertive of their identities and their divergent interests.

The state, as traditionally imagined, lies within clearly defined boundaries, with its armed forces defending its integrity and its sovereignty through what are described as 'blood and iron wars', when necessary. This has been the case for centuries though borders have shifted, as has the nature of weapons and war. Against this backdrop of relentless strife, Walter Lippman describes the essence of national security:

> A nation has security when it does not have to sacrifice its legitimate interests to avoid war, and is able, if challenged, to maintain them by war.[5]

We have long seen war as a dichotomy, a presence or an absence. We are either at war or at peace. Today, India celebrates long years of 'peace', decades over which military force, or at least overwhelming or decisive military force, has not been necessary to resolve our conflicts with neighbours.

But war is being reinvented; enormous sources of power are being deployed by India's adversaries. While manifest military violence between states, and particularly in the Indian neighbourhood, may have declined, warfare has entered into every aspect of human activity as political, economic, environmental and technological violence escalates. The state's capacity to defend its legitimate interests—the essence of national security—is being systematically challenged and eroded by new ways of warfare.

Decades ago, strategists of the Maoist revolution in China imagined a slow process of attrition, using all available instrumentalities of power, in their concept of 'protracted conflict': 'The strategy of protracted conflict postpones the decisive battle and calibrates its challenges to a calculus of risks—until the balance of power has shifted overwhelmingly to the side of the revolutionary forces.'[6] This is a process of 'nibbling expansion',[7] of exploiting the vulnerabilities and eroding the strengths of the adversary system. The entire strategy is based on the idea that military and political instruments are interchangeable in the execution of one vast and integrated strategic plan. The premise, moreover, is that 'victory, in the protracted conflict, will indeed go to the side able to preserve its position the longest'.[8]

This revolutionary strategy of protracted conflict has been vastly refined, again by Chinese strategists, into a contemporary dynamic of what has been described by two People's Liberation Army Officers, Colonel Qiao Liang and Colonel Wang Xiangsui, as 'unrestricted warfare'.[9] Unrestricted warfare is based on the premise articulated in the Maoist slogan 'Using the inferior to defeat the superior', and has broadly been framed as a strategy targeting American global hegemony. However, it is deployed not just against the USA, but globally—and India is already a visible target.

The first rule, and among the most prominent assumptions of unrestricted warfare, is that there are no rules; nothing is forbidden.[10] The doctrine of surprise, misdirection and deception is paramount, and the strategy also employs civilian technology as military weapons 'without morality' and with 'no limits' to break the will of democratic societies.[11] Other aspects envisaged under this strategy include the following:

High tech computer hackers, irregular forces and a range of newly empowered actors have ensured that 'boundaries between soldiers and non-soldiers have now been broken down'.[12]

The traditional practice of urban terror warfare is a means to impose 'a huge psychological shock to the adversary'.[13] Conventional state sponsorship of terrorism and proxy war retain their salience, but within a much wider strategy of employing all instrumentalities of power, kinetic and non-kinetic, against the adversary.

The strategy seeks to provoke overreaction and overreach on the part of the adversary. Thus, a particular offense or operation, such as the 9/11 attacks in the USA, for instance, can cause an adversary that uses conventional forces and measures as its main combat strength to 'look like a big elephant charging into a china shop'.[14] The 9/11 Commission estimated that the 9/11 attacks on the World Trade Centre and Pentagon cost Al-Qaeda between US$ 4,00,000 and US$ 5,00,000.[15] In its reaction, the US government has already spent more than an estimated US$ 5.4 trillion on its 'war on terrorism'.[16]

The components of unrestricted warfare include,[17] but are not exhausted by,

- financial warfare;
- cyber warfare;
- smuggling warfare: throwing markets into confusion and attacking economic order;
- cultural warfare: it is useful, in this context, to examine the proliferation of China's Confucius

Institutes across the world, and the US decision to shut several of these down on its soil;[18]

- drug warfare;
- media and fabrication warfare;
- technological warfare (gaining control of or having an edge in particular vital technologies that can be used in both peace and wartime);
- environmental warfare;
- terrorism; and
- political subversion: 'The legislatures of countries with representative forms of government cannot evade encirclement by lobbying groups.'[19]

It is important to remind ourselves that war is essentially a process of taking the adversary society apart so that it submits to your will. In classical war, you did this with swords and spears and, as technology advanced, with guns, bombs and missiles, and you did it across a fairly clearly defined border. But any instrumentality that can inflict damage on the target system is just as good, and contemporary social organisation offers a wide range of such instrumentalities which do not need a single shot to be fired or any territorial boundaries to be forcibly crossed.

The truth is, in many ways, that even as state identities harden, the 'world without borders' has come to pass. Not in the benign sense that Lester Brown intended, but in a malefic avatar. What we have is not a *world without borders*, but *wars without borders*; neither war nor peace. *Unrestricted Warfare* notes, 'The war god's face has become indistinct.'[20] Walter Wriston, writing about the revolution of the Information Age, notes that 'sovereignty, the power of a nation to stop others from interfering in its internal affairs, is rapidly eroding'.[21] There is, then, not a benevolent but a malevolent erosion of borders and state systems, inclining toward chaos, empowering the most malicious of actors, both state and non-state.

In *Unrestricted Warfare*, Qiao Liang and Wang Xiangsui speak of 'ten thousand methods combined as one', and of 'combinations that transcend all boundaries'.[22] In other words, unrestricted warfare.

There is now a progressive breakdown of distinctions between military technology and civilian technology, and between the professional soldier and the non-professional warrior. The battlespace overlaps with the civilian realm. Virtually every space is endowed with battlefield significance. It is 'even possible to start a war in a computer room or a stock exchange ... soldiers no longer have a monopoly on war'.[23] Further, 'Non-lethal weapons can effectively eliminate the combat capabilities of personnel and equipment without loss of life.'[24]

In May 2019, Hamas launched a barrage of missile attacks against Israel. In its response, Israel not only targeted Hamas military infrastructure, but, crucially, bombed and partially destroyed a building in Gaza because it was allegedly the base of an active Hamas hacking group. An Israel Defense Forces (IDF) tweet proclaimed, 'HamasCyberHQ.exe has been removed.' The media reported this action and reaction as a manifestation of contemporary 'hybrid warfare'.[25]

Compared to the warfighters of this new way of warfare, 'professional armies are like gigantic dinosaurs which lack strength commensurate to their size in the new age. Their adversaries ... are rodents with great powers of survival, which can use their sharp teeth to torment the better part of the world.'[26]

We have already seen this evolving in the Indian theatre, first and most visibly as terrorism and proxy war. It is not necessary to dwell at any length on this aspect. It is a familiar theme, and its principal architect has been Pakistan and its strategy of 'death by a thousand cuts'.[27] But note the carte blanche that Beijing gives to Islamabad on this. Despite loud proclamations of supporting the war against terrorism everywhere, China has implicitly protected Pakistan's relentless mischief in India. Crucially, the Chinese imprint is certainly visible from time to time, even in the weakening movements of India's troubled north-east.

Explicit proxy war is now being refined through a range of innovations, including forms of indirect incitement that include leaderless jihad[28]; stochastic terrorism or acts 'indirectly enabled by conspiracy theories' circulated in the mass media, especially by high-status political or religious leaders[29]; and 'scripted violence', where 'a high-status political or religious leader publicly identifies and demonises a specific group of people alleged to be conspiring to ruin the ideal nation'[30] but leaves it to listeners to carry out consequent violence. Each of these overlapping patterns of incitement results in potential 'lone-wolf' or 'wolf-pack' actions.

Despite the tremendous suffering and cost that terrorism and insurgency, often backed by foreign powers, have inflicted on India, these are relatively easier to fight—particularly because they are identifiable threats and the atrocities they perpetrate steel the national will to react, albeit fitfully. The instrumentalities of unrestricted warfare are, on the other hand, often celebrated by the target society, even as they destroy the fundamentals of social, economic and state power. It is useful to examine some contemporary trends within this context.

Data from 2018 showed India's trade deficit with China falling by US$10 billion, mainly because of a sizeable increase in exports from India. Trade watchers cheered. But there was a disproportionate increase in Hong Kong's exports to India of the same goods that New Delhi buys from Beijing. China was using Hong Kong to camouflage the real size of its exports to India.[31] India's trade deficit with China in 2017 was US$59.3 billion, dropping to US$57.4 billion in 2018. However, combined figures for China and Hong Kong showed that the deficit had, in fact, expanded from US$55.4 billion in 2017 to US$60.1 billion in 2018. India's import of mobile phone spares from China fell by 34.1 per cent in 2018, but rose from Hong Kong by 728 per cent during the same period. Similarly, import of LAN adapter cards from China fell by 32 per cent, but import from Hong Kong increased 173 per cent. The import of digital monolithic integrated circuits from Hong Kong increased by 6,017 per cent.[32]

Further, in its report of July 2018, the Parliamentary Standing Committee on Commerce noted that Chinese manufacturers were rerouting their products through markets of other countries with whom India had a Free Trade Agreement (FTA). Members of the Association of Southeast Asian Nations (ASEAN) served as hubs for Chinese exporters to circumvent anti-dumping and countervailing duties. The report observed, 'Chinese imports have thrown a spanner in the wheel of India's economic progress *per se*, and the industrial sector in particular.'[33] And further, that 'unscrupulous imports from China are also on account of influx of under-invoiced Chinese goods, goods brought in through misdeclaration and outright smuggling'.[34] Between April 2014 and December 2018, the Committee noted, a total of 4,133 cases of seizure of smuggled Chinese goods were recorded, with a total value of over ₹13.8 billion.[35] It is useful to note here that seizures of smuggled goods are only the tip of the iceberg, and this is borne out by the vast volumes of Chinese goods openly available in 'grey markets' across the country.

The impact on the economy can be illustrated with a single high-profile example. In 2016, it was estimated that two out of every three mobile phones sold in India were 'domestically produced', and that, by 2020 almost 96 per cent of the mobile phones to be sold in India would be 'locally manufactured'.[36] This should certainly be cause for celebration; except that local value addition in 2016 was a meagre 2.6 per cent and was expected to rise to 6.2 per cent by 2019.[37] In essence, Indian 'manufacturing' was stuck at the level of 'screwdriver technology', with 'limited capabilities across various processes of manufacturing value chain...resulting primarily in last mile assembly'.[38] This is the model of 'manufacturing' to be found across a wide range of sectors of Indian industry.

While traders and 'screwdriver manufacturers' profit, and gross domestic product (GDP) figures are inflated by this burgeoning trade with China, few realise the enormous costs inflicted on the long-term prospects of Indian state power. If you go out to buy an India flag today, it is likely to have been manufactured in China. The market is flooded with cheap Chinese goods of progressively improving quality. What does this mean for the Indian economy? For Indian industry? For employment in India? 'Manufacturers' are shutting down; or are rebranding Chinese goods and selling them as Indian products; increasing proportions of Indian manufacture are on the spectrum of screwdriver technology. Over time, Indian industrial capacities, Indian skills, research and development efforts and allocations, Indian entrepreneurship and Indian human resources profiles are being inexorably eroded. It is not just that India manufactures less and less. The country's infrastructure, the capitalisation, the skills, and the entrepreneurial attitudes and networks are slowly but surely disappearing. India can no longer efficiently manufacture even what she earlier could.

This is not a process impacting India alone. China has successfully acquired, stolen or developed the technological capabilities, and created the industrial capacities, to undermine manufacturing across the world. While it is entirely possible to look at this as a purely economic process driven by China's purposeful strategy to improve its economy, it is necessary to remind ourselves that the Chinese strategy welds all instrumentalities of power to a clear and sustained national purpose, which includes the promotion of

Chinese military–cultural–economic hegemony, both within the Asian region and across the globe.

The intention here is not to claim with any authority that China is engaged in a campaign of unrestricted warfare against India. But it is critical to note that the Chinese leadership does have such a strategy in mind. Indeed, the ambiguity of intent and purpose is integral to the nature of this strategy. It is the very complexity and opacity of globalising processes that give this strategy its power, and rob victim societies of the capacity for targeted response.

Equally, it must be understood that the Chinese intent is not the most significant, or even a relevant, variable here. Even if China is simply pursuing its own economic interests, without political–cultural–territorial hegemonic designs, the outcome remains the same in terms of the impact on Indian power and capacity.

India's policy trajectory has been tragically distorted by adherence to half-digested theories borrowed from the West, and the past decades have seen a shift from what can best be described as 'idiot socialism' to 'idiot capitalism'. Incoherence, opportunism and corruption, rather than adherence to either 'model', have dominated the Indian economy. It is crucially important to understand that there is no pure 'model' of either socialism or capitalism in the real world. In our new-found love for capitalism, we fail to recognise the very wide spectrum between, say, the Scandinavian model of welfare capitalism, and the predatory capitalism that dominates the USA. It is largely the rapacious US model that India has borrowed from, compounding its voracity with rampant corruption and crony capitalist practices. It is also important to note here that US capitalism is not, in any measure, 'pure'. It is deeply overlaid with 'socialist' practices, such as massive subsidies to certain sectors. In 2019, for instance, agriculture alone received a total subsidy of US$22.42 billion.[39] The USA has seen no conflict of ideology in adopting protectionist policies where it sees its competitive advantage shrinking. 'Pure' capitalism is something that is strongly recommended to other countries, particularly where profit-driven practices would benefit the dominant powers of the world. But interests of state, and not theory, overwhelmingly define the practices of these powers themselves.

Despite the rhetoric on the power and centrality of the private sector, the 'capitalist' Western states have never relinquished decisive control over certain economic and developmental processes. In particular, leading Western states have played a pivotal role in technological development, particularly through their funding and direction of defence research. Indeed, an overwhelming proportion of technological innovations of the last and current century—including virtually all dominant 'civilian' technologies—has been the result of government-funded defence research. This includes areas such as jet aircraft, rocketry, microwave devices, global positioning systems, wireless communications, the internet, virtual reality, computer networking, and satellite communication and surveillance, among a host of others. It was the 'spinoffs' of defence research that generated vast capacities for wealth creation in the wider economy.[40]

State support to science and technology was conceptualised as a control of 'command technology',[41] a notion reminiscent of the Nehruvian idea of the 'commanding heights' of the economy. While the failure of the Nehruvian vision is greatly emphasised by commentators today, what is forgotten is that Jawaharlal Nehru, in pursuit of this vision, laid the groundwork not only for India's ailing 'public sector' (undermined and corrupted by succeeding regimes) but also for whatever exists today as the country's lead scientific and technological infrastructure as well as the institutional framework for most of the country's best educational and research establishments.

Indeed, few among India's leaders have displayed any understanding of the true dynamics of state power. Western states have long operated on the premise of the centrality of the military–industrial complex, but this does not stand alone. Industrial competitiveness is based on sustained technological innovation, and this, in turn, on the country's scientific infrastructure. This last must be fed by outstanding educational institutions harnessing the best talents of human resources that have, themselves, been given the opportunities to grow across the entire national human resource pool. The national human resource profile, and consequently the education, healthcare and welfare complex that ensures its optimal development, is thus a crucial component of the dynamics of state power. Mere GDP growth, even if it is sustained over decades, cannot ensure the consolidation of state power as long as it continues to be marred by extreme inequalities and inequities, deteriorating standards of general education and the overwhelming burden of a poor and, crudely put, backward population.

The Western 'capitalist' economies persist with the policy of providing critical financial resources for the development of emerging technologies, particularly where these require massive investments and have long gestational cycles, as well as in horizon scientific research. The American 'Third Offset' strategy is a case in point. This is a programme that is intended to maintain military–technological superiority by supporting research and development in machine autonomy, artificial intelligence, quantum computing, enhanced digital communications and other technologies that would help dominate the future.[42]

China, similarly, seeks to establish technological leadership in a number of critical civilian and defence sectors.[43] China already accounts for 20 per cent of the world's research and development spending,[44] with a critical focus on semiconductors, quantum computing and artificial intelligence.[45] By 2017, China was spending 2.15 per cent of its far greater GDP on research and development, as against India's 0.6 per cent of GDP.[46] The widening gap between India and China can be imagined on this last parameter alone. In the absence of radical transformations in state policy, practice and investment across a wide spectrum of issues, prominently including education, research, technology development and transfer, India's ambitions as an 'emerging great power' are no more than delusional.

What needs to be understood, moreover, is the dramatically changing nature of power, and of power projection, across the world. Globally, power has become increasingly unstable, diffuse and fleeting. A global leadership void is complicating the ability to develop effective responses to mounting policy challenges. The shifting balance favours aggressors and abusers of traditional sources of power. Moreover, any direction, measure, group or person can be a source of threat to national security,[47] and establishing intent and responsibility for harm has become increasingly difficult for the victim state.

Crucially, it is not hostile states alone that exercise this power. The nation state no longer embodies the monopolies over power as was the case in the past. Today, an entire spectrum of transnational, private and non-state entities has the capacity to challenge national authority, national interests and national will. Such entities may, moreover, conspire with hostile states to undermine national systems.

Much of the new way of warfare involves means that appear bloodless—to the extent that explicit violence, the old 'blood and iron warfare', is not employed. But the consequences are no less devastating, and can bring ruination and death across vast populations; 'War is still as brutal as it has always been.'[48]

The West has, for decades, celebrated China's rise and enjoyed the fruits of cheap labour and the cheap goods it brought to Western shores. It is only now that there is an incipient realisation of the colossal price that has been imposed, the progressive erosion of Western power and capacity, and the relentless consolidation of the Chinese.

Moreover, the West is already in what has been described as a 'high technology trap involving the endless waste of limited funds and an arms race', as a result of which 'weapons to defend the country actually become a cause of national bankruptcy'.[49] Qiao Liang and Wang Xiangshu note, 'Based on weight, the B-2, which runs $13–$15 billion each, is some three times more expensive than an equivalent weight of gold.'[50] As mentioned earlier, the USA has spent trillions in conventional wars to respond to the low-cost terrorist attacks on their soil.

It is useful to recall that the break-up of the Soviet Union was, in fact, a direct consequence of the application of protracted war principles by the USA, resulting in the collapse of the Soviet Empire without a single shot being exchanged—at least, directly. There is now increasing consensus that the Soviet Union lost the Cold War because it was defeated by non-military means employed by its adversary, using psychological, political, informational, social and economic attacks against the Soviet state.[51] And yet, despite their experience with the Soviet Union, the Americans appear to be following in the footsteps of their erstwhile adversary.

Across the world, today, we find that few among those who actually run and administer the state comprehend how global power is being deployed, shaped and exercised. Never before has the adage 'knowledge is power' been truer or more urgent. And rarely before has the knowledge that underpins the efficient deployment of power been accessible to so few.

In India, there has been increasing awareness of the need for synergy, of a 'whole of government approach' to security. But this has not translated well into policy, practice and institutional evolution. Institutional cultures of government, and more so of the specialised agencies concerned with security and intelligence—where such synergy is even more urgently needed—militate against the shared environments, responsibilities, infrastructures and ethos that are necessary in the borderless, indeed, often formless wars that we must contend with. If India is not to fail, it is now imperative that we forge our own strategy of 'ten thousand methods combined into one'.[52]

12

# Non-traditional Neighbourhood Challenges Impacting Indian Security

TILAK DEVASHER

Any traditional analysis of national security challenges begins with a country's geographical construct and threat perception. For example, in Pakistan's case, there is a flat terrain coupled with several of Pakistan's population centres being close to the border with India. Even before the creation of Pakistan, the Cabinet Mission Plan of 16 May 1946 had stated clearly: 'The two sections of the suggested Pakistan contain the two most vulnerable frontiers in India and for a successful defence in depth the area of Pakistan would be insufficient.'[1] As a consequence of its geographical construct, Pakistan has always seen its threats in territorial terms and security primarily in military terms. This is equally true of other countries. Analysts have pitched in with comparison of nuclear arsenals, conventional military capabilities, use of non-state actors as force multipliers and so on with a missile for missile, tank for tank, division for division, aircraft for aircraft and ship for ship comparison between countries.

In this framework, conventionally, while talking about India's national security challenges the focus is on three elements: military, including nuclear challenges; terrorism, encompassing both territorial and transnational as well as ideology and the growth of radicalisation in and from the neighbourhood; and diplomatic, especially the role that our biggest neighbour, China, has started playing in the neighbourhood. Included in such discussions would be the new emphasis on the Indo-Pacific, the Belt and Road Initiative (BRI), the China–Pakistan Economic Corridor (CPEC) and so on.

Today, there has been a shift away from the exclusive stress on traditional security due to a variety of challenges faced by nation states. This has led to the evolution of the concept of 'national security' rather than 'military security' alone. National security essentially involves the capability of the state to overcome multidimensional threats to the well-being of its people and its survival as a nation state. This would encompass: energy security, food security, water security, economic security, environmental security and societal security.

An understanding of these non-traditional threats would make it easier to understand where India's neighbourhood is headed and what threats it could pose to us in the future, in addition to the traditional military, terrorist and diplomatic threats that we face.

In my first book, *Pakistan: Courting the Abyss*,[2] I had coined an acronym for these non-traditional threats—the WEEP factors, which stood for Water, Education, Economy and Population. Let me try and frame India's non-traditional security challenges in this framework.

## Water

A country is considered water stressed if the per capita availability of water falls below 1,700 m3/per annum, water scare if per capita availability falls below 1,000 m3/pa and absolute water scarce if it falls below 500 m3/pa. In our neighbourhood, Bangladesh, Nepal and Sri Lanka are very well placed and water abundant. China is above the water stressed mark with 1,971 m3/pc/pa while India is below the water stress level with availability around 1,450 m3/pc/pa.[3] In Pakistan, the availability has dropped to about 860 m3/pc/pa or a situation of water scarcity. According to the Pakistan Council for Research in Water Resources (PCRWR) the availability will fall below 500 m3/pc/pa by 2025,[4] that is, Pakistan will become an absolute water scarce country by 2025—in half a decade from now. This means drought-like conditions in parts of the country.

One reason for this is that Pakistan's productivity per unit of water and land is one of the lowest in the world. Its productivity per unit of water is 0.13kg/m3 only, one-third of India's and one-sixth of China's. Similarly, Pakistan's productivity per unit of land is half of India's.[5] Second, according to the International Monetary Fund, Pakistan's water intensity rate—the amount of water, in cubic metres, used per unit of gross domestic product (GDP)—is the world's highest, which means that Pakistan's economy is more water intensive and water dependent than any other country in the world. It is also indicative of the inefficiency of water usage. Its per capita water withdrawal is the third highest in the world.[6]

The United Nations (UN) estimates that water demand in Pakistan is projected to rise from the current levels to 274 million acre-feet (MAF) by 2025 while total water availability by 2025 is not likely to change from the current approximately 200 MAF. This gap of about 74 MAF is almost two-thirds of the entire Indus River's current annual average flow of about 91 MAF.[7] The IMF report 'Is the Glass Half Empty or Half Full?' takes the figures of water availability at 191 MAF and so projects a water shortage at 83 MAF by 2025.[8] There is no additional Indus River so where does Pakistan get this water from?

One indication of the impending crisis is calculating water withdrawal as a percentage of total renewable water resources (TRWR). According to the Food and Agriculture Organization (FAO), the pressure on national water resources is considered high if the TRWR value is above 25 per cent. Pakistan's water pressure amounts to a staggering 74 per cent. This pressure is exorbitant even compared with neighbouring high-pressured countries, including India at 34 per cent and Afghanistan at 31 per cent.[9]

An immediate impact of the water crisis would be on food production. Pakistan had the same water resources in 1951 when its population was 32.5 million. In 2017, it was 207 million and could increase to over 220 million by 2025. To feed this population at current production rates, 'Pakistan could have a food-grains shortfall of 16 million tonnes by 2020, increasing to 28 million tonnes by 2025. This would necessitate a 31 per cent increase in water availability to meet requirements of the population in 2025'[10]—an availability that is just not possible.

One of the most destructive consequences of the inefficiency of water usage has been the devastation of the Indus Delta. 'With the reduction of the historical flow of water into the delta region to barely 0.50–0.70 MAF per year, the sixth biggest mangrove forest in the world has been reduced from 0.6 million to 0.25 million acres.'[11] In addition, the drying up of the Indus Delta has led to sea intrusion up to 225 km. The two tehsils of district Thatta, that is, Kharo Chan and Keti Bander, have almost been eliminated from Pakistan in the past three decades and now only a few thousand fishermen reside along the coastal belt of Keti Bander and Kharo Chan.[12] Likewise, hundreds of villages in Badin district have been deserted and around 3,50,000 people have been forced to migrate to some other areas in search of livelihood. Apart from traditionally at-risk districts of Thatta and Badin, even districts such as Sanghar, Umerkot, Mirpurkhas, Nawabshah, Naushehro Feroz and parts of Hyderabad in Sindh have also been classified as being at risk of increasing soil infertility as a result of salinity due to seawater intrusion. This is the accumulated 'environmental debt' (a term used by the World Bank) that Pakistan's future generations will have to pay.

It is obvious that Pakistan's precarious water situation will pose a challenge and a threat to it but it is a threat for India too. For one, it is very likely that potential water refugees in the tens of thousands would start coming into India across the Sindh or south Punjab border due to drought-like conditions there and shortage of food. The water situation has already started impacting Indo–Pak relations with India being accused of water terrorism and with calls being made in Pakistan to review the Indus Waters Treaty. Such rhetoric will only increase.

Though China's per capita availability is above the water stress level, it has a serious problem of distribution. Simply put, China's agricultural core is in the north, providing two-thirds of Chinese agriculture but with only one-fifth of its water. Of China's water supply, 80 per cent lies in southern China. In the north, 12 Chinese provinces that account for 41 per cent of the population, 46 per cent of industry, and 50 per cent of its power generation face water scarcity. In fact, eight of these provinces are currently experiencing acute water scarcity, while in four provinces water is 'scarce' and two provinces are largely desert. As many as 400 Chinese cities now face water shortage, while 110 cities face severe water shortage.[13] The scale of the problem can be imagined by the fact that the 112 million people living in Beijing, Tianjin and the surrounding province of Hebei manage with less than the per capita annual water consumption of Saudi Arabia.[14]

Ground water availability too has become problematic. Nationally, groundwater usage has almost doubled since 1970 and now accounts for one-fifth of the country's total water usage, according to the China Geological Survey Bureau. It was believed in the late 2000s that the aquifer in northern China may be drained within 30 years.[15] According to a hydrologist quoted by the *New York Times*: 'The rate of decline is very clear, very well documented. They will run out of groundwater if the current rate [of extraction] continues.'[16]

Water shortages are thus China's (like Pakistan's) greatest threat both economically and politically. A report by the USA's National Intelligence Council described Chinese water and food shortages, predicted to occur by 2030, as a threat. [17] The problem is likely to be get further aggravated with annual water demand expected to rise to 545 MAF by the early 2020s. It is believed that if by 2030 drastic changes are not implemented the water crisis may no longer be containable. Moreover, 300 million people are estimated to be drinking water that is severely contaminated, and 190 million cases of illness are considered to result from this fact.[18]

The other problem is of climate change. China's lifeline is the glacial melt from the Qinghai-Tibetan Plateau that feeds the Yangtze and Yellow Rivers; the Yangtze alone supports 584 million people and serves an economic zone that constitutes 42 per cent of GDP. According to the State Laboratory of Cryospheric Sciences in China, run-off into the Yangtze decreased by 13.9 per cent during the 1990s.[19] Across the Yellow River basin region, water availability has been halved in the past 50 years. In 1997, the Yellow River dried up for 226 days, severing the river's connection to the Bohai Sea. [20]

A water crisis in China will lead to economic instability with significant political implications. It will also have an impact regionally and globally since

China's economy is predicted to account for 17.2 per cent of global GDP by 2025. In 2011, winter drought in China's eastern wheat-growing province forced it to purchase vast volumes of wheat from international markets.

The main thrust of the Chinese solution is engineering—the very high-profile South–North Water Transfer Project (SNWTP), inspired by Chairman Mao. In 1952, Mao stated, '[The country's] South has lots of water, the North has less, if it were possible, it could borrow a little.' The core of the project is a 1,200 km canal from the Yangtze to Beijing. The SNWTP is a US$62 billion project to funnel more than 12 trillion gallons northward every year along three routes from the Yangtze River basin. The full project is supposed to be completed in 2050. Of the three routes, the eastern and central are in various stages of construction/completion while the western one is mired in controversy due to environmental concerns. Analysts believe that this will only temporarily avert a crisis because it addresses the symptoms rather than the causes and may ultimately not resolve the problem in totality.

As the water crisis intensifies, it is quite possible that China would turn its attention to the Himalayas. This region is the source of Asia's great rivers: not only the Yangtze and Yellow, but also the Indus, Ganges, Sutlej and Mekong. Its ice fields are the third largest in the world, after the two poles. The impact of any such disruptions would not only be felt in India but also in Pakistan, Nepal, Bhutan, Bangladesh, Myanmar, Thailand and Vietnam.

For India, it is important that the Sutlej originates in China in the Kailash Mountain range. It has a catchment area of 75,369 sq km, of which 70 per cent is in India. According to a report by the FAO, the total inflow from China to India in the Indus River basin is estimated at 148 MAF. The mean annual inflow into Pakistan from India through the western tributaries, considering the Indus Waters Treaty, amounts to 138 MAF.[21] Thus, a water diversion/stoppage by China would certainly be a net loss for India but even more for Pakistan, if India were to develop the necessary infrastructure to divert water from Pakistan.

There is also the threat about the Brahmaputra due to reports about the Grand Western Water Diversion Plan (GWWDP). This is based on China's water crisis getting so serious that it will divert water flow from the Brahmaputra river to its dry north. This would be catastrophic for downstream countries. It is also significant that China has so far been disinclined to sign any binding agreement with downstream countries over transboundary rivers.[22] Some analysts, however, believe that the GWWDP is not technically feasible in the foreseeable future.

## Education

Education provides the road map for future generations and has two elements: quantitative, that is, the number of children in schools and, conversely, out of school; and qualitative, that is, what is taught in schools—the curriculum.

In our neighbourhood, Sri Lanka is best placed in this regard with just 1 per cent (12,000) children out of primary school and a literacy rate of 92 per cent. Nepal and Bangladesh, too, are not doing badly, each with 5 per cent (1,60,000 and 7,50,000 respectively) children out of primary school. The literacy rate is almost 60 per cent in Nepal and 73 per cent in Bangladesh. In India's case, 2 per cent (almost 2.9 billion children are out of primary school and literacy rate is close to 70 per cent. China has 11 per cent (14 billion) children out of primary school though its literacy rate is 95 per cent.[23] Once again, it is Pakistan that is the joker in the pack.

The Pakistan Education Task Force 2011 described the situation in Pakistan as an 'education emergency',[24] primarily because the country's education system is among the least effective in the world. Pakistan ranks 113 out of 120 countries in the Education Development Index. Nearly 50 per cent or 25.02 million children are out of school. Of these, over 5 million are at the primary level. The report estimated that one in ten of the world's not-in-school children in the primary age group lived in Pakistan (globally placing it second worst in out-of-school children rankings). Furthermore, even those admitted to schools suffer from massive drop-out rates before they reach class 5:63 per cent of boys, 77 per cent of girls in 2011. The proportion of out-of-school children increases with the rise in the level of education.[25]

While the country needs to spend 4 per cent of GDP on education just to be on track for the Millennium Development Goals (MDGs), its budgetary allocations have been abysmally low, hovering between

1.5 per cent and 2.1 per cent during the last 15 years with an even lower rate of actual expenditure.[26] According to a 2001 study, the government spent 3.3 per cent of GDP more on defence than other countries of its comparable income level, and that the overspending on defence was roughly equal to the sum of the underspending on health and education as a percentage of GDP.[27] Increasing education spending to 4 per cent of GDP would be next to impossible for the Pakistan Tehreek-e-Insaf (PTI) government given the precarious state of the economy.

Even more critical is the distorted curriculum in Pakistan. According to a Pakistani study,[28] curricula and textbooks of government schools include incitement to militancy and violence, and encouragement of jihad and *shahadat*, a glorification of war and force; encouragement of prejudice, bigotry and discrimination toward fellow citizens, especially women, religious minorities and other nations. Its conclusion was

> *Madrassas are not the only institutions breeding hate, intolerance, a distorted worldview, etc. The educational material in the government run schools does much more than madrassas.* The textbooks tell lies, create hatred, inculcate militancy, and much more.... [T]he curriculum encourages ideas that are incompatible with the ideals of Pakistan as a forward looking modern state committed to equal rights and equitable treatment for its citizens.[29]

Or, as a noted Pak intellectual put it: 'The greatest threat to Pakistan may be its abysmal education system.

Pakistani schools—and not just madrassas—are churning out fiery zealots, fuelled with a passion for jihad and martyrdom.'[30] Another 2016 report pointed out that in the curricula 'Hindus were portrayed as "enemies", while Christians were portrayed as "agents" of the West.'[31]

Given such a curricula in government schools, let alone madrasas, the radicalisation in Pakistan is hardly surprising.

The net impact of huge numbers being illiterate and semi-literate and infused with radical ideology is that the type of jobs they can do are at best low end; also, given their ideology the one attractive avenue would be to join the jihadi ranks. Cumulatively, this will act as a huge handicap on Pakistan emerging as a moderate and democratic state.

An uneducated or a poorly educated population imbued with hatred for India and Hindus (as also Christians and Jews) in a stagnant economy would be cannon fodder for the various jihadi organisations in Pakistan, most of whom have been programmed with an anti-India agenda. This, again, would pose a major security challenge to India.

## Economy

In macro terms, South Asia has just 2.7 per cent of global trade compared with East Asia's 30.1 per cent, 2.2 per cent of global foreign investment compared with East Asia's 48.1 per cent and 4.0 per cent of global GDP compared with East Asia's 30.2 per cent, while they account for 23.9 per cent and 30.7 per cent of the global population respectively.

Coming to specifics, the GDP growth is the highest in Bangladesh at 7.9 per cent, followed by China at 6.6 per cent, Nepal at 6.3 per cent, Sri Lanka at 3.2 per cent and Pakistan at 3.3, with the last expected to be at 2.4 per cent in the current financial year.[32] The poverty headcount ratio is also the highest in Pakistan at 33 per cent, followed by Nepal at 25 per cent and then Bangladesh at about 22 per cent. Sri Lanka is at about 4 per cent and China at 3.1 per cent. Applying a multidimensional poverty index (combination of the levels of education, health and standard of living), the Oxford Department of International Development showed that in 2012–2013, 44.2 per cent of Pakistanis were poor, 23.7 per cent were in severe poverty and 15.1 per cent were vulnerable to poverty.[33]

Due to poverty levels, according to the World Food Programme (WFP), 43 per cent of the population in Pakistan was food insecure, with 18 per cent facing a severe shortage; about 15 per cent of the population under the age of five was acutely malnourished; and close to 43 per cent children face stunting (low height for age) and were chronically malnourished. The World Health Organization (WHO) puts the number of stunted children in Pakistan at 50 per cent.

Pakistan Vision 2025, a document prepared by the Planning Commission of the Government of Pakistan in May 2014 explains the situation succinctly:

> Pakistan is currently facing serious challenges on various fronts. These include the combination of

> low growth and high inflation, which is one of the major factors leading to the perpetuation of poverty and unemployment. Energy shortages have posed great problems to the citizens as well as businesses and agriculture. Social indicators reflect serious deficiencies in education, health and population, gender equity and social services. The law and order situation in the country poses a critical threat to security as well as the economy. The decade-long struggle against terrorism and extremism continues to impose immense social, economic, and human costs.[34]

The World Economic Forum (WEF) held that Pakistan was especially weak on macroeconomic environment, health and primary education, higher education and training, labour market efficiency, institutions, infrastructure, technological readiness, innovation and market sophistication. It was ranked 139 out of 140 countries in business costs of terrorism, 132 in organised crime, 130 in business costs of crime and violence, and 126 in reliability of police services.[35]

The basic reason for the inconsistent performance of the economy is the structural weaknesses that have not been rectified over the decades and will not be rectified by ad hoc, Band-Aid type of solutions. The key among these structural weaknesses are poor governance, the high dependence upon external factors such as foreign assistance, exports and workers' remittances instead of internal drivers of growth, high burden of debt repayment, inadequate measures to raise the rate of savings and investment, low investment as a percentage of GDP in the social sectors such as health and education, a very high defence burden, a skewed land policy, revenue shortages and so on. The result of these structural flaws has been low rates of growth, poor infrastructure, unscientific agricultural practices, lack of industrialisation, a widening trade gap, high incidence of poverty, low social development indicators, a low standard of living, a low literacy rate and an unskilled workforce. Being a consumption economy, Pakistan has been heavily dependent on imports. This coupled with declining exports and inflation has led to rising debt servicing obligations and severe foreign exchange problems. Resultantly, there are inadequate funds available to invest in long-term assets for the well-being of the people.

As Stephen Cohen put it,

> Pakistan now barely survives on its own income and most social services are paid for by foreign countries. Were aid to cease, as it has in the past, the government would again be faced with financial failure. That happened in 2001, and it was only US intervention after 9/11 that came to the rescue of the fiscally bankrupt state. Both Pakistan's leaders and foreign donors know that given its current tax structure and weak export capability, Pakistan will remain dependent on foreign assistance indefinitely.[36]

## Population

Finally, population. Population of China is growing at 0.5 per cent, India and Sri Lanka's are growing at 1 per cent, that of Bangladesh at 1.1 per cent and Nepal's by 1.7 per cent.[37] Here again, it is Pakistan that is out of sync with the rest of South Asia with its population growing by a whopping 2.4 per cent. It was 207 million in 2017 when the last census was held. Incidentally, at present fertility levels, Pakistan's population could be as high as 335 million by 2050,[38] it could be even higher at 395 million in case of one additional birth per woman and as low as 266 million in case of one birth less.[39]

Numbers apart, the most critical aspect of population is age structures because countries with a larger proportion of working-age population relative to the young and elderly dependents have the potential for a demographic dividend. This potential has to be harnessed to lead to an economic spurt; if not harnessed it could lead to massive unemployment and its attendant consequences.

Bangladesh, India, Nepal and Pakistan have a growing working-age population: Bangladesh is at 67 per cent (63 per cent in 2010), India is at 66 per cent (64 per cent in 2010), Nepal is at 64 per cent (58 per cent in 2010) and Pakistan is at 61 per cent. China and Sri Lanka have a declining working-age population. In the case of China, the working-age population is estimated at 71 per cent, a decline from 74 per cent in 2010; in Sri Lanka's case it is 66 per cent, a decline from 67 per cent in 2010.

In Pakistan's case, the age structure of the population has been calculated as given in Table 12.1.

TABLE 12.1 *Population of Pakistan by Broad Age Groups (in Millions/ Percentage)*

| | 0–19 | 20–64* | 65+ |
|---|---|---|---|
| 2010 | 80.8/47 | 85.3/49 | 7.5/4 |
| 2030 | 91.9/38 | 136.8/56 | 14.5/6 |
| 2050 | 89.9/30 | 178.5/60 | 29.5/10 |

Note: * *The Economic Survey 2015–16* takes the age group of 15–64 as the benchmark and notes that 60.4 per cent of Pakistan's population falls in this age group. Likewise, it holds the dependent population of children under the age of 15 as 35.4 per cent.

Source: Asif Wazir, Anne Goujon, and Wolfgang Lutz, 'Education and Population: Closely Linked Trajectories for Pakistan', in Sathar, Royan and Bongaarts, *Capturing the Demographic Dividend.*

Pakistan's working-age population of 15–64 years crossed 50 per cent in the early 1990s and is currently estimated to be at 61 per cent, creating the possibility of a demographic dividend. This current share of 61 per cent would peak at 68 per cent around 2045 by when it will start ageing and move out of the working-age group.

Thus, the once in a lifetime window for Pakistan for a 'demographic dividend' is roughly between 1990 and 2045. Of these 55 years, 28 have already passed without any visible pick-up in economic activity.

To actualise demographic dividend the basic question is whether those entering the labour market can be absorbed productively against the backdrop of an increasingly globalised and technologically advanced world. A GDP growth of 5 per cent has been generating employment for less than 1 million persons per year. Based on population projections, 3.1 million persons are expected to enter the labour force every year over the next four decades. Thus, what Pakistan needs is a sustained GDP growth of over 7 per cent to generate employment to absorb these numbers. It would have to grow even faster if the current unemployment rate of 6 per cent is to be reduced.[40] However, Pakistan's economy grew at 3.3 per cent in 2018–2019 and is expected to grow at 2.4 per cent in 2019–2020. Hence, the employment generated will be around half a million. Moreover, more than half of the new entrants to the labour force will be either illiterate or poorly educated.

Table 12.2 shows the distribution of labour force by level of education, as calculated by an economist.

TABLE 12.2 *Distribution of Labour Force by Level of Education*

| Year | Illiterate | Primary | Middle | Matric | Intermediate | BA+ |
|---|---|---|---|---|---|---|
| 1990–1991 | 53 | 22.7 | 10.9 | 9.6 | 3.0 | 1.7 |
| 2001–2002 | 36.7 | 25.7 | 15.9 | 14.6 | 4.7 | 2.3 |
| 2010–2011 | 35.3 | 26 | 16.4 | 13.8 | 5.3 | 3.3 |

Source: Rashid Amjad, 'Why Has Pakistan Not Reaped Its Demographic Dividend?', in Sathar, Royan and Bongaarts, *Capturing the Democratic Dividend.*

What this shows is that over 61 per cent of the labour force was either illiterate or had only primary education and 3.3 per cent was graduate and above. What this means in an increasingly technologically advanced world can well be imagined.

Given the structural problems in the economy there are few signs of optimism in the key economic indicators or that the GDP growth would pick up significantly in the short to medium term. So what happens to the 2–2.5 million young people who year on year for the next three decades will be entering the labour market and will be unemployed?

If the demographic dividend is not realised, and it looks unlikely that it will in Pakistan, the massive 'youth bulge' could pose a serious threat to law and order, including, in Pakistan's case, of terrorism. The danger for Pakistan is that without sustained economic growth and without investment in education the demographic dividend would degenerate into a 'demographic horde' with all its attendant consequences of radicalisation, frustration, alienation and violence.

The other problem with an unrealised demographic dividend is that an unproductive population would pose huge pressures on resources such as food, water and energy. One sign of an unrealised demographic dividend is already visible. According to the National Nutrition Survey '... approximately 60 per cent of the country's population is facing food insecurity and nearly 50 per cent of the women and children are malnourished'. It warned, 'The growing population in Pakistan poses a significant threat to food security, Pakistan's development and social indicators and stability.'[41] The Planning Commission of Pakistan and the WFP in a report titled 'Minimum Cost of Diet in Pakistan' put the figure of lack of access to proper recommended nutrition at 67.6 per cent of the households across the country. This was particularly prevalent in the rural areas of Balochistan, where as many as 83.4 per cent households were unable to pay for adequate nourishment, closely followed by that in Sindh (70.8 per cent), Khyber Pakhtunkhwa (67.4 per cent) and Punjab (65.6 per cent).[42]

To conclude, India's neighbourhood challenges seen in terms of non-traditional security get focused on Pakistan, just as the military, nuclear and terror-related threats do. While military, nuclear and terrorist threats can be countered by developing our own capabilities, non-traditional security challenges are in a different league altogether. There is very little that India can do to counter such challenges in Pakistan, such as its increasingly diminishing water supplies, an uneducated horde of young people, an economy on the drip, demographic pressures and a growing radicalised population. The one thing that India can do, of course, is to ensure that its own parameters on such issues are in good shape and not deteriorating.

Pakistan faced an emergency situation in all these four areas about a decade ago. Today, it should be in the disaster management mode, but there are no signs that it is. Consequently, neither the army, nor nuclear weapons, nor non-state actors and neither Chinese assistance will help Pakistan overcome these hydra-headed problems. Pak leadership will have to demonstrate vision, understand the non-traditional security threats the country is faced with and be prepared to take resolute action to tackle each of the problems. For the moment, this is just not happening.

We will have to factor in the fact that India may not be able to escape the consequences of Pakistan's vulnerabilities and this, to my mind, could be among our dominant national security challenges in the future.

## Stop Press

The COVID-19 pandemic has impacted the neighbourhood as adversely as it has impacted India.

The consequences of this are still working themselves out at the time of writing. Hence, it is difficult to assess what the end result would be for the neighbouring countries. However, one thing is definite: a lot would depend on the intrinsic strength of each country to be able to bounce back, on the shape of its economy and the resilience of its people to put the devastation of the pandemic behind them and look ahead. Countries such as Pakistan, that were already on a slippery slope even before the pandemic, have been more severely impacted than the others in the neighbourhood. Assessments indicate that its GDP growth has slipped into the red with estimates varying up to minus 2.4 per cent. Given poor leadership and the deteriorating state of play of its relations with one of its key benefactors—Saudi Arabia—Pakistan is likely to face an extremely uphill task in reviving the economy in the months ahead.

13

# Combating Left-wing Extremism

PRAKASH SINGH, IPS

The Communist Party of India (Maoist) was ranked fourth among the top ten most active non-state armed groups of the world in 2013 by *Jane's Global Terrorism and Insurgency Index*. The then Prime Minister Manmohan Singh described it as the greatest threat to the internal security of the country.

## Early Phase

The Naxal movement, as it was originally called, had its beginnings in 1967 in a small village called Naxalbari at the tri-junction of India, Nepal and Bangladesh (then East Pakistan). Three persons shaped the course of events—Charu Mazumdar, the ideologue, Kanu Sanyal, the organisational mastermind and Jangal Santhal, who mobilised the tribals. The movement was crushed by the West Bengal police, but the sparks flew to different parts of the country. The idea that there should be a revolutionary struggle with bases in the rural areas, that these should be expanded to encircle the urban centres and that a people's liberation army should be organised to bring about a democratic revolution in the country caught the imagination of the people. The movement spread in ever-widening circles to different parts of the country. Charu Mazumdar was, however, arrested in 1972 and he died soon thereafter.

During the last 50 years, the movement had its ups and downs, but the trajectory of violence remained at a fairly high level and, according to an estimate by the Ministry of Home Affairs, about 12,000 lives have been lost during the last 20 years.[1]

In 2004, the two largest components of the Naxal movement, the People's War and the Maoist Communist Centre, coalesced to form the Communist Party of India (Maoist). At the Party Congress held in 2007, the party stated that its objective was to bring about a New Democratic Revolution with agrarian revolution as its axis, and that this would be achieved through

- protracted people's war,
- establishing base areas,
- strengthening the People's Army,
- broadening the mass base and
- militant mass movements.

The strategy and tactics of the party were defined in the following words:

> The central task of the Indian revolution is the seizure of political power. To accomplish this central task, the Indian people will have to be organised in the people's army and will have to wipe out the armed forces of the counter-revolutionary Indian

> state through war and will have to establish, in its place, their own state—the People's Democratic State and will have to establish their own political authority. The very act of establishment of the state machinery of the people by destroying, through war, the present autocratic state machinery—the army, the police, and the bureaucracy of the reactionary ruling classes—is the central task of the People's Democratic Revolution of India.

In 2010, the movement touched a peak, when a total of 2,213 incidents of Naxal violence were reported from across the country in which more than a thousand people were killed. More than 200 districts were affected, particularly in Andhra Pradesh, Bihar, Chhattisgarh, Jharkhand, Madhya Pradesh, Maharashtra, Odisha and West Bengal.

## Government Efforts to Contain It

The Indian government has all along been trying to contain the movement. P. Chidambaram, then Home Minister of India, sent battalions of the Central Armed Police Forces to all the Naxal-affected states in early 2010. His strategy was summed up in three graphic words: *clear*, *hold* and *develop*. It implied that the Naxals should first be cleared out of their swamps by undertaking counter-insurgency operations and, in the second stage, the civil administration would establish itself in the areas cleared; finally, in the third stage, economic development shall be undertaken in those regions. The sheer presence of security forces in strength and the operations undertaken by them brought the level of violence down. A number of politburo and central committee members were put in charge of the areas. The NDA government has been broadly continuing with the same policy though, in 2017, it came up with the concept of SAMADHAN—which implied smart leadership, aggressive strategy, motivation and training, actionable intelligence, dashboard KPIs (Key Performance Indicators) and KRAs (Key Result Areas), harnessing technology, action plan for each theatre and no access to financing.

Presently, the government is following 'an integrated and holistic approach' to deal with the problem of Left-wing extremism (LWE). It is pursuing what is called a 'National Policy and Action Plan',[2] which involves a multipronged strategy in respect of security, development and ensuring the rights and entitlements of local communities.

The security related measures include the following:

- Providing Central Armed Police Forces
- Sanctioning India Reserve Battalions
- Modernising and upgradation of state police
- Reimbursing security-related expenditure
- Strengthening and sharing of intelligence
- Fortifying police stations
- Providing helicopters for counter-insurgency operations
- Facilitating interstate coordination.

The Government of India has also launched special schemes to improve the basic infrastructure in areas affected by LWE. These include road and telecom connectivity and skill upgradation. Priority is also being given to implementing the Forest Rights Act, 2006, especially the provisions relating to allotment of title deeds to individuals and communities.

Table 13.1 shows the total number of incidents and deaths in various states from 2013 to 2018 and the figures are illustrative.

It can be seen that there has been a significant decline in LWE violence. There was a decline in the total number of violent incidents (1,091 to 833) and also in casualties (310 to 244). As compared to 2017, the year 2018 saw a decline of 8.3 per cent in violent incidents and 8.7 per cent in the number of deaths. Casualties of security forces also fell by 10.7 per cent (75 to 67) during this period while there was a 65.4 per cent increase (136 to 225) in the number of Maoist cadres eliminated.

Chhattisgarh remained the worst affected state followed by Jharkhand, Bihar, Odisha and Maharashtra. In fact, Chhattisgarh and Jharkhand together accounted for 71.7 per cent of the total number of violent incidents and 81.7 per cent of deaths.

During 2019, there were a total of 302 fatalities. These included 99 civilians, 49 security forces personnel and 154 Naxalites.

During 2020, according to data compiled by the South Asia Terrorism Portal, there have been a total of 61 fatalities (18 civilians, 25 security forces personnel and 18 Naxalites) in LWE-linked violence till 19 April 2020.[3]

The geographical spread of LWE violence has also shrunk considerably. In 2018, LWE violence was

TABLE 13.1 *Total Number of Incidents and Deaths in Various States, 2013–2018*

| State | 2014 | | 2015 | | 2016 | | 2017 | | 2018 | |
|---|---|---|---|---|---|---|---|---|---|---|
| | Incidents | Deaths | Incidents | Deaths | Incidents | Deaths | Incidents | Deaths | Incidents | Deaths |
| Andhra Pradesh | 18 | 4 | 35 | 8 | 17 | 6 | 26 | 7 | 12 | 3 |
| Bihar | 163 | 32 | 110 | 17 | 129 | 28 | 99 | 22 | 59 | 15 |
| Chhattisgarh | 328 | 112 | 466 | 101 | 395 | 107 | 373 | 130 | 392 | 153 |
| Jharkhand | 384 | 103 | 310 | 56 | 323 | 85 | 251 | 56 | 205 | 43 |
| Madhya Pradesh | 3 | 0 | 0 | 0 | 12 | 2 | 3 | 1 | 4 | 0 |
| Maharashtra | 70 | 28 | 55 | 18 | 73 | 23 | 69 | 16 | 75 | 12 |
| Odisha | 103 | 26 | 92 | 28 | 86 | 27 | 81 | 29 | 75 | 12 |
| Telangana | 14 | 5 | 11 | 2 | 7 | 0 | 5 | 2 | 11 | 2 |
| Others | 8 | 0 | 10 | 0 | 6 | 0 | 1 | 0 | 0 | 0 |
| Total | 1,091 | 310 | 1,089 | 230 | 1,048 | 278 | 908 | 263 | 833 | 244 |

Source: Ministry of Home Affairs Annual Report, 2018–2019, pp. 10–11.

reported from 60 districts spread across 8 states as compared to 76 districts spread over 10 states in 2013. The arc of violence, according to the Ministry of Home Affairs (MHA), is now restricted to 30 districts of the country only, accounting for 89 per cent of the LWE violence.

Surrenders have further eroded Maoists' strength.[4] While replying to a question in the Rajya Sabha, State Home Minister G. Kishan Reddy stated that 1,442 Naxals had surrendered in 2016, followed by 685 in 2017 and 644 in 2018. In 2019, according to South Asia Terrorism Portal (SATP), the figure of surrenders was at least 340.

Concerned over the weakening of the movement, the Naxals replaced Muppala Lakshmana Rao aka Ganapathy, the 71-year-old 'General Secretary' of the CPI (Maoist), on 5 November 2018 with his second-in-command, Nambala Keshava Rao aka Basavaraj (63 years). Keshava Rao was heading the military wing of the People's Liberation Army and is said to be an expert in military strategy. There has been a recrudescence of violence ever since his taking over.

Rajnath Singh, the former Home Minister of India, expressed his optimism on 23 April 2019 that the Naxal problem will be rooted out from the country by 2023.[5] In this context, it is worth placing on record that P. Chidambaram as Home Minister had also asserted on 29 July 2010 that, 'The Centre was confident of overcoming the ultra-left problem in the next three years through its existing two-pronged policy—development and police action—to deal with the menace in the affected areas.'

Addressing a meeting of Chief Ministers of the affected states,[6] Home Minister Amit Shah said on August 2019 that the government was committed to uprooting Left-wing extremism and urged all the states to adopt a focused, time-bound approach to completely eliminate the problem while also ensuring all-round development of the Naxal-affected areas. He laid particular emphasis on intelligence-based and technology-aided operations, and stressed on implementing central welfare schemes, setting up local Eklavya model schools and providing banking facilities. On 28 November 2019, Home Minister Amit Shah, while campaigning for the assembly elections in Jharkhand, asserted that Naxalism shall be 'buried twenty feet under the ground'.[7] The claim is not borne out by the situation prevailing on the ground.

## Naxal Threat Continues

The Naxal threat to the Indian State, notwithstanding the government's claims, continues. It is true that there has been a depletion in their strength; it is also true that they are having difficulty in attracting fresh recruits and that they have retreated from some areas where they were well entrenched. But, the fact remains that they still have the capacity to launch lethal attacks on security forces. In Chhattisgarh, a Bharatiya Janata Party (BJP) Member of Legislative Assembly (MLA), Bhima Mandavi, and four police personnel were killed in an IED (improvised explosive device) explosion in Dantewada while they were returning in a bulletproof vehicle after electioneering on 9 April 2019. In Maharashtra, 15 policemen of the Quick Response Team of C-60, Maharashtra Police counter-insurgency commando unit, were blown up when Maoists triggered an IED in Gadchiroli on 1 May 2019. In Jharkhand, at least 26 CRPF (Central Reserve Police Force) and Jharkhand Armed Police personnel were injured when Maoists exploded a series of IEDs in Seraikela-Kharsawan district on 28 May 2019. An important newspaper commented in its editorial that 'clearly, the Maoists sent out a message that they still possess the firepower to take on the security forces and establish territorial dominance'.[8] There was also a report in October 2019 that the Naxals have perhaps acquired unmanned aerial vehicles (UAVs)/drones. According to the CRPF spokesman, drone-like objects were seen flying over the CRPF camps of Palodi and Kistaram in the jungles of Sukma district of Chhattisgarh.[9]

In 2020, the CPI (Maoist) cadres ambushed a police party in the dense forests of Elmaguda in Sukma district of Chhattisgarh, killing 17 security forces personnel (12 District Reserve Guards and 5 Special Task Force) and injuring another 15. The Maoists also looted at least 15 weapons including 12 AK47 assault rifles.

The Maoists are meanwhile trying to expand their influence in certain new areas. They have infiltrated parts of the north-east. They are also attempting to increase their influence in the three southern states of Tamil Nadu, Karnataka and Andhra Pradesh. Increased Maoist activity has been noticed at the tri-junction of these states. Besides, they have made a dent in some urban areas, where a sizeable number of intellectuals support their ideology. In this context, it may be recalled that the former state government of Maharashtra had arrested 10 urban Naxals in what is now famously known as the Koregaon-Bhima case in 2018; five (Surendra Gadling, Shoma Sen, Mahesh Raut, Sudhir Dhawale and Rona Wilson) were arrested on 6 June and another five (Sudha Bhardwaj, P. Varavara Rao, Gautam Navlakha, Arun Ferreira and Vernon Gonsalves) on 28 August from different parts of the country.[10] They were charged with inciting violence between the Dalits and upper castes on 1 January 2018 and certain other offences including a plot to assassinate the Prime Minister. The People's Union for Civil Liberties criticised the arrests as 'a concerted attempt to crush human rights interventions and silence voices of dissent'. The present state government is reviewing the case.

In the rural areas of several states, the Maoists have formed organisations opposed to the establishment under different names. Thus, there is the Pathalgadi movement in parts of Jharkhand and Chhattisgarh, Sarvahara Jan Andolan in Maharashtra, Jai Adivasi Yuva Shakti in Madhya Pradesh and Majhi Pargana Mahal in West Bengal.[11] The slogan of the Pathalgadi movement is *Na lok sabha, na vidhan sabha, sub se bada gram sabha* ('neither parliament nor assembly, the highest is *gram sabha*'). These groups have been exploiting agrarian discontent among the peasantry in their respective states.

The CPI (Maoist) has, according to a recent report,[12] formed a new Central Committee with 21 members, out of whom 10 are from Telangana, 4 from Jharkhand, 2 each from Andhra Pradesh, Maharashtra and West

Bengal, and 1 from Bihar. The strength of the People's Liberation Guerilla Army was estimated in June 2018 at around 6,000. According to another recent report, it plummeted to 3,500 in 2019.[13]

## Movement Resurrects

The Naxals may be in a sort of a tactical retreat. It would, however, be naïve to conclude that the government is in the process of vanquishing the LWE. Taking a historical overview, the movement has shown a remarkable capacity to reorganise and reinvent itself after a period of setback. Twice before, the government was lulled into a feeling that they had knocked out the Naxals. It happened in the late 1970s when Charu Mazumdar was arrested and died in police custody and there were serious inner party differences. The movement, however, revived with the formation of the People's War Group in 1980. Later, after Kondapalli Seetharamaiah, leader of the People's War, was arrested and there were successful counter-insurgency operations, the government was again under an illusion that they had seen the end of the problem. The movement again revived—with much greater ferocity and violence—with the merger of the People's War and the Maoist Communist Centre (MCC), two major components of the movement, and the formation of the CPI (Maoist) Party in 2004. The CPI (Maoist) has since emerged as the leading Naxal formation wanting to bring about a new democratic revolution in India as part of the world proletarian revolution.

Any assessment that the Naxal problem is going to end in the next few years is completely misplaced. There are periods when the security forces are able to establish their dominance and the Maoists suffer reverses. The movement, however, always resurrects in a new avatar for the simple reason that the basic socio-economic reasons, which gave rise to it and continue to sustain it, remain largely unaddressed.

## Socio-Economic Factors

India is today one of the fastest growing economies of the world. The country is expected to overtake Germany to become the fourth-largest economy in 2026, and Japan to become the third largest in 2034.[14] However, it is said that we have moved from the British Raj to Billionaire Raj. The country has the fourth-highest numbers of billionaires after USA, China and Germany. But there are glaring inequalities. According to a latest Oxfam report,[15] which was released on the eve of World Economic Forum meet in Davos (January 2020), in India, the top 1 per cent of the wealthy, roughly 13 million people, hold 42.5 per cent of the national wealth as against 2.8 per cent held by the bottom 50 per cent or about 650 million of the poorest citizens. Another report, *The World Social Report, 2020: Inequality in a Rapidly Changing World*[16] by the United Nation's (UN's) Department of Economic and Social Affairs has also painted a gloomy picture of the widening income gap.

> Without appropriate policies and institutions in place, inequalities concentrate political influence among those who are already better off, which tends to preserve or even widen opportunity gaps.... Growing political influence among the more fortunate erodes trust in the ability of government to address the needs of the majority. This lack of trust, in turn, can destabilise political systems and hinder the functioning of democracy.

In the Global Corruption Index, India has slipped two spots according to Transparency International's report released early this year.[17] India's rank was 78 in 2018; it is 80 in 2019. Land reforms are not on the agenda of any state government. Farmers continue to commit suicide in large numbers. According to The National Crime Records Bureau (NCRB) data, at least 10,349 people working in the farming sector ended their lives in 2018, accounting for 7.7 per cent of the total number of suicides in the country. The employment scenario is also bleak and, according to Azim Premji University, unemployment among the youth and educated is at 16 per cent.

Our approach to development has, in fact, some basic flaws. An Expert Group appointed by the Planning Commission (2008), of which the author was also a member, observed as follows[18]:

> The development paradigm pursued since Independence has aggravated the prevailing discontent among marginalised sections of society. This is because the development paradigm

> as conceived by the policy makers has always been imposed on these communities, and therefore it has remained insensitive to their needs and concerns, causing irreparable damage to these sections. The benefits of this paradigm of development have been disproportionately cornered by the dominant sections at the expense of the poor, who have borne most of the costs. Development which is insensitive to the needs of these communities has invariably caused displacement and reduced them to a sub-human existence. In the case of tribes in particular it has ended up in destroying their social organization, cultural identity, and resource base and generated multiple conflicts, undermining their communal solidarity, which cumulatively makes them increasingly vulnerable to exploitation.

The tribals who constitute the backbone of the Naxal movement are today a disaffected lot. Two factors—land alienation and their displacement—have mainly contributed to their disillusionment with the establishment. An Expert Group constituted by the Ministry of Rural Development of the Government of India, which studied the problem in depth (2004),[19] concluded that land alienation was rampant in all the states, and it noted with anguish that such alienation was taking place 'despite the existence of an umbrella of protective legislation since the 19th century'. The Expert Group went on to observe that in the process of alienating land from the tribals, it seemed 'as if private individuals, derelict revenue officers including Deputy Commissioners, unscrupulous lawyers, ignorant civil courts and even the better-off tribals themselves have all joined hands, as it were, to deprive the tribal communities of their land'. The tribals, as a result, were feeling 'totally exhausted, impoverished and traumatised'.

A large population of tribals has also been displaced from their habitat because of development projects—irrigation dams, power plants, industrial and mining projects, declaration of sanctuaries and national parks and so on—undertaken in the area. There are no official figures of the total number of tribals displaced. However, some unofficial studies, particularly by Dr Walter Fernandes, peg this figure at around 60 million for the period from 1947 to 2004.[20] Tribals constitute only about 8 per cent of the country's population, but they are 40 per cent of the total displaced persons due to the projects. The rehabilitation and resettlement of these tribals have been inadequate. No wonder that they are bitter with the government.

The tribals are also unhappy over the implementation of the Forest Rights Act. Fortunately, the Supreme Court, on 28 February 2019, stayed its earlier order of eviction in 16 states of tribal families whose claims to forest land had been rejected.

Governance is also a major factor. There are areas which are poorly governed, there are areas which are badly governed and there are areas which are not governed at all. The result of bad governance is seen in the multiple insurgencies that we face in different parts of the country, particularly in the north-east and on our northern borders. According to the Expert Group (2008), areas in Central India where there is unrest are 'minimally administered' and that state interventions both for development and law and order had been fairly low. As a result, there is a kind of administrative vacuum in these areas that is exploited by the armed insurgent groups. In Chhattisgarh, Abujmarh in Narayanpur district was beyond the pale of administration even 70 years after Independence. It is a 4,000 sq km area comprising 260 villages inhabited by tribals, particularly of the Maria group. The terrain is no doubt difficult, but there could be no justification for the area not having been surveyed and the absence of any regular revenue or police administration in the region. It is hardly surprising that the Maoists established a 'liberated zone' in Abujmarh.

As long as these factors continue—extreme inequalities of income, unemployment on a large scale, neglect of land reforms, rampant corruption, significant groups of tribals feeling disaffected, poor state of governance—and there being no indication yet of the aforesaid factors disappearing in the foreseeable future, the Naxal movement would continue to haunt the Indian State and pose a formidable challenge to the law enforcement agencies

## Way Forward

Tackling the movement calls for a 'whole of government' approach. It is necessary that all the government departments contribute their bit to addressing the grievances and needs of the people belonging to the lower strata of society. Unfortunately, this is not happening, and there is a tendency to look upon the Maoist problem as essentially a law and order problem and pass on the buck squarely to the police. This mindset will have to change if the battle against the Maoists is to be won.

It is also disconcerting that every Chief Minister views the problem from his own perspective. The Chief Minister of Bihar believes that development is the right approach and not counter-insurgency operations. In West Bengal, Mamata Banerjee was, in the initial stages, inclined to mollycoddle the Maoists until they started attacking Trinamool Congress cadres. The present Chief Minister of Chhattisgarh believes that Naxalism is a socio-economic problem and there is 'need to initiate a dialogue with the affected people, mainly of Bastar, and all the other stakeholders on how to bring an end to violence'.[21] It is absolutely necessary that there is a national policy to deal with the LWE problem and all the state governments are on board with that policy.

It would also be necessary to build the capabilities of the state police forces and strengthen their intelligence network. The Supreme Court's directions on police reforms must be implemented. The requirements of manpower, better transport, improved communications and adequate forensic facilities for the police forces must be addressed. Several Chief Ministers look upon LWE as an all-India problem and, therefore, the Centre's baby. The states will have to understand their constitutional responsibility in the matter and contribute substantially to containing the Maoist problem. The Centre can play a useful supporting role, but it is the states and their forces that will have to be at the forefront of any assault on the Maoists. Interstate coordination in counter-insurgency operations will have to be ensured.

The socio-economic factors, which contributed to the growth and expansion of the movement, will have to be tackled in a sincere and sensitive manner. The provisions of the Forest Act must be implemented in letter and spirit.

The government should also consider initiating peace dialogue with the Maoist leadership. This seems to be an opportune moment for holding out the olive branch. If the government can have talks with the Naga rebels for more than the last two decades, if it had no problem in having talks with the Hurriyat leaders of Jammu and Kashmir in the past, there is no reason why it should have any reservation in holding talks with the Maoist leaders.

There are enough indications that the Maoists are losing influence in their strongholds across the country. There are few takers of their ideology, their base area has shrunk, recruitment has almost dried up and desertions and surrenders have corroded their strength.[22] Their ageing leadership is finding it difficult to sustain the momentum of the movement. The time is ripe for making right and decisive moves. The government should, while maintaining pressure on the law and order front, send feelers for a peace dialogue. Above all, it must address the grievances of the aggrieved sections of people, especially the tribals.

The Naxal movement has seen a lot of bloodshed. It is time that the gory chapter is brought to a close. The Indian State should show large-heartedness in meeting the legitimate demands of the Naxals and initiate steps to bring them into the national mainstream. The Naxals should adjust themselves to the present environment 'where the space occupied by the left is gradually shrinking and Marxism–Leninism–Maoism is ceasing to have any significant relevance'.[23]

14

# India's Approach on Jammu and Kashmir after Revoking Article 370

LIEUTENANT GENERAL SYED ATA HASNAIN (RETIRED)

The most flogged subject in India's strategic circles, Jammu and Kashmir (J&K), is also everybody's favourite. From the politician to the academic and from the layman to the tourist, everyone has an opinion; that is how it should be. However, policy and strategy are not made on the basis of half-baked conjectures. That should be based upon meticulous background knowledge and solid evidence of what has earlier worked, to some extent, in J&K or fully elsewhere in the world in the context of sponsored proxy hybrid conflict, the conflict system which is in vogue there. Besides precedence, it is prediction that is necessary to develop the strategic needs to handle such a situation. This essay is an attempt to place the conflict situation in J&K in better perspective, away from the simplistic understanding with which most of our countrymen appear to view it. It is a complex affair in which there is need to discard misnomers and strengthen understanding so that the Indian public can realistically support the Indian narrative to strongly secure J&K

to India. None of this can be done without at least a minimal background narrative; and the starting point of that is 1971. The period 1947–1971 quite obviously forms an important part but events of that period have been overtaken by history.

## Brief Background

Let us start with a basic assumption that many of our countrymen overlook or nonchalantly dismiss. Pakistan is no pushover. It is a nuclear-armed nation with a 6,50,000-strong army. No doubt it was comprehensively defeated on the battlefield in 1971, but today it cannot be wished away as weak, poorly administrated and capable of being divided or split up. It occupies a very important geostrategic space which all the big powers find significant for their strategic interests. So even as Indian diplomacy achieves much in garnering international support for our nation, no one is going to turn around and just dismiss Pakistan or blindly support Indian narratives. In fact, most of the big and middle powers do engage Pakistan in pursuit of their interests although most of them also do not support its policies on J&K. In addition, the common Indian citizen's wishful thinking about resolving the J&K issue through conventional war is passé. Contemporary experience in the light of various alternative strategies has proven that smaller and weaker nations may be comprehensively defeated but, many a time, without achievement of war aims. Iraq and Afghanistan are two prime examples. So if we want the world to support us we have to adopt the right strategy and execute the right actions in J&K and correctly project them; the moral aspect of the narratives too must be sound and backed by effective communication.

The current situation has a complex history which is not addressed here. However, just a few reminders to get the context and narratives in right order. First is that the territory of J&K is claimed by us on the basis of the Instrument of Accession signed by the Maharaja of Kashmir ceding J&K to India on 26 October 1947. Pakistan contests it on the plea that it was signed under duress. Second is the fact that we hold only a percentage of J&K's original territory, the rest being occupied by Pakistan (and China); the borders currently rest on unstable lines—the Line of Control (LoC) and the Line of Actual Control (LAC). Third, India went to the United Nations (UN) with sincerity as it wished to get on with the business of nation building and not get mired in armed conflict right at the outset of its journey as a nation in 1947–1948. The UN resolutions have been un-implementable because they call for withdrawal of Pakistan's forces before a plebiscite can be held; Pakistan will not do that. Internationally, Pakistan continues to harp upon the resolutions without being questioned on its responsibility towards the slated withdrawal. The Indian standpoint changed after 1972, when the Shimla Agreement was signed post the Indo–Pak conflict of 1971. The agreement introduced bilateralism as the means of conflict resolution without intervention or mediation by any third party. That made the UN resolutions irrelevant although we did not officially pursue that line at the UN. Year after year, Pakistan has internationalised the issue by raising it in the UN and other forums against the spirit of the Shimla Agreement. Fourth, India, with a lack of strategic insight, hoped that J&K would be resolved early; on that assumption it gave no thought to the special constitutional status that it accepted and accorded to J&K under Articles 370 and 35A. These provisions were progressively hollowed out, but the psychological perception of J&K not being fully integrated dictated the narrative among the local people, primarily the Muslims. Although strongly debated by many, these provisions also kept the conflict potential alive with hope of *azadi* (freedom); a notion Pakistan exploited to promote separatism for eventual integration with its territories.

## Pakistan's Conflict Initiation in 1989

India roundly defeated Pakistan in 1971, created Bangladesh, but failed to remove J&K as a bone of contention. With 93,000 prisoners of war in its hands it could have abrogated both special constitutional provisions at that juncture; although international realpolitik of the time may have prevented it.

The Pakistan Army's intent towards retribution against India for the events of 1971 was insufficiently monitored or assessed in India. It was armed by the USA and financed by Saudi Arabia to lead the fight against the Soviets in Afghanistan from 1980 to 1989. There it built a repertoire of experience in proxy war and, by the end of 10 years, was battle ready for J&K through a more prudent war strategy—sponsored hybrid war. That put at rest India's conventional military superiority; Pakistan's undeclared acquisition of nuclear weapon capability also neutralised the asymmetry to some extent. With India in a state of weakness in 1989, when its comprehensive national power was perhaps at its lowest, Pakistan launched what it termed a 'war by a thousand cuts'. It was designed to bleed India, prevent it from achieving its true aspirations as a nation and avoid Pakistan being de-hyphenated from India which could render it strategically less relevant. Pakistan's conflict initiation without a thought toward conflict termination involved a sponsored uprising in J&K, reinforced by infiltration of foreign fighters and dedicated efforts to set up systems and structures which could sustain such a campaign. It is pertinent to mention here that India's efforts for the integration of J&K were tardy, it's governance of the state mired in severe corruption and its political management contingent upon the whims of local political personalities for whom self-aggrandisement was the priority. With that the state continued to be wracked by separatist trends given impetus by the demands for autonomy even by mainstream political elements. The Indian effort toward political stabilisation was ill-conceived leading to gross mistakes such as the alleged rigging of the state elections of 1987, which became the trigger for mass alienation and handed Pakistan the initiative for the launch of its proxy hybrid war.

Indian strategic thinking on hybrid wars was based upon the experience of the insurgencies of north-east India and the then recent experience against the Liberation Tigers of Tamil Eelam (LTTE) in Sri Lanka.

Hybridity was minimal in these and the campaigns were fought from the angle of the military against the militants, kinetic subjugation being the aim and the focus of strategy. What Pakistan progressively built in J&K was an ecosystem which could keep separatism alive even under the most adverse circumstances to itself. It is important to understand this ecosystem if India has to appreciate its own success and failure through the 30-year experience since 1989 and evolve workable counter-strategies.

## The Hybrid War Ecosystem and Its Ingredients

When militaries are ordered and deployed to handle a separatist situation in a sub-region anywhere in the world, the common refrain is to come out with all guns blazing, the kinetic option being perceived as the most optimal one. Even if that succeeds it is usually a pyrrhic victory because it only postpones the resistance to another time in the future. If state intervention of this variety fails, it gives an impetus to resistance. Thus, in either case it's the state which is the loser; the kinetic approach alone is thus never recommended. What the hybrid ecosystem does is to combine different domains which give resistance a more comprehensive colour. In the case of J&K, the ecosystem comprises the following:

- Human resources: These consist of terrorists (both locally recruited and foreign infiltrated under the garb of being non-state), ideologues, separatists, mainstream politicians, bureaucrats or government servants, over-ground workers (OGWs) from different professions, youth and lawyers, all wedded together. Many are fence sitters. It also has the Pakistani deep state in support at all times.

- Information resources: Very early in the campaign, a well-conceived communication strategy was put into place using information and disinformation, aided by social media as the same developed after 2009. The print media in J&K has played a major role in giving anti-national elements (ANEs) the right platform to disseminate information and build perception as per need. In Srinagar alone, 30 English newspapers and 20 or more Urdu ones are published daily. The voice of the print media in the Jammu region has supported national narratives but that voice is insufficiently strong.
- Material resources: This consists material necessary to wage war against security forces (SF). It includes weapons, improvised explosive devices (IEDs), grenades and communication equipment. The transportation and induction of these to the theatre is essential to keep armed resistance alive.
- Financial resources: No such campaign can last beyond a finite period without a steady and assured flow of finances. Ironically, even the advent of a cashless economy has ensured financial security for the ANEs through financial networks. Money flows by even legitimate means into the coffers of ANEs. At one time, pensions were being paid for families of neutralised terrorists. The Pakistani High Commission in Delhi was known to provide cash to separatists in their exclusive meetings within

the High Commission premises. Fake currency played a major role and continues to a lesser extent till today. The J&K Bank, otherwise a rare but major corporate success story of the state, has been exploited to bring it within the fold of such networks.

- Ideological resources: A simple phenomenon rarely explained by strategic analysts is the fact that Sufi Islam largely followed in J&K has always been in sync with Indian secularism and tolerance. Introduction of bigoted radical religious ideology ensured that a generation of people grew up swearing by more obscurantist beliefs, thus changing the minds of the Kashmiri youth in particular, bringing them in line with radical thinking attempting to dominate the Islamic world.
- Wedded together with this is a clandestine system which can be activated for demonstrated support at short notice and depends much on manipulation, always awaiting opportunities created by the mistakes of the SF. These incidents are then given out of proportion coverage for absorption by the local environment and the world. The system is structured down to the tehsil and *halqa* levels and is well networked to instantly respond.

## India's Inability to Develop a Comprehensive J&K Strategy

For 30 years, India has fought against a dynamic proxy effort by Pakistan. While it never reached the proportions of being an existential threat to India, the continuous focus on fighting the designs of the adversary did create conditions counter to our interests as a peaceful nation seeking high economic growth and betterment of the lot of our people. The strategy employed by our adversaries followed a pattern of testing our will by causing internal strife, increasing the alienation of the people of J&K against India and creating sufficient triggers to project the feasibility of a war between two nuclear-armed neighbours with a hope of some international mediation. India stuck steadfastly to a counter-strategy of neutralising the armed elements that attempted to create mayhem, drastically reducing their strength through a combination of continuous military operations and engagement with the people by the Indian Army. However, the much awaited political initiative to exploit the sizeable military gains proved largely elusive. Separatism continued to survive while democratic principles that India ceaselessly followed were exploited by the adversaries. The strength of terrorists was successfully reduced from a high of 7,000–8,000 to a low of just 300. In that process, many strategies were also experimented with by Pakistan.

The one strategy Pakistan heavily relied upon was the projection that little or no space existed for India to go to conventional war in response to Pakistan's sponsorship of high-profile acts of terror. In the bargain the lack of Indian military response to events, such as the attack on the Parliament on 13 December 2001, the Mumbai terror attack on 26 November 2008 and the series of lower-level terror-related incidents in Jammu and the Valley, appeared to reinforce the perception underlying the

Pakistan strategy. Although Prime Minister Vajpayee for various other reasons did not permit the crossing of the LoC as response to the Kargil intrusion in 1999, it too appeared to strengthen Pakistan's belief.

India did develop the Cold Start strategy in 2003 for a quicker conventional response to Pakistan-sponsored, big-ticket, terror-related incidents or any other triggers demanding such response. Pakistan then deployed tactical nuclear weapons (TNWs) to target Indian battle groups seeking entry into Pakistan territory and once again presumed that deterrence had been achieved. This is a faulty deduction because a reasonable space exists for Indian-triggered conventional escalation in response to an errant act sponsored by Pakistan; it has been sufficiently proven in the period 2016–2019. There always appears to be an absence of projection that India too is a nuclear weapon power; Pakistan's strategy often reflects an absence of the realisation that India too has nuclear weapons.

While terror-related activity inside J&K and mass agitation in the streets aimed to keep alive the hope of those who form part of the ecosystem, the LoC at the periphery too has its own dynamics. First, the crossing of the LoC is an essential element of infiltration by Pakistan-based terror groups such as the Hafiz Saeed-led Lashkar-e-Toiba (LeT, also referred as Jamaat-ud-Dawa or JuD) and the Masood Azhar-led Jaish-e-Mohammad (JeM) and others. Their numbers in J&K are contingent upon successful infiltration across the LoC. Over time, the Indian Army has developed an effective counter-infiltration grid with sufficient depth of deployment and an integrated anti-infiltration obstacle system (AIOS). However, given the constraints of terrain and climate, ensuring zero infiltration is not always possible. By 2011, infiltration was brought down to double-digit figures after the average annual four-digit figure of infiltration between 1996–2003. The other element of the LoC is the military deployment to ensure its sanctity. It is an alignment along which intense military activity takes place; exchange of artillery, support weapons and small arms firing, trans-LoC raids and strikes against patrols. Pakistan's intent in ratcheting up and calibrating violence here is to keep international attention focused on J&K with the potential for escalation of uncontrolled violence in a nuclear weapon zone. Indian response, and many a time proactivity, is designed to attain a certain moral ascendancy at the LoC. For almost 10 years after 2003, the LoC remained relatively quiet with a ceasefire agreed upon by both nations even as infiltration efforts continued. The same was broken in 2014 after Pakistan realised that the strength of terrorists in the hinterland was not fetching it the dividends of keeping the proxy war sufficiently alive; the LoC was then reactivated alongside the Pakistani strategy to enhance concerns of the international community.

## Situation between 2014–2020: Generational Transition and the Change of Indian Government

The tragedy of the Indian approach to securing J&K more firmly to the rest of India was the inadequate understanding of the way the ecosystem worked. Effective neutralisation of terrorist strength and its erosion down to much lower levels needed a follow-up with simultaneity of action in all other domains. From 2009 the Delhi–Srinagar disconnect left too much in the hands of J&K's political community, with Delhi not sufficiently exercising its authority except on rare occasions. The problem also lay in the deep cleavage between the people of the respective Jammu and Kashmir regions. It has existed historically but the carnage against the Kashmiri Pandits in 1990 made this worse and the 2008 Sri Amarnath Shrine agitation brought it to a head when the roads into Kashmir were blocked at Jammu. It gave opportunity to Mufti Mohammad Sayeed's Jammu and Kashmir Peoples Democratic Party (PDP) to demand the opening of trade with Pakistan Occupied Kashmir (PoK), a follow-up to the weekly bus service on the Srinagar–Muzaffarabad road introduced in April 2005 by Mufti. The trade facility so opened received lesser attention than desired, even though it was a transactional effort at best. Its nuisance potential often reported by the army continued to persist, providing more facilitation for the rapidly improving ecosystem. The ability to smuggle in mobile SIM cards, fake currency and the like along with the adoption of under-/over-invoicing in accounting facilitated the separatists in their financial networks.

The inability of the Centre to adopt any J&K strategy and allow the system of drift led to such demands as the abrogation of the Armed Forces Special Powers Act, 1990 (AFSPA). This was endorsed by the local mainstream political parties without any consideration of the fact that nothing except the strength of terrorists had changed in J&K. No doubt militancy had been largely wiped out from the Jammu region and the tracts in the south of the Pir Panjal, but a revival was always possible. In 2011–2012, to its credit, the Centre stood its ground and retained AFSPA although it continued its transactional approach in all other matters.

In 2013–2014, another conflict transformation of sorts took place. The penetration of mobile internet progressively facilitated better coordination and control by terrorists. It also brought in better means of propaganda and influence. Pakistan's Inter Services Public Relations (ISPR) wing enhanced its influence capability adding capacity to the hybrid war effort. This was just about the time when a generational change in leadership of the terrorist movement was taking shape. The nature of proxy hybrid conflict started to change. The local Kashmiri terrorist cadres of the Hizbul Mujahideen (HM) were from a different generation. Led by Burhan Wani and his cohorts, they were reluctant to listen and even less to be under the control of elements across the LoC. With reduced Pakistani presence in the hinterland, especially in north Kashmir, the traditional hunting ground of the FTs suddenly found itself bereft of leadership. Big-ticket capability started to wane and with loss of control Pakistan's deep state started to panic. This coincided with three other events: the arrival of the National Democratic Alliance (NDA) government at the helm in India in May 2014; a brief period of an attempt at normalisation of India–Pakistan relations; and the deeper involvement of the Pakistan Army in its internal security duties against 'unfriendly terror groups', Operations Zarb-e-Azb and Radd-ul-Fasad.

Even under the new Indian government the kinetic route adopted by the Indian SF was accompanied by nothing else to counter the ecosystem which time and again had restructured itself and helped calibrate Pakistan's strategy. The year 2016 was an important one. Panic stations within the deep state on the potential loss of momentum in J&K led to a surge of actions closer to the LoC and the international border (IB) in the Jammu sector. It started with the Pathankot attack (31 December 2015), went on to the Uri terror attack (18 September 2016) and ended with the Nagrota incident (29 November 2016). It also saw the Indian government take ownership of a surgical strike across the LoC in September 2016, which initiated a new muscularity in approach. Pakistan vehemently denied the Indian strike but the operation, when seen in conjunction with the raid against the NSCN (K) camp in Manipur in June 2015, gave the Indian government and the army a new confidence in striking and controlling escalation.

Post the surgical strikes, Operation All Out was launched early in 2017 and a robust policy resulted in a fair clean-up. What was missing in the Indian strategy was the proverbial 'all of government approach', an essential aspect of counter–hybrid war strategy. The information domain remained unaddressed, finances remained in the hands of the separatists and the rabid radicalisation continued unabated.

It was finally sometime in 2017 that the first strains of a new strategy started to emerge with the National Investigation Agency (NIA) going after the financial networks and dismantling much of them. The OGWs started to feel the heat; good times for the ecosystem appeared to be coming to an end as media houses too started feeling the heat. Simultaneously, New Delhi worked on finding the loopholes and legal infirmities in the constitutional provisions of Articles 370 and 35A, and drew a plan for the second term of the NDA government, NDA 2.0.

The Ministry of Home Affairs (MHA) had reported to the Parliament that in the first six months of 2019 the situation in the state of J&K had witnessed improvement with terror-related incidents seeing a 28 per cent decline, infiltration reducing by 43 per cent, local recruitment declining by 40 per cent and neutralisation of terrorists increasing by 22 per cent. To a casual observer this should have been a time for celebration with deduction that the back of the resistance and the support from Pakistan had both been effectively neutralised. To an experienced practitioner it was time to analyse deeper to see what it would take to sustain the apparent stability achieved. The results were due to a combination of Operation All Out which commenced in 2017 and the focused targeting of parts of the ecosystem. For the first time in years, a synchronisation of effort was leading to a 'partial implementation' of the all of government approach. There were two major domains yet missing in this approach. First was the absence of anything transformational to win back the sentiment and loyalty of the people of Kashmir. A sub-part of this was the lack of understanding and inability to neutralise the growing footprint of radicalisation, which in turn helped drive alienation. The second aspect that remained unaddressed was the inability to turn around the governance of J&K. The state continued to languish under severe corruption, nepotism, bureaucratic apathy and perception of mismatch of deployment of resources between the three sub-regions. This trend needs a complete turnaround if India is to finally claim that it has resolved much of the J&K issue after 5 August 2019.

The error that Pakistan committed in 2019 was that it assessed that unless it could sponsor a spectacular terror-related event in Kashmir by early 2019 the comprehensive Indian approach toward conflict management initiated since 2017 could effectively prevent Pakistan from further calibration of the situation there. The age-old element of irrationality continued to remain an element of Pakistan's policy; that is how the Pulwama incident happened leading to the next calibration by India in the form of the Balakote strike on 26 February 2019 with escalation still under its control. The successful phase of control over J&K displayed in the first half of 2019, the Bharatiya Janata Party's (BJP's) return to power at the Centre with enhanced majority and the inability of Pakistan to further respond emboldened the Indian government to take the decisions of 5 August 2019.

## The Decisions of 5 August 2019: Abrogation and Restructuring of the Administrative Set-up

It should be clear to the reader that the decisions of 5 August 2019 were a form of conflict transformation and a path towards internal resolution and stability; it was not a final solution. The build-up to the transformation had commenced in end 2016. If the constitutional and administrative domains had not been addressed this conflict transformation too would have ended up in only neutralising terrorists and the situation would have awaited a fresh initiative from Pakistan and the separatists. So how was it different this time?

The long-awaited political initiative finally came on 5 August 2019 but in an unexpected way. The special constitutional status was removed but Kashmir came under a lockdown, which it can be claimed was temporarily necessary to cater to the anticipated violence; none took place. With no money and leadership, the internet not functional, and enough police on the streets the situation remained under control. Although distasteful, detentions took place as precautionary on the basis of past experience when Kashmir had seen major turbulence on the streets in 2008–2010, deliberately instigated by exploiting triggers. Prominent leaders were detained primarily because no effort toward political consensus had been made; the state of politics in India had created undesirable schisms and the threatening utterances of Kashmir's mainstream political leaders were not helpful. Of course, this entire exercise could have been done differently in a different context; by a government campaign over several years, to explain the benefits of full integration to the people. That did become difficult, not impossible, due to the ongoing proxy war sponsored by Pakistan and the disinformation campaign so astutely put in place by Pakistan's Inter-Services Public Relations (ISPR).

A final political solution of the J&K issue with Pakistan does not appear anywhere on the cards, especially now, after the reiteration of the 1994 Joint Parliamentary Resolution which clearly demands the return, to India of the territories of J&K under occupation of Pakistan and China. What the abrogation of the two constitutional provisions has achieved is the removal of the perceptional doubt that there existed scope for separatism because J&K was yet being treated as a special entity, a virtually disputed one. With the security situation under a fair degree of control and the terror ecosystem under dismantlement, India has nine essentials which must be included in its strategy:

- A clear projection to the international community that J&K is not disputed and is an integral part of India; that past UN resolutions are passé. As part of its future bargaining strategy India will need to reiterate that PoK, Gilgit, Baltistan and Aksai Chin remain unrecovered territories for which India will continue to work and aspire.
- An immediate adoption of an efficient system of governance with high level of transparency and accountability to assuage feelings in both the regions, Jammu and Kashmir. This can be done through a large-scale revamp of the administration with infusion of fresh talent without the baggage of the past system. Any change has to be transformational and its effect felt early. A recommended domain to focus upon for early delivery of results and positive perception is the winter management of Kashmir. Much of the population suffers the winter due to unimaginative administration resulting in

shortages of essentials, poor medical support and infrastructure breakdown.

- A top-down adoption of a communication strategy with sufficient research and academic backup to achieve three things. First is the formulation of clear Indian narratives on J&K which must be transmitted to the international community through various formal and informal instruments of diplomacy. It must include the full training of the diplomatic corps, employment of think tanks and the garnering of media support. Second is the communication of the advantages of J&K being part of India to the Muslim population. Third is the adoption of a clergy-backed counter-radicalisation and de-radicalisation programme to neutralise the hold of the radical elements who have garnered psychological space in J&K.
- As a subset of the communication strategy, an outreach programme to touch various segments of J&K's society is necessary. This must not be limited to Kashmir's Muslims but equally applied to the Kashmiri Pandits and the citizens of Jammu irrespective of their faith. This programme must aim for grassroots contacts, public meetings with elders, youth and women in informal settings, public meetings and seminars to absorb the public sentiment, deliver the Indian narrative with adequate explanation and reinforce the good intent with small-scale administrative decisions on the spot. These must be undertaken by teams of fully aware Indian citizens, high-profile personalities

from all walks of life and must also comprise people from the political community.

- The media in J&K needs to be engaged to come on board and be an instrument of integration rather than one of divisiveness.
- The perception that Kashmir's demography is about to undergo change under the new constitutional dispensation must be firmly put to rest.
- A long-term intra-state people's dialogue between the people of the Jammu and Kashmir regions must be initiated through many meetings. These meetings can be arranged in groups with some similarity and affinity between them: business people, youth and sportspersons, lawyers, teachers and panchayat leaders. A mutual adoption of towns and cities may commence with an adoption between Samba and Anantnag, and Udhampur and Baramula. Joint seminars by the universities in both sub-regions could pave the way for more joint academic collaboration.
- A review of AFSPA to remove the perception about it being draconian may be undertaken. Only two sections out of the seven are recommended to be retained; one, on the empowerment of the army and the second, its protection from prosecution for inadvertent mistakes made in the line of duty, with a time-based clause for the Central government to decide its action. The remaining sections which remain explanatory must be reworded and included as explanatory notes along with the Supreme Court's dos and don'ts of 1997, the concept of Operation Sadbhavna as humanisation of conflict adopted

in 1997 and the standard operating procedures of Northern Command for the conduct of antiterrorist operations.

- The Indian Army's Operation Sadbhavna, which encompasses a tactical-level military civic action programme, needs to be adopted by the Government of India and the state government to bring a strategic all of government approach to the hearts and minds programme.

What India needs to be mindful of is the fact that while it's undoubted that her international status is at a high there is no permanence in such support. Pakistan's diplomatic and information-based efforts have for a change come cropper but it has managed to throw up the J&K issue internationally even if it has not gained traction in support of its cause. Yet, it is not as if the entire world has come to our support. The 57-member Organisation for Islamic Cooperation (OIC) has shown no propensity to support Pakistan and the Gulf countries have largely ignored Pakistan's pleas for support. However, a fuller understanding of the nuances of the Indian stand does not appear to have permeated the perception of these countries or of many others. For example, the Indian standpoint that the Shimla Agreement of 1972 has overridden the UN resolutions of 1949 and that a plebiscite is not an option are rarely understood by most observers. Our narratives do not explain this and the essence of bilaterism being the only way forward abjures Pakistan from sponsorship of terror, which it has pursued for 30 years.

Organised visits to Kashmir, of the European Union (EU) political community and Delhi-based diplomats have not drawn visible positivity in the international media. For the right international messaging detainees need to be released and the political opposition must be taken into confidence, with its visit permitted with due precaution. Some semblance of political activity must return through outreach programmes on the lines recently witnessed with Delhi's political community's visit, but this must include the opposition. The most important factor for projection of normalcy is the functioning of mobile internet. Its nuisance potential also being high; the same should be calibrated. Yet, nothing projects normalcy as the emanation of communication activity from a region; this must be kept in mind.

Return of mainstream politics will always assist in returning normality. Panchayati Raj, which seems to be finding its feet quite well, may not be a replacement for mainstream politics. However, the recent efforts by Kashmir's political parties to jointly resist and agitate for restoration of Articles 370 and 35A may act as dampeners towards normality. On the political front, a final decision toward carrying out an exercise in delimitation to redraw borders of electoral constituencies will need to be taken. It is yet uncertain whether this will be on the basis of the 2011 Census or the one in the offing in 2021. If the latter, we may expect no elections in the Union Territory till at least 2022. This is a fairly long period without an elected government but equally it gives the Central government enough time to impact the lives of the people in a positive way.

The international support that India's Balakote strike garnered, the run of military success against terrorist cadres post Pulwama–Balakote and the added political stability at the Centre gave the Indian government the requisite confidence to execute the long-awaited political initiatives on 5 August 2019. Pakistan's attempt to gain greater relevance from the USA for its Afghan policy and President Trump's ill-informed offer for mediation on J&K acted as triggers for the decisions of 5 August 2019 to rescind the special constitutional provisions for J&K. Now with the Financial Action Task Force (FATF) remaining unrelenting with demands on Pakistan to do more to dismantle the terror infrastructure, Pakistan's economy causing major concern and focus shifting to management of the US interests in Afghanistan with a shaky deal, Pakistan finds itself in a dilemma. Internal demands from civil society to wind up terror networks are increasing. All this could have pointed toward Pakistan adopting a more rational course in J&K and preventing triggers from creating a situation which it will clearly be in no position to handle. However, the importance of the Indian Army remaining deployed is an imperative. The temptation to dilute the army's presence will be an invitation for the return of turbulence. No stability or peace in J&K is permanent in nature unless it lasts an optimum period.

## The Standoff in Ladakh and Its Effect

While on security, it is also essential to take stock of the likely effect of the situation which has developed at the northern borders with China since May 2020 and the impending possibility of a new international balance of power post the COVID-19 pandemic. India has been proactive in its external psychological operations to the extent that there have been frequent references by political leaders on the need for reintegrating PoK and Gilgit-Baltistan, the territories of J&K, currently under occupation of Pakistan. There have been muted references to Aksai Chin (under Chinese occupation) too. Based on reports from the Indian Meteorological Department (IMD), India's official television channel Doordarshan and All India Radio have commenced weather bulletins for Gilgit-Baltistan and PoK. Indian social media accounts increasingly carry a public desire to see the integration of all these areas with J&K. The cumulative effect of the 5 August 2019 decisions and the progressive psychological pressure placed by India probably have both Pakistan and China worried about the future of the China–Pakistan Economic Corridor (CPEC) which passes through this area. Among the reasons being ascribed to China's sudden provocation in Ladakh has been the increasing Indian proactiveness on the reintegration of Gilgit-Baltistan and PoK with J&K. This may not be entirely true but may be counted as one of the inputs which indicated India's growing strategic confidence with which China has been uncomfortable. In fact, India's progressive handling of the post 5 August 2019 situation in J&K and Ladakh with renewed confidence and the inability of Pakistan to find options to retrieve the situation in J&K may have partially contributed towards instigating the Chinese action. Ladakh offers the best ground for a limited Sino–Pak collusion to pressure India militarily at a time when the pandemic has also impacted the Indian economy. Pakistan was reported to have moved approximately 20,000 troops to Gilgit-Baltistan as a sympathetic gesture of support for China. Chinese coercion may last the campaigning season of 2020 with Pakistan making increasing efforts to retrieve lost control over the situation in J&K. This is the reason why there must be no dilution in efforts to prevent resurgence of instability in J&K and all options must be war-gamed for a potential 'big act' by Pakistan-sponsored elements in J&K. As things stand on the Sino–Pak front, India needs to be prepared for a long haul of Chinese coercion that will also aim at obtaining an advantage for Pakistan in J&K. Yet, the international community in the COVID-19 situation and perhaps beyond is veering away from China. India needs to ensure its diplomacy is right to garner more of the already available support.

We expected that the summer of 2020 in J&K would be stable. However, till August, 150 terrorists were eliminated in largely one-sided encounters. India must maintain a tight control over infiltration, prevent the ecosystem's potential for revamp and remain prepared for all eventualities. The future course of the J&K proxy conflict situation remains as unpredictable as ever except that it has shifted in India's favour much more comprehensively. Absence of violence must not be construed as normality and even if violence returns in spurts the larger strategy of integration outlined in this essay must remain the dominant approach. In principle, holding the periphery by the army and other

SF while the integrative process is hard at play may finally deliver an era of stability, leading to the Indian government then having the choice to accept talks with Pakistan and determine a way forward. That choice need not be exercised unless a decided advantage is pursued for the future. We have to create that advantage to be in the rider's seat, now and in future.

15

# Emerging Security Scenarios and Role of Intelligence

VIKRAM SOOD

## The World Ahead

For more than 200 years, Anglo–US policies for the world had assumed that the West's domination over the world would continue although this might ebb and flow at times. This presumption is changing, and along with other factors, explains the present turbulence the world is experiencing. Global ambitions for dominance and control, rising powers, economic ambitions of the hitherto deprived peoples, ideological battles, rising nationalism and Islamist terror constitute some of the main reasons for these uncertainties.

Situated as India is with two nuclear weapon powers on our boundaries, we need to find space for ourselves in a world that is full of increasing uncertainties. India's emergence in the new world order is taking place during a time of global turbulence and uncertainty. This is happening at a time when the increasing perception is that of a USA that is withdrawing from its global commitments, with its massive military, economic and technological capabilities unable to secure the results it has sought since the end of the World War II.

The Cold War also did not lead to the former Soviet Union disappearing as a perceived threat to the West; instead, there has been a resurgent Russia after the end of the Cold War. Russia remains a power to be reckoned with and it would be unwise to write it off. There never was an end to the Cold War; it merely morphed into another version in the 1990s when the USA tried to dismantle not just the Soviet Union but also Russia. Today, the world stares at a more virulent form of the Cold War with the USA and China poised against each other. Mutual interdependence between China and the USA in economic and financial arrangements has prevented a full-blown Cold War but once this mutual interdependence breaks—as it appears now is a case of 'when' and not 'if'—the new Cold War could turn nasty.

Technological blitzkrieg, unhindered globalisation and now virulent pandemics have diffused national boundaries, creating new threat perceptions, priorities and needs. Sovereign states are no longer the sole authorised wielders of instruments of violence. State-sponsored jihad is now privatised and there is 'copycat jihad' being replicated in other parts of the globe. The world has entered the Second Cold War or the Colder War as it is sometimes called. The struggle for energy and control of the land mass between Russia and the Red Sea, most of it Islamic and resource rich, will continue. The Russian giant, itself resource rich, sits like a huge canopy from the Pacific to the Atlantic, with the Arctic becoming increasingly navigable due to global warming. America's Central Command is coterminous with this resource-rich region as well. China will be one of the cold warriors. China, with its overweening ambition, will remain adversarial to India; terrorism will become increasingly Islamist and internet-centric. A global struggle for resources and markets will exacerbate, where the influence of the USA will decline and China will hold a monopoly over 80 per cent of strategic raw materials. There is turbulence and upheaval within the Muslim world and Islamist terrorism against the rest of the world is spreading rapidly. National security now has a far wider dimension than in the past.

The future, with all its possibilities and dangers, is upon us. We are looking at plans to have Islamic Caliphates and Virtual Caliphates in a zettabyte era and in the coming age of artificial intelligence. One wonders if we are ready to handle this. The unfortunate truth is that the future is usually upon us sooner than we anticipate, and a future spanning 50 years is far too short. There was a steady predictability about the wars of the previous century and even the Cold War. The combatants were more identifiable and had territorial boundaries with extraterritorial and ideological ambitions. The way technology has transformed human life and national prowess in the last 20 years would give us some indication of the shape of things to come. The world still does not know how and when technology will change direction in the future. Wild predictions are possible but reasoned intelligence assessments are going to be difficult.

The US National Intelligence Council in its report 'Global Trends 2030' did make some predictions: according to the council, there will be no global hegemon by 2030.[1] The global economy will be crisis prone; there will be governance gaps, especially in our neighbourhood, as well as potential for increased conflict and wider regional instability. New technologies will by themselves also impact security. India and its neighbours will have massive youth bulges that cause demographic dislocations and instabilities. The traditional threats will remain and new threats such as innovative terrorism and emerging technologies will display a scope and speed of change never seen before. There was no prediction about a pandemic.

Chinese leaders regard themselves as being a major force in the entire land mass between the Western Pacific and the Atlantic Oceans—east to west—and from the Arctic to the Indian Ocean—north to south. China has its dreams of grandeur with the Belt and Road Initiative (BRI) indicating its long-term geostrategic vision, its desire to protect its trade interests and to be politically relevant globally, with the China–Pakistan Economic Corridor (CEPC) being a subset of that dream. The Indian Ocean will have a permanent Chinese commercial and naval presence. In any post-pandemic phase, China will make sharper economic inroads into Pakistan and elsewhere as economies collapse. Indian intelligence should have its work in the neighbourhood planned out for the next few decades.

The USA has begun to understand that military force alone is not enough to control events, even when the ability to destroy has grown exponentially. Possibly, China sees that its moment in history has come, with a decline in the abilities and interests of the USA and a renewed suspicion of Putin's Russia that has begun to re-emerge and assert itself. Its postures at Doklam in

June–August 2017 were an indication of the growing impatience in Beijing. China, and not Pakistan, will remain the biggest threat to Indian security, interests and prosperity. China will coerce when suitable and trade when convenient but will not concede on core issues such as territory or give space when in search of resources and markets or entry into the United National Security Council (UNSC) or the Nuclear Suppliers Group (NSG).

The animus that Pakistan has for India will endure. Pakistan is not about to give up the weapon of state-sponsored terrorism as a force equaliser against a stronger India. Pakistan's drift toward Islamic radicalism is now a certainty, with the army and Islamic radicals using the same curriculum and slogans in their training academies and battalions. The Pakistani deep state will find it difficult to shake this off without trauma. Its close bonds with China may turn into bondage but it need not be any consolation to India, as it would also mean that we would have China on our western flanks as well. It would be prudent for Indian policymakers to remember that Pakistan was created for a certain purpose and its leaders now believe that their salvation and existence lie in perpetual enmity with India.

We were gifted the Afghan jihad as a fallout of the first Cold War. Al-Qaeda morphed into the ISIS in West Asia and now the Islamic State of Iraq and Syria (ISIS, now officially known as the Islamic State [IS]) will surely be reborn elsewhere in another form and create ripples all over, India included. Al-Qaeda will most certainly rediscover itself. Besides, demobilised, out of work jihadis need a home. Intelligence agencies will have to cope with the mountains of data that will continue to be downloaded by technology. It will be impossible to make sense of this, given the near certainty of inadequate analytical capabilities.

There is a strong link between narcotics and human trafficking and the smuggling of precious minerals, piracy and terrorism. Unravelling the financial support to terrorism will remain an almost insurmountable challenge. Currency wars, the decline of the dollar and the rise of the yuan will add to other kinds of instabilities. Regionally, Iran, Afghanistan and our own immediate neighbourhood will remain important for India. Old traditional threats with newer threats showing up in different ways will be on the menu. Intelligence will simply have to get smarter.

There is another grim news. It is highly unlikely that the globe can sustain a population of 10 billion if all of us continue to devour resources the way richer societies are doing today, even as the vast majority is not even above the poverty level. Climate change and refugees from disasters and epidemics will cause their own demographic pressures and instabilities. Uneven economic growth, poverty and hunger in our neighbourhood will add to pressures, strife and instabilities.

The quest for fossil energy resources, despite alternative renewable sources, and water will continue. The search is for not only meeting domestic consumption but also control over production and distribution. This means the entire Eurasian belt, the Middle East and Africa will be zones of competition and conflict of energy interests of outside powers, regional rivalries and religious battles among Muslims and against the rest.

India–US relations may be at their best in decades, but the USA will remain unreliable. It defines its self-interest far too strongly and Americans are poor losers. The USA will push its own agenda and look the other way when we are in trouble. It is not in the USA's interests to continually support an Indian cause. In the American lexicon, strategic partnerships and alliances mean securing American interests first and the convergence of interests usually means that the other partner must acquiesce to US interests.

The Cold War diminished the Soviet Union into non-existence, but in its current avatar Russia has become extremely active in West Asia, aggressive in the USA and Europe, and is making inroads into Pakistan. It has been a steadfast friend in the past, and unlike the USA and the West, never imposed restrictions on India over policy differences. The present Russian leadership has shown an ability to bounce back and hold its own despite negative propaganda in the West. It would almost seem as if the USA needed an enemy of the Russian kind for its military–industrial–intelligence–technology complex to thrive. However, it would be a mistake to assume that Russia will be India's permanent friend.

National ambitions, sharp sectarian differences, regional rivalries and extra-regional interests in the Islamic world involve complicated matters. The turmoil in West Asia shows no sign of abating, and the kinds of Islamist terror that result will continue to be of concern to intelligence agencies. It would be of vital interest to

Indian intelligence to know which combination of an extra-regional power along with a local regional power eventually becomes ascendant in West Asia. The main regional players from the Islamic arena are Iran and Saudi Arabia.

The two world wars did not bring permanent peace. Europe and the West may have averted conventional wars on their territories, but they have not escaped terrorism. Yet, the growth of the military–industrial complex into a military–industrial–intelligence–technology complex of the current era only means that wars will remain profitable and peace an illusion. Dominance and control will be the goal of major powers and they will build their narratives to suit their goals. Future wars are less likely to be about militaries against militaries. They are going to be systems versus systems, fought at high speed, maybe just on video screens, and not be about glorious tales of numbers of tanks or aircrafts knocked out. It is the adversary's capability to make war that is important, which means linkages to the economy, technology, intelligence and infrastructure.

## Technology as the Newest Means to Control

New technologies are undoubtedly a boon to humans, particularly in medicine, engineering and communications, but there is a dark side. We are in the midst of the next Industrial Revolution, also known as the Information Revolution. This has massive but unrealised implications for our personal and global security because it is like the proverbial train that is leaving the station but this one is gathering speed at an exponential rate. Just over the horizon are newly emerging technologies, including robotics, artificial intelligence, genetics, synthetic biology, nanotechnology, 3-D manufacturing, brain science and virtual reality. All of this will make today's cybercrime seem like child's play. These innovations have begun to play essential roles in our daily lives, yet there is no in-depth analysis that will make mankind understand the risks these technologies and capabilities pose.[2]

Given the growth of technology, scientists Ray Kurzweil predicted in his first book *The Age of Intelligent Machines* that in the first half of the 21st century machine intelligence would become indistinguishable from its human creators. Few have thought about the implications of this merger between our biological thinking and the one we are creating. It is this destiny of the human civilisation to become indistinguishable from machines that Kurzweil describes as 'the Singularity' in his latest book *The Singularity Is Near*.[3]

Kurzweil's thesis underlying the impending singularity is that the pace of change of our created technology is accelerating and its powers are expanding at an exponential rate. At today's rate of progress, we will see doubling of progress every 10 years, which will be equivalent to a century's progress. This means that software models that can emulate human intelligence will be readily available in the years to come.

With both hardware and software ready to emulate human intelligence, computers will be able to pass the Turing test by 2025, which means that artificial intelligence will be indistinguishable from human intelligence by the end of the 2020s. When this happens, computers will be able to combine the traditional strengths of human intelligence with that of machine intelligence. Given that there are no limits to human creativity, to the power of ideas and to human depravity, the use of this power will have wide consequences for mankind.

The world will have to contend with the weapons of tomorrow, of a robotised world and miniaturised weapons. Writing about 13 years ago, Ray Kurzweil said that smarter weapons that 'think', designed as precise missions to maximise damage and minimise own casualties, would be the trend.[4]

Future battlefields could be under the sea, in space and cyberworld-based, using information, artificial intelligence and fully automated robots. There is always the fear that artificial intelligence can make mistakes, go rogue or fall into rogue hands. The ethical issue here would be whether weaponised robots should be fully automated. Consequently, warfare will be much faster, while democracies will remain slow, creating an inherent contradiction. New weapons mean new ambitions and new strategies.

The imagery defining future wars is going to be different. Battlefields will not be clearly defined. These could be the streets of a city or news feeds on Facebook, messages sent on WhatsApp and other encrypted messenger services or even pandemics used by terrorists. There may be weapons with combatants but also computers, smartphones, and other satellite-connected gadgets. There may not be uniforms but young men and women in jeans and T-shirts controlling the scene from a basement. Perhaps that time has not come for India but there is need to think about this, as it is inevitable.

## The Need for Smart Secret Intelligence

Exponential growth of technology has tremendous inbuilt uncertainties. These could leave present institutions of governance hopelessly out of their depth unless they are able to think fast and act as much pre-emptively as possible. It is necessary to have an assessment about the sort of power we will want to be, the route we will have to take and the obstructions and pitfalls that we will face from our adversaries and even friends along the highway. Added to this, we live in an age of digital jihad and rising Islamist supremacy where terrorists use technologies as force multipliers. Having determined our goals and obstacles, we must ask ourselves whether we have or will have an intelligence agency that will deliver 30 years from now under changed circumstances. Intelligence agencies and officers have a long gestation period, as there is no off-the-shelf intelligence protocol nor an app that can be downloaded for immediate use. If we do not plan now, then intelligence is doomed to fail.[5]

For the development of intelligence agents with diverse kinds of expertise, intelligence networks, like military strengths, are also built in peacetime and not when a crisis is upon us. Area, language and subject expertise must be built over a long time. Only this gives an intelligence officer the ability to analyse and assess. Operational intelligence requires another sort of skill sets and aptitudes. Since secret intelligence is not available at the click of a button, a nation's internal political health and security gets neglected if its rulers neglect the functioning and output of intelligence.

Intelligence agencies and governments must continually assess the kind of human capabilities that will be required in the future, whether the existing pattern of recruitment and compensation are adequate and will remain so in the times ahead. The organisation must continue to get the appropriate kind of human material to form the core of the agency to deal with emerging threats, and it must have access to external expertise from time to time.

The worst thing that can happen to an intelligence agency is that it becomes just another bureaucracy: stiff, unimaginative and risk averse. Any intelligence organisation that is manned by careerists who are either too old to be moulded or are risk averse is on a sharp downhill slope. The government of the day must guard against this because faulty or inaccurate intelligence is far more dangerous than no intelligence.

It would be suicidal to fight 21st-century threats with 20th-century techniques and skills. To prepare an intelligence organisation that will continue to deliver in the future, course corrections have to be applied in the present. There might be an increasing reliance on technical aids and algorithms for intelligence collection and assessments but the essential work to prepare the final output of intelligence has to be done by human beings and not by robots or artificial intelligence. Sources have to be spotted, cultivated and handled by human agents. Intelligence officers have to conduct translations and hostage negotiations; analysis and interpretation of the spoken or written word need an experienced human being.

What has changed is the environment of work and the speed with which threats surface and spread, not knowing when and where. The nature and volume of work has been changing over the decades and now more rapidly so. Economic activity of target countries, treaties, trade arrangements, investments and explorations for resources and their control remain vital today and will be much more in the future as they become scarce. China, one hears, has cornered vast quantities of rare earth and strategic minerals. It could end up being the world's sole monopolistic supplier of these materials, leaving the rest subject to manipulation and blackmail.

Technology may be king in almost all our activities but in the world of intelligence, human intelligence will continue to be the most important factor in determining the outcome of the campaign against terrorism. Despite the superiority of the State in numbers, material and technological resources, international jihadi terrorists do not show any signs of withering away. Terrorism cannot be tackled without human intelligence just as no missile-related intelligence can be handled only by technological means. The quality of the human element that agencies have at their disposal would substantially determine this ability for controlling or preventing threats and enabling the state to prevail.

There must be a revolution in intelligence culture and tradecraft or operating techniques. The existing tradecraft served adequately in the past for penetrating systems of State adversaries to collect human intelligence (HUMINT). The same methods are inadequate, if not unsuited, for penetrating terrorist set-ups, crime cartels and related violators such as narcotics smugglers, gun and human traffickers, as many now operate on the principle of autonomous cells. The progress toward the evolution of new tradecraft and new techniques has been unsatisfactory. A revolution in intelligence culture also calls for effective networking of national and foreign intelligence agencies and the sharing, without inhibition, of all relevant intelligence. Intelligence and counterterrorism networking need to be as effective as the networking by terrorists.

A civil service examination is no longer the best source of recruitment into intelligence agencies as it does not test aptitudes and other skills. Intelligence agencies need language (colloquial and dialect) skills and interrogation skills, ability to deal with hostages, and area and issue expertise apart from operational skills of a specialised kind. They also need expertise in economic and financial matters, cyber and cryptanalysis, and military and scientific matters. The regular civil servant, however bright, just does not necessarily have these skills or the aptitude.

Besides, with the corporate sector opening, the civil services are no longer the career of first choice for most. There is no option for intelligence organisations in India but to emulate the pattern followed elsewhere in the world—recruit from the open market through advertisements. Intelligence agencies need more professional intelligence officers assisted by a never-ending supply of qualified economists, scientists, computer whiz-kids, mathematicians and experts in international banking and finance. Area and subject expertise are built in-house over a period. The COVID-19 pandemic and its implications mean that this too needs to be seriously looked at from the security point of view. Such talents do not come cheap; nor is security or preservation and enhancement of the country's interests inexpensive. Recruitment should be from the open market and offer competitive remunerations, fast tracks for the efficient and an exit for others.

The clear aim is to have an external intelligence agency that keeps the government best informed of looming threats, provides inputs that can direct policy formulation and is an aid in the government's process of decision-making. It is necessary to have periodic reforms to ensure that the country has the best intelligence apparatus it can afford. What is the price a government is willing to pay a band of men and women who sacrifice their individuality for anonymity and go against the grain of human nature that seeks self-adulation is a question that the government has to answer if it does not want to be surprised in the future that stares at us.

Choices will have to be made repeatedly between security and privacy, and between security and freedom of speech and expression. The argument for intelligence agencies is straightforward. If the country needs intelligence that makes it secure, then agencies need to be able to access personal information along with other relevant information to be able to determine patterns of behaviour and interest. This information could be vital for protection against terrorist attacks and serious crime as heinous as terrorism. While safeguarding freedoms and privacy, the state will have to ensure that agencies are not denied necessary access in real time to intelligence because of excessive restraints imposed on them.

The work of intelligence is not a standalone exercise and is related to the larger question of security, national interests and the evolving situation. Sound and professional intelligence does its own in-house forecasts and SWOT (strengths, weaknesses, opportunities, threats) analyses to work out possible scenarios and responses regardless of what the government of the day might contemplate for the future.

Artificial intelligence and its applications and other new technologies growing at an exponential rate will create new threats that one can only speculate about and yet must be prepared to handle them. American generals have begun to demand that new guns be equipped with artificial intelligence. Terrorists and others will have access to this too. Financial systems with the technology of block chain will be another major shift that will complicate the life of an intelligence officer tracking illicit money transactions.

Intelligence organisations cannot compete with information about events, tragedies or threats that occur every day. The electronic media, the internet and communications take care of that. Intelligence agencies would need to operate in dealing with cyberspace and terrestrial threats, moving in great volumes, at times with lightning speed and coming from state and non-state sources. They will also have to continue to deal with immediate and long-term threats. This means having to deal with the present and prepare for the future all the time in a world where reality will be increasingly virtual.

Our global standing would be determined not by our efforts to make peace and appease but by visibly defending our interests. This ability requires secret intelligence acting through enhanced traditional methods of espionage to protect the nation, technological prowess to collect and assess intelligence and being able to exercise the covert option where needed. Warfare has moved from the trenches of World War I through the mushroom clouds of Hiroshima to the present trenches of cyber terror and cyber warfare. Any intelligence agency that does not adapt to the new methods of classical intelligence collection and operations will be a loser.

It is generally assumed that the current context of global affairs that we live in is the most unstable period in our history. Imagine, however, the world of the 1940s with social media and the internet, or similarly so the Cold War years. The world would have looked far more unstable and unpredictable. Yet, many take solace in the frozen stability of the Cold War as the two superpowers assured a tense peace through the concept of mutually assured destruction. This stability was mostly in the Western world while the USA and the Soviet Union battled for supremacy using their surrogates in Asia and Africa. The collapse of the Soviet Union in 1991 did not mark the end of history as many predicted. Instead, globalisation and the spectacular rise of China marked the post–Cold War years of the 1990s. The 21st century had a violent beginning with the terror attacks in the USA; suddenly terrorism became a global threat, but selectively so. It needed global responses and the USA led with ill-advised and badly executed military campaigns in Afghanistan and Iraq—wars that lasted well into the second decade of the century. The limitations of pure military power became evident and many began to predict the beginning of the end of an era of American dominance. This was happening at a time when China was becoming gradually but perceptively more assertive. A massive technology surge at the beginning of the century changed long-established concepts and shibboleths. A new power in Asia had risen challenging the existing world order. It was going to be a battle between a status quo power and the challenger. Trade, financial control, environment and climate change, scarce water and energy resources, strategic control of territory for global dominance and global terrorism were the issues and apart from conventional military means, technology, including cyber, and now even biology, was weaponised by the first half of 2020. Pandemics could well be the new weapon except that this would have few means of controlling the direction of the effect. COVID-19, whether planned or otherwise, has shown that despite all the military and economic strength even the mightiest are vulnerable. We have been fighting a mostly unmentioned two-front war with Pakistan and China, both exhibiting hostility in different ways, ever since Pakistan parcelled out Shaksgam in northern Kashmir to China in 1963. For long, the political establishment never adequately fashioned this into the long-term security implications of this possibility and did not plan accordingly. Hope and haphazard planning have been the policy.

For India, the old threats will remain, and new ones will arise in unimaginable and unpredictable ways. Any intelligence service that begins to understand what lies ahead and what should be done now to prepare itself for the uncertain future will have better chances of providing answers. India will have to assert itself internationally if it wishes to achieve what it has set out to do. This would require a combination of traditional diplomacy, sharpened intelligence and effective military activity accompanied by a massive national socio-economic effort. All these instrumentalities would need constant updating. Any government keen on staying ahead of the competition and thwarting threats would need a first-rate external agency manned by men and women of honour who care for the organisation to which they belong.

One of the prerequisites for such a victory is a smart intelligence agency that provides adequate advance intelligence.

16

# Indian Journalism: The Fourth Pillar of Our Democracy?

SEEMA MUSTAFA

> Many journalists now are no more than channelers and echoers of what George Orwell called the 'official truth'. They simply cipher and transmit lies. It really grieves me that so many of my fellow journalists can be so manipulated that they become really what the French describe as 'functionaires', functionaries, not journalists. Many journalists become very defensive when you suggest to them that they are anything but impartial and objective. The problem with those words 'impartiality' and 'objectivity' is that they have lost their dictionary meaning. They've been taken over ... [they] now mean the establishment point of view.... Journalists don't sit down and think, 'I'm now going to speak for the establishment.' Of course not. But they internalise a whole set of assumptions, and one of the most potent assumptions is that the world should be seen in terms of its usefulness to the West, not humanity.[1]

So wrote John Pilger, an Australian journalist, respected and highly regarded by journalists across the world. This quote although long, just about touches upon what is wrong with journalism today, and why is it that at the time of an information revolution, journalism has lost the sheen of honesty, courage and independence. The situation is complex, it is not sudden even though it appears to be and has reduced the media to a propaganda tool of establishments.

I remember as a young cub reporter in *The Indian Express* I was chasing a story on the film being made then *Gandhi*. It was for the first time that the government of India had given the then princely sum of ₹50 million to a foreign enterprise to make a film on the Father of the Nation. And naturally, there was considerable anger and protests across the country. Richard Attenborough's film thus became a hush-hush mission, which I as a passionate reporter given full play by the editors of *The Indian Express* at the time, made it my job to expose.

We carried almost a story a day, with the photographer and I often jumping over walls to get the shots and the verbal picture. A lady who was handling the production in India started calling me directly and telling me to stop or else.... The direction made us even more determined and clearly the coverage hurt those in charge. She called one day, told me that the owner of *The Indian Express*, Ramnath Goenka, was a great friend of hers and she would report me to him. I told her she could do what she damn well pleased, and slammed down the phone. Remember, there was no television and no mobile phones those days. I narrated the same to one of our editors at the time, Arun Shourie, who was extremely supportive throughout.

One morning, after a particularly scathing expose he came to the reporters room saying, 'I am sure this story will bring her here.' And sure enough, after a while he came back saying, 'Goenka wants to see you.' There was silence in the room as Goenka rarely sent for a lowly reporter, and if and when he did, it spelt disaster—for the reporter, of course. Shourie accompanied me to Goenka's little cabin, where the lady was sitting beside him.

To cut a long story short he told me, in so many words, that I could get her version and told her that she should make sure she receives my calls. And then the old man said, 'Young girl, you will find along the way that many will come to you and say they know me and try and stop you from writing a story; as long as you are sure of your facts, just go ahead.' The lady left upset and angry, and I sailed out on cloud nine as with those words the jute baron, as he was referred to even by the journalists, had restored my faith in the profession that I was so passionate about.

That there were several sides to Goenka was apparent to those journalists more political than I in those days. And that he, along with the owners of other major newspapers, represented business control over news. But then he had also taken a stand against the Emergency, and had not allowed an authoritarian leader of those times to browbeat him into censorship as had the proprietors of the other newspapers on New Delhi's 'Fleet Street' at that time. Kuldip Nayar, who was also one of the editors at the time, was jailed for defying the Emergency. The point is that at the first sign of the whip most of the media succumbed and crawled without the hint of a spine.

Post emergency, there was a sense of shame though in the media. And while Goenka walked tall, other corporate owners were named and shamed. Journalists, young and old, entered the 1980s with a sense of pride, anger and irreverence that was demonstrated through a determined refusal to allow government censorship again. Every hint of it had journalists on the roads in protest, be it against the Press Bill introduced by Gundu Rao in Karnataka and Jagannath Mishra in Bihar; or walk outs from press conferences where the minister was seen to have been rude or impolite to a scribe; or boycott of Parliament for similar reasons. The 1980s saw the resurgence of a fairly independent media, where the establishments were put in the dock, where the police quivered at daily press conferences in Delhi, and where for every journalist cosying up to politicians in power there were at least three others grilling them on acts of omission and commission.

It was a golden period, even though the decade of the 1980s cutting into the 1990s was also a period of violence. But such was the freedom that we reporters in the field were able to come back with the stories confident that these would be published in their entirety. I personally was in travel mode through the decade, covering the violence in Assam, Punjab, Kashmir, Uttar Pradesh, Bihar and of course Delhi that lit up in flames with thousands of Sikhs killed and injured, but through it all the one thought—will my story be published or not—did not cross my mind. I remember during the anti-Sikh violence where very few reporters were out on the streets, we heard through the rumour-charged atmosphere that trains were coming in from Punjab carrying dead bodies of Hindus. I rushed to the railway station, and indeed the trains were rolling in with burnt bodies—but not of Hindus but only Sikhs. On the basis of this rumour mobs had collected on the outskirts of Delhi, were stopping the trains, and in an act of 'revenge' pulling out the Sikhs, killing them and putting the bodies back in. I myself counted 200 bodies during the course of the day. I went back to the office and of course it was going to be a top banner story, but the headline being given by the desk was '200 killed…' as in those days journalist ethics did not allow you to identify communities by religion. This time I insisted on the need for identification saying that the headline would feed into the rumour, not dispel it. The editors went into a huddle, and came out of it with '200 Sikhs…';. This cut the rumour, and stopped further massacres. A lowly reporter had a say and the dignity and respect of the newsroom came into full play.

Business houses continued to own the newspapers, but the owners had to take a back seat for some years as journalists under professional editors asserted their rights. But not for long. Media expanded from the print to television, the business became huge almost overnight, and the old business houses started appearing small in comparison. Besides, the old owners who came from a 'respect the media' stable started handing over their little empires to their sons and daughters who, as time revealed, did not share the respect for a free and independent media. Money replaced news, Target Rating Points (TRP) became the driving force, and the money bags were encouraged to enter the business with television channels mushrooming across India with amazing rapidity over the next many years.

The power of television was felt by all, with big corporates and political parties investing heavily in the same. No rules were set, no ground ethics established. Anyone with interest and money opened television news channels in Delhi and in the state capitals, with journalism turning from a profession into a business in front of our eyes. Slowly, as the business started earning money, professional editors who still cared about the verification of news and independent, honest journalism were replaced by those whose only visible qualification was their ability to say 'yes' to the owners and their mentors.

Mentors is a word I am using deliberately here, as by this time ruling parties had realised that the way to control journalists and news was to control the owners through their business interests. So the nexus of government–owner–news was quickly established, with the governments able to exercise censorship by squeezing those who owned the media.

In the process, there was no real need for direct censorship. One call to the owners was enough to ensure that news was blacked out by all. It goes without saying that the business community's interdependence on those in power is deep, and since the advent of big television channels had made media a business it came under scrutiny and increasing control.

Unfortunately, the few journalist bodies that did exist, such as the Editors Guild of India, tried to frame laws and rules to ensure that the rapidly expanding media world was made aware of its responsibilities and remained accountable to the people it reported for, even as it retained its independence insofar as the owners and the politicians were concerned. Editors at the time suggested that every television channel should carry a scroll announcing the name of the owner and the websites should have details of all funding. It was also proposed that editors should declare their assets to offset rumours of journalists moving from rags to riches in remarkably short periods of time. All this was scoffed at by the newbies seizing the strings of media power, and this unfortunately remained a failing effort at best. Over the years, even the feeble last effort has capsized with particularly television now under the complete control of those who own it, and of course those who own the owners.

Journalism is a proud profession. It is characterised by adjectives some of which I will mention here—courageous, bold, honest, independent, irreverent. It is a watchdog of society, the fourth pillar that keeps a close watch on the other three pillars of a democracy—executive, legislature and judiciary. It does so by accepting the Constitution and the Law as its bible, and by being trained to speak for the people, for the most vicitimised, harassed and discriminated souls. It is in existence not to rub shoulders with the rich and the powerful, but to carry the voices of the poor to the corridors of power for remedial action. It is there to warn and alert through direct reportage, with the safety and security of knowing that governments in power in democratic countries know and realise the importance of free and impartial news to keep nations strong and vibrant.

Sound journalism keeps the pillars of democracy firmly on the rails, using public pressure to ensure that the judiciary remains honest, the executive responsive and the legislature sensitive to the tenets of democracy. Rogue journalism, as is becoming increasingly visible now, plays havoc with democracy and her people and weakens nations, often beyond repair.

This happens when money and power turn journalism into a publicity machinery, a public relations exercise where anchors propagate for their owners and the politicians they are serving at any given moment. Governments have realised the importance of this, in fact even more so than journalists themselves. They know the power of the messenger, even as they officially deride it, and every dispensation has done its little bit to control it more and more. The methods used are many—instructions are sent out to television channels on how to report or not to report important news, threats are issued to individual journalists and smaller networks, advertisements are stopped, taxes are scrutinised, scribes are arrested, sometimes killed as in the case of Gauri Lankesh and Shujaat Bukhari in recent times, and pressure exerted to make the messenger conform.

The effort by increasingly insecure governments across the world is then to manufacture consent. And the media is an important tool in this exercise that comes from the 'repeat a lie often enough it becomes the truth' principle, with scholar Noam Chomsky nailing the entire complicated methodology being used by democracies to keep their hands clean while using the messenger along with other controlled institutions to manufacture consent. This consent is unhealthy, against the interests of the country and yet legitimised and acceptable because it comes under the guise of 'consent'. It seeks to legimitise propaganda and criticise dissent.

This also comes from the argument used by politicians and political parties, at times, to identify themselves with the nation. In India, we first heard it through D.K. Barooah's 'India is Indira, Indira is India' slogan, but subsequently it has been used in the same kind if not exactly similar words over and over again. The effort to make the voter link the ruler with the nation, manufacturing consent that the two are linked, is a political exercise that those in power use all the time across the world. It needs a vigilant media to debunk the claim, and to separate the two in democracies such as India. Otherwise, it gives a carte blanche to the government or the individual to rule with no questions asked, a procedure that is detrimental to the very concept of democracy per se no matter how good the party in power or the individual heading it.

By controlling the media, questions are prevented from being asked. Facts are obfuscated, truth is hidden. The result is that the people are not informed and take decisions based on half-truths, or even outright lies. This weakens democracy in the long run, as it gives carte blanche to governments in power to function according to their own will, and not the people's will. Simply because the people's will is not heard, as the messenger has been controlled.

Noam Chomsky put it rather well in his *Media Control: The Spectacular Achievement of Propaganda*, where he wrote,

> The picture of the world that's presented to the public has only the remotest relation to reality. The truth of the matter is buried under edifice after edifice of lies

> upon lies. It's all been a marvellous success from the point of view in deterring the threat of democracy, achieved under conditions of freedom, which is extremely interesting.[2]

In the process, journalism, even while pilloried by some when it reports the truth, is losing respect. And doing so rapidly. The journalist is seen often as a sellable, purchasable commodity. The media house as an entity that can be silenced with one phone call. Those who toe the power line are rewarded with access, those who do not are threatened with abuse.

The counter view that is increasingly propagated by those in power is that the media, if not controlled, tends to run amok and trashes all achievements in its supposed quest for truth. It hence comes in the way of India's rise to power. There are different versions of this argument forwarded by governments, depending on the language used, but this remains the crux of it. So gradually, the reader or the viewer has been seduced to accept the lie as the truth without questioning it for the national interest—that is the new seductive mantra to justify both silence and propaganda.

This is highly dangerous for a democracy. It allows institutions to subvert democracy in the knowledge that no questions will be asked. It creates a system where the poor are marginalised, largely because they take away from the propaganda value of the rich and beautiful circle and do not bring in TRPs that makes them worth the while. This is one of the main reasons why the poor have disappeared from the media map of India, with the migrants leaving the cities on foot during the pandemic disappearing as suddenly as they appeared. And why thousands of workers can walk through the national capital without even a passing mention in the media.

This puts a pressure lid on problems and challenges, be these of external security or internal security. Both tend to erupt from time to time in the form of encounters, protests, skirmishes—conflicts that leave the nation battered and bruised, and democracy dented.

This might not be visible in the short term but such bruising makes itself evident with time, when democracy itself is endangered as the institutions propping it up collapse.

A person who can string a few words together is not a journalist. Journalism is a profession grounded in the field, woven by professionals practising the art of news gathering and fact checking, and brought together for the people through independent media houses that refuse to sell to the highest bidder. And as it is for and by the people, journalism has to be independent enough to report the truth without fear, courageous enough to say it is as it, and compassionate enough to be sensitive to the news it brings. It has to temper news gathering with compassion, accountability and responsibility. It has to learn from the Constitution of India even as it ensures that this is implemented by every institution of democracy. It has to have respect for the law, even as it reports the judiciary freely and fairly; it has to have a good understanding of the legislature and parties even as it keeps a distance from the politician; it has to write on the executive without seeking favours, boldly and honestly.

This comes from professional editors, an atmosphere that encourages good and not pliant journalism, and a realisation that journalists are not CEOs of public relations companies but representatives of the fourth pillar without which democracies can crumble.

17

# COVID-19: Global Challenges and Indian Responses*

MANISH TEWARI[1]

Nothing focuses the mind more intensely than the thought of impending death. That is exactly what the world is going through currently. From a borderless world, humanity is transitioning to one where borders are at the doorstep of our homes. The physical world has come to a halt, while the cyber world is in a corresponding overdrive.

It is interesting to recall what I have articulated ad nauseam: that a brick and mortar civilisation evolved over the millennia and a virtual civilisation is now evolving. The future of humankind lies at the intersection of these two civilisations. Social distancing is the new sovereignty.

## The Post-COVID World

With the number of reported COVID-19 infections touching 24.8 million across 196 Westphalian entities at the time of writing, this pandemic is truly global in every sense of the word. However, there will be a post-COVID-19 global architecture that no one is currently contemplating. What will it be like? Is the current pandemic the first inflection point of the 21st century? These are questions that need to be examined at some length.

However, stop and think for a moment. What if the virus was airborne? What if the virus did not respect the new sovereignty called social distancing? What if it was non-impervious to the new border that is your doorstep? What if hand washing were not the temporary solution ? What if another variant were to get airborne in the not too distant future? Where would that leave humanity? Precisely where the Spanish Flu left us a 100 years earlier with 50 million dead. They did not know a virus then, we do not know the coronavirus now. The only known unknown is that there is no vaccine so far and all cures are hit and miss trials.

The 20th century had *five* major geostrategic crossroads: World War I from 1914–1918; World War II from 1939–1945; the subsequent demise of imperialism and colonialism, and the rise of newly liberated nations across Asia, Africa, Latin and South America; the Cold War between 1945 and 1991 and the division of the world into blocs, with some nations professing non-alignment; and finally, the end of the Cold War in 1991 and the rise of unipolarity and globalisation underpinned by the Washington Consensus.

Each of these events were epochs in themselves with a before and an after. Often one dovetailed into the other or the latter was the consequence of the former. However, each of these events profoundly influenced the course of history, with or without bloodshed.

Historians will remember the COVID-19 epidemic as such a similar moment.

This is certainly not the world's first modern pandemic. There was the Spanish Flu from 1918–1920, the Asian Flu in 1957, the Hong Kong Flu in 1968, the Severe Acute Respiratory Syndrome in 2002, the 2009 H1N1 flu pandemic, and the West African Ebola virus epidemic of 2016–2018. However, none of these were ever elevated to the level of a geostrategic event. Why, then, is COVID-19 different even though fewer people may ultimately succumb to the disease than what is anticipated?

COVID-19 is different because it is truly universal, with known cases in 196 countries and territories around the world. The previous five pandemics had a more localised influence. Five of the eight billion people on planet Earth have gone through one or another form of an unprecedented lockdown. More than 100 nations around the world have put their people under some form of punitive restrictions or the other. Global travel has all but stopped and supply chains stand disrupted. The most primitive form of disease prevention 'stay away from each other'— under the chic new nom de guerre, social distancing—seems to be the only weapon available to governments. Medical practitioners have been experimenting with what is colloquially called 'hit and trial' to save the most critical.

The first and the biggest failure has been the lack of any substantive global leadership to pre-empt or prevent the proliferation of COVID-19. What are the known knowns at the moment? On 20 March 2020, the World Economic Forum reported,

> Sometime in December 2019, 27 of the first 41 people hospitalized (66%) passed through a market located in the heart of Wuhan city in Hubei province. But, according to a study conducted at Wuhan Hospital, the very first human case identified did not frequent this market. Instead, a molecular dating estimate based on the SARS-CoV-2 genomic sequences indicates an origin in November....

However, it was only on 31 December 2019 that China notified the World Health Organization (WHO) of several cases of an unusual pneumonia in Wuhan. Several of the infections were linked to the Huanan Seafood Wholesale Market, which was shut down the following day.

As late as 9 and 11 January 2020, the WHO put out bizarre tweets either downplaying the situation or trying to undercut travel advisories that were anticipated. On 9 January 2020, the official WHO Twitter handle had this to say at 11.58 pm: 'Novel coronavirus emerge periodically as we have seen. SARS emerged in 2002 and MERS emerged in 2012. Several known coronavirus are currently circulating in animals that have not impacted humans.'

On 11 January 2020, WHO followed it up with a travel advisory as follows: 'WHO does not recommend any specific health measures for travellers to and from Wuhan China. It is generally considered that entry screening offers little benefit, while requiring considerable resources.' Even entry screening of passengers from Wuhan or China was discouraged.

It would be interesting to find out how many passengers travelled to and from Wuhan before the city was finally locked down. It was only on the 20 and 21 of January 2020 that WHO conducted its first field visit to Wuhan. It is apparent from a perusal of the summary of the report that the full impact of the epidemic was not grasped even three weeks after China had notified WHO. It took another five weeks until, on 11 March 2020, the Director General of WHO, Dr Tedros Adhanom Ghebreyesus, declared COVID-19 a pandemic.

It also calls into question WHO's failure to question China about the whistle-blower doctor Li Wenliang, who in early December 2019 had privately warned his colleagues that a new SARS-type illness had started manifesting—nearly a month before China grudgingly informed WHO. It is another matter that this brave whistle-blower is ostensibly dead because of the same COVID-19 that he had exposed.

What is truly bizarre is that despite gross negligence, if not malfeasance, China's response to the pandemic has won influential but notorious admirers. 'The Chinese government is to be congratulated for the extraordinary measures it has taken,' declared Tedros Ghebreyesus. The WHO representative in China, Dr Gauden Galea, outdid Dr Ghebreyesus in his praise. He declared as early as 16 March 2020, 'It is an epidemic that has been nipped as it was growing and stopped in its tracks. This is very clear from the data that we have, as well as the observations that we can see in society in general.' This obtuseness was on display even as large parts of the world were entering lockdown. In fact, India's lockdown commenced only on 24 March 2020.

It is therefore clear that there has been gross failure on part of the WHO leadership. It was negligent, if not complicit, in the initial cover-up and therefore needs to be investigated by a special investigation unit under the joint auspices of the International Court of Justice (ICJ), International Criminal Court and the United Nations Security Council (UNSC). If the bureaucratically top-heavy UNSC was to argue that these bodies do not have the mandate to carry out such an exercise, then the UN General Assembly should amend their remit to investigate its own organs for criminal culpability.

Wuhan has already reopened its so-called wet markets, where the virus allegedly first jumped from animals to humans. However, there is an overwhelming body of opinion, if not evidence, that believes that the virus is in fact lab-driven and the wet markets theory was only an exercise in obfuscation.

As far as China is concerned, given its opaque system the truth may not ever emerge. However, the whole episode warrants an international in-depth investigation either by the International Criminal Court invoking the principle of motu proprio as China is not a state party to the Rome Statute or under an internationally mandated special investigation team especially constituted for this purpose. China obviously will not give access to information for such an investigation, but based on whatever is known an enquiry is imperative. Under no circumstances should WHO be given this remit. Nothing evidences China's culpability more than the manner in which it has used the rotating presidency of the United Nation's security Council that it currently occupies to block even a discussion on COVID-19.

The second is the failure of the UN leadership itself. The UN Secretary General has been extremely slow in coordinating a global response to the situation and has all but abdicated the organisation's responsibilities. Kaysie Brown and Megan Roberts had this to say in a Council for Foreign Relations blog post on 24 March 2020:

> The coronavirus crisis is unfolding against a historic backdrop, the seventy-fifth anniversary of the UN Charter, signed in San Francisco in June 1945. As part of the UN 75 commemoration, Secretary-General Antonio Guterres had launched a global discourse, in the hopes of 'crowding in' ideas about the UN we want and the United Nations we need. It is a timely effort, ever more so now. The United Nations, after all, was established in a moment of crisis, as was the Global Fund for AIDS, Tuberculosis, and Malaria in 2002 and the G-20 in 2008 in the face of the global financial crisis.

However, exactly the opposite seems to be happening. As Colum Lynch, the senior diplomatic reporter of *Foreign Policy* wrote on 18 March 2020:

> The U.N. Security Council, meanwhile, has essentially stopped meeting in its chamber around its iconic horseshoe table and is unlikely to reopen for the foreseeable future, issuing its edicts from a remote computer. One council diplomat said that

> sensitive closed-door meetings that are critical for hammering out differences would be put off for the 'foreseeable future'.[2]

With China vetoing a UNSC meeting on COVID-19 and Estonia's call for transparency on the issue, no further evidence is required of the failure of the UNSC at this critical moment in time.

Some missions have shut shop and others have gravely reduced their footprint when global leadership is sorely required. If the UN is going to be conspicuous by its absence when it is required the most then it would be legitimate to question its efficacy or even continuance. The time has perhaps come to move the UNSC to a safer location where it can keep functioning when most required. The reform of the UNSC should be the first item on the global agenda, including and not limited to doing away with this invidious veto power.

The third has been the failure of even the G-20. Created in the wake of the global financial crisis of 2008, it had its first virtual summit on 26 March 2020—a full 11 weeks after the initial report to WHO. So far, all the responses have been national if not nationalistic. Most countries and cities have tried to isolate themselves to insulate their populaces. This is also the result of sustained assaults by the right wing on globalisation and the neoliberal global order at whose heart lies an increasingly frail UN system.

The fourth is a call for immediate action. The ninth Review Conference of the Biological Weapons Convention (BWC) is scheduled for November 2021.

The date must be brought forward and the conference convened at the earliest to assess as to how the COVID-19 situation evolved from the biological weapons standpoint.

As a background, it would be interesting to recap that the BWC is a legally binding treaty that outlaws biological arms. After being discussed and negotiated in the UN's disarmament forum in 1969, the BWC was opened for signature on 10 April 1972, and came into force on 26 March 1975.

The BWC proscribes development, stockpiling, acquisition, retention and production of biological agents and toxins

> (1) ...of types and in quantities that have no justification for prophylactic, protective or other peaceful purposes;
>
> (2) weapons, equipment or means of delivery designed to use such agents or toxins for hostile purposes or in armed conflict.[3]

It also prohibits the transfer of or assistance with acquiring the agents, toxins, weapons, equipment, and delivery vehicles described earlier.

The convention further requires states parties to destroy or divert to peaceful purposes the 'agents, toxins, weapons, equipment, and means of delivery' described earlier within nine months of the convention's entry into force. The BWC does not ban the use of biological and toxin weapons but reaffirms the 1925 Geneva Protocol that prohibits such use. It also does not ban biodefence programmes.

The time has come for a complete and total ban on any kind of bio-offence or bio-defence weapons. In fact, the BWC Secretariat is grossly understaffed and needs to be strengthened so that it can strictly monitor both developments and research in the biotechnology sectors in both government or private domains.

In the post-COVID-19 world, the UN General Assembly must meet in an extended session. It must divide itself into special committees consisting of Permanent Representatives to the UN or their equivalents to review the functioning of each and every institution of the UN that has been tasked with a role or otherwise during the current crisis.

Similarly, other global governance institutions will have to be revisited and remodelled so that they have the ability, efficiency and nimbleness to respond swiftly to global challenges. Moreover, countries and institutions will have to be held accountable for practices, whether deliberate or inadvertent, that put humanity at risk and test the resilience of national healthcare systems.

## Lessons for India—an Absent Legal Framework

Both in the developed and the developing world, healthcare paradigms and national economic priorities, especially social safety nets for the most vulnerable sections of society, will have to be reimagined and re-budgeted, because what will follow COVID-19 is a deep economic recession.

However, from a legal standpoint, the ongoing COVID-19 pandemic (caused by the novel coronavirus or SARS-CoV-2) has exposed glaring gaps in India's domestic laws. In the absence of a rationally structured legislation to fall back on, the Union government in March advised states to invoke the Epidemic Diseases Act (EDA) of 1897 to tackle the pandemic in their jurisdictions. The 123-year-old colonial law, however, does not even define what a disease is, let alone an epidemic or a pandemic. Indeed, a Public Health (Prevention, Control and Management of Epidemics, Bio-Terrorism and Disasters) Bill had been drafted in 2017, intended to replace the EDA of 1897. The bill is yet to be tabled in Parliament

### *The Epidemic Diseases Act, 1897: Limitations*

The colonial-era EDA of 1987 is India's solitary law that has been historically used as a framework for containing the spread of various diseases including cholera and malaria. On its own, however, the EDA—comprising four sections in one page—might be insufficient to deal with the ongoing pandemic of COVID-19.

Democratic countries such as Australia, Canada, England, and the United States of America (USA) have in place more comprehensive and updated legislations to deal with public health emergencies such as the ongoing pandemic· These countries continuously adapt their existing laws to contemporary needs, enabling them to customise their responses to evolving emergencies. In contrast, the Indian government appears to have a limited arsenal comprising the EDA, the battered Section 144 of the Indian Penal Code, which prohibits public gatherings, and the Disaster Management Act of 2005.

The EDA came into effect on 4 February 1897, amidst the outbreak of the bubonic plague in Bombay (now Mumbai). The law proved inadequate and the plague soon spread to Bangalore (now Bengaluru) and other parts of India.

This Act authorises the Central and state governments to take 'exceptional measures and prescribe regulations' to be observed by the citizens to contain the spread of a disease. Over the years, no standard or model rules and regulations have been prescribed as a corollary to the law. The law merely outlines a set of rudimentary elements, including travel restrictions, examination and quarantine of persons suspected of being infected in hospitals or temporary accommodations and statutory health inspections of any ship or vessel leaving or arriving at any port of call. The law specifies consequences that will be faced by those violating the remit of the Act, with penalties being pari passu with Section 188 of the Indian Penal Code, which is the law that deals with acts of disobedience to a government order.

The EDA is deficient for three key reasons. First, the law fails to define 'dangerous', 'infectious' or 'contagious diseases', let alone an 'epidemic'. There is no elaboration in the Act on the extant rules and procedures for arriving at a benchmark to determine which disease needs to be declared a epidemic. The law is silent on the steps to categorise an epidemic as 'dangerous' based on variables such as the scale of the disease, the distribution of the affected population across age groups, the possible international spread, the severity of the malady or the absence of a known cure.

The second limitation is that the EDA contains no provisions on the sequestering and the sequencing required for dissemination of drugs/vaccines, and the quarantine measures and other preventive steps that need to be taken. Third, there is no underlying delineation of the fundamental principles of human rights that need to be observed during the implementation of emergency measures in an epidemic. The Act emphasises only the *powers* of the Central and state governments during the epidemic, but it does not describe the government's *duties* in preventing and controlling the epidemic, nor does it explicitly state the *rights* of the citizens in the event of a significant disease outbreak.

It does not help that India's existing healthcare apparatus is highly regimented, with separate institutions in charge of primary, secondary and tertiary healthcare. Such a siloed approach is a serious impediment to the country's efforts at tackling any epidemic such as the current COVID-19 one. The imperative is for the formulation of a seamless approach.

By way of example, in India's medical template, the Integrated Disease Surveillance Programme (IDSP) units are in charge of early detection. The medical officer stationed in the primary health centre, the community health workers and field workers function in close coordination with the District Chief Medical Officer and the designated district-level teams for the prevention and containment of disease outbreaks. When a system already exists, especially with regard to disease reconnaissance, the provision in the 1897 EDA for devolution of power to 'any' person makes little sense; in an exigency, the biggest challenge would be to break hierarchies and establish seamless coordination. Except for providing for anodyne supervisory directions for different levels of the government machinery, the 1897 Act does not mention any scientific steps that are required to prevent or contain the spread of an epidemic.

The punishment prescribed in terms of Section 3 of the Act that is pari passu with Section 188 of the Indian Penal Code also needs to be revisited. Section 188 provides for a fine of ₹200 and imprisonment of one month for violating an order of a public servant.

India has a number of laws that can be applied during a public health emergency. There is, for instance, the Indian Ports Act, as well as the Livestock Importation Act and the Aircraft Rules and Drugs and Cosmetic Act, which all contain provisions that can be used during a situation such as the COVID-19 pandemic. The requirement is for these provisions to be harmonised into a single overarching legislation.

### *The Imperative of a Holistic Law*

Ideally, contemporary legislation should clearly provide both the trigger and the caveats in empowering the state to curtail or restrict certain rights of the citizens such as to liberty, privacy, movement and property. This would then lead to predictable and transparent decision-making. India's EDA fails in this regard; similarly, it fails to address the human aspect of healthcare. Indeed, the Union Ministry of Health and Family Welfare had drafted a Public Health (Prevention, Control and Management of epidemics, bio-terrorism and disasters) Bill in 2017 to fill these gaps. Jointly prepared by the

National Centre for Disease Control (NCDC) and the Directorate General of Health Services (DGHS), it also tried to address—albeit in a limited manner—the need to empower local government bodies given the peculiarities of each emergency situation. It was expected that with the implementation of this law, the old EDA, 1897, would be repealed. However, for reasons that remain unclear, the bill has not been tabled in Parliament.

The key pillar of a national epidemic law must be equal access to healthcare services. The EDA fails on this count, too. The obligations of healthcare professionals and other workers, juxtaposed with their rights and the safety standards that they would be entitled to, also need to be delineated, along with the responsibilities of civil society during such a crisis. After all, India is familiar with incidents such as an Air India crew returning from rescue missions of Indian citizens stranded in other countries being ostracised by neighbourhood associations rather than being feted.

In the past, there have been attempts to draft statutes predicated on community health such as the Model Public Health Act of 1955, updated in 1987. The Union government, however, has been unable to convince states to adopt the law since health is a state subject. Many Indian states have had their own epidemic disease acts since the colonial era, such as the Madras Public Health Act of 1939 and the Malabar Public Health Act of 1939. More recently, states such as Karnataka and Gujarat have drafted their own public health legislations.

The National Health Bill, 2009 was similarly targeted for providing an overarching legal framework for the provision of essential public health services by recognising health as a fundamental right of the people. It also provided for a response mechanism for public health emergencies by outlining a collaborative federal framework. However, none of these initiatives ever fructified as states considered it as an encroachment on their domains.

When push comes to shove, India, with its bare-bones legislative structure, will find it hard to find an enabling legal framework that will allow an efficient lockdown of entire cities, the quarantining of people, the temporary closure of business and the distribution of medicines. There is anecdotal evidence of travellers who, upon returning from abroad, have been reported as unwell by their neighbours and consequently picked up by the police.

In a recent discussion on the COVID-19 pandemic in the Lok Sabha, some members raised the legal 'anomaly' with regard to the pandemic, urging the government to rectify the situation and bring about emergency legislation while Parliament was in session. The suggestion has not been heeded.

With little or no legal backing for the government's actions, it has had to resort to the much-maligned Section 144 of the Indian Penal Code, curfews, and other draconian measures to limit the spread of COVID-19. One must bear in mind that other countries of the Commonwealth that have analogous legal provisions in criminal law such as Section 144 are not compelled to invoke them to control the spread of an infectious diseases due to well-structured and sensitive contemporary legislation on public health situations.

## Learning from Global Best Practices

Certain lessons can be drawn from contemporary laws that exist in advanced democratic countries such as Australia, Canada, Britain and the United States of America (USA).

### *Canada*

In Canada, emergency measures and emergency management requirements at the federal level are governed by the Emergency Act of 1988 and the Emergency Management Act, 2007. Most provinces also have their own health acts that clearly delineate measures that are to be implemented in case of a health emergency. However, there is a comparatively higher bar for the federal government to take the lead in the situation of a health emergency. Therefore, most health crises in Canada are handled at the provincial level, in close coordination with the Central government.

The Public Health Agency of Canada Act of 2006 led to the creation of the Public Health Agency of Canada (PHAC), which is responsible for the promotion of health, prevention and control of chronic diseases, prevention and control of infectious diseases, and preparation and response to public health emergencies. The Public Emergency Act gives the power to the Federal government to regulate movement of people, regulate requisition and disposition of property, to regulate distribution of essential goods, to establish emergency hospitals, and to impose fines. Moreover, the Quarantine Act of 2005 'authorises the Minister of

Health to establish quarantine stations and quarantine facilities anywhere in Canada, and to designate various officers, including quarantine officers, environmental health officers, and screening officers'. Indeed, the provincial governments have greater powers to quarantine and impose penalties.

### *Australia*

In Australia, the National Health Security Act, 2007, lays down processes and structures to pre-empt, prevent and, in any eventuality, deal with national health emergencies. Designated entities provide coordination and oversight at the national level, with the provinces applying their own laws, jurisdictional responses and coordination processes. The National Health Security Arrangement, 2008, supports the National Health Security Act, 2007, and the National Health Security Regulations, 2008. Both of these give effect to WHO's International Health Regulations (2005). These regulations required Australia to 'develop multi-level capacities in the health sector to effectively manage public health threats and to develop, strengthen and maintain the capacity to detect, report and respond to public health events'.

The National Health Security Arrangement is primarily concerned with strengthening Australia's public health surveillance and reporting system. It spells out the responsibilities of entities at the national and state levels of government with regard to surveillance and reporting of communicable diseases and responding to significant public health events. The National Health Emergency Response Arrangements, also called the

Nat-Health Arrangements, 'articulate the strategic arrangements and mechanisms for the coordination of the Australian health sector in response to emergencies of national consequence'. The document further provides structure for information flows during a health emergency, while also providing a governance structure for coordination, command and control.

Apart from having sophisticated legislation, Australia has also set up coordination entities such as the Australian Health Protection Committee, National Health Emergency Management Subcommittee, Communicable Diseases Network Australia, Public Health Laboratory Network and Australian Medical Assistance Teams. They respond to and coordinate efforts during disease outbreaks. Furthermore, the Federal Quarantine Law clearly defines what a quarantine is and lays out for what purposes people can be quarantined along with punishments for those who fail to comply. The keystone of this administrative superstructure is transparency. The Department of Health, through the National Notifiable Diseases Surveillance System, provides information on notifiable diseases that is updated three times a week and is online and publicly available. Summary data going back to 1991 is available online, along with data disaggregated by region and disease.

### *England*

The Public Health (Control of Disease) Act of 1984 was brought into force with the aim of creating specific functions for different authorities in response to a national health emergency. This Act provides for a clear hierarchical chain in which the primary, secondary and tertiary responders need to operate when dealing with a health challenge. Responsibilities from the local level up till the national level are clearly defined in the Act. Not only does England have laws in place to deal with an outbreak of the magnitude of COVID-19, but it is updating these laws to adapt to current challenges.

A Coronavirus Bill was introduced on 23 March 2020 in the House of Commons; it is currently being debated in the House of Lords. The provisions include empowering the police to enforce isolation for those who are symptomatic, and to shut down ports. The bill provides for a host of capacity-building measures for the National Health Service (NHS) such as return of retired staff, reduced paperwork for discharge of patients and extra employment safeguards for volunteers to allow them to suspend their jobs for up to four weeks.

### *The USA*

While the guiding US legislation is dated (The Public Health Services Act, 1944), it is comprehensive enough to facilitate necessary action and creates an administrative framework through which any public health emergency can be channelled. It even foresees the need for supplemental personnel by creating a reserve corps. The law was last amended in December 2019. President Donald Trump has also invoked the Defense Production Act, 1950, to battle the pandemic.

## The Way Forward

The COVID-19 public health emergency provides the Union government a rare opportunity to update the country's laws; otherwise, this legislative and policy gap could soon prove to be India's Achilles heel.

An approach paper on a new public health act[4] proposed by a Task Force put together by the government in 2012 had suggested that laws needed to be an integral part of a robust public health system. The paper contended that deficiencies in the public health system's legal preparedness found generally in relation to planning, coordination and communication, surveillance, management of property and protection of persons during a public health emergency needed to be addressed by the proposed new public health act.

Even the law that has been invoked to deal with COVID-19 and order a curfew underpinned by a 21-day lockdown, which was then extended—the Disaster Management Act of 2005—was never designed to cater to health emergencies. This is evident from the definition of 'Disaster' in Section 2-(d) of the said Act.

> (d) 'disaster' means a catastrophe, mishap, calamity or grave occurrence in any area, arising from natural or man-made causes, or by accident or negligence which results in substantial loss of life or human suffering or damage to, and destruction of, property, or damage to, or degradation of, environment, and is of such a nature or magnitude as to be beyond the coping capacity of the community of the affected area.

This definition does not allude to a medical emergency, except perhaps by a loose interpretation. Similarly, the two sections of the said Act under which notifications have been issued, namely Section 6 (2) I and Section 10 (2) I, are both supplemental sections to the substantive provisions of this Act.

Further, Sections 6 (1) and (2) read as follows:

> 6. Powers and functions of National Authority.—
>
> (1) Subject to the provisions of this Act, the National Authority shall have the responsibility for laying down the policies, plans and guidelines for disaster management for ensuring timely and effective response to disaster.
>
> (2) Without prejudice to generality of the provisions contained in sub-section (1)
>
> and sub section i reads as (i) take such other measures for the prevention of disaster, or the mitigation, or preparedness and capacity building for dealing with the threatening disaster situation or disaster as it may consider necessary.[5]

Similarly, Section 10 (2) I states:

> (i) evaluate the preparedness at all governmental levels for the purpose of responding to any threatening disaster situation or disaster and give directions, where necessary, for enhancing such preparedness.

This analysis of the lacunae in the existing 1897 law, and the illustration of global best examples, make it clear that India is short of a legal architecture to effectively fight a pandemic such as the COVID-19 one. Without an updated and comprehensive law on health emergencies, the state governments are resorting to the use of Section 144 of the Indian Penal Code and other draconian laws. Once the COVID-19 crisis abates, the country's lawmakers should use this opportunity to repeal the colonial law and pave the way for a new one that can better address health emergencies that India might face in the future.

18

# A New Frontier: Digital Insecurity and India

SAMIR SARAN AND AKHIL DEO[1]

## Introduction

Breakthrough technologies have driven political, economic and security change through the millennia. From the development of gunpowder to the launch of Sputnik, new technologies, new actors and new military doctrines have disrupted strategic stability. The 21st century is no different: the emergence of unevenly governed spaces in the technology and digital domains have become new theatres of military and economic confrontation, creating new vulnerabilities and opportunities for states, businesses and malicious actors to exploit. To understand how these processes are implicating international security, a wide-ranging assessment of political, economic and strategic factors that are shaping the deployment of emerging technologies is essential.

Even as we do this, it is necessary to acknowledge that the global community is at a critical juncture. It is a moment when the neat distinctions between the real and the virtual are rapidly collapsing. We are witnessing in its place a phenomenon what has earlier been described as the 'platformization of everything'.[2] In other words, social, political, economic and security relationships are increasingly being mediated—to varying degrees of extent—through digital means, and perhaps it is fair to paraphrase Mcluhan and suggest that 'technology is now the message'.[3] Computational systems, individual behaviour and social forces are increasingly intermingling, creating a global society where politics, trade and conflict are often disconnected from sovereign jurisdictions, and take place, instead, on an amorphous 'cloud state'. The outbreak of the novel coronavirus will only accelerate these processes, as states, businesses and communities increasingly rely on digital technologies.

This process is underway even as states around the world are reasserting their sovereign powers. The heady days of global integration at the turn of the century—where countries were willing to sacrifice national control for the sake of a 'global village'—is fast coming to an end. In the coming decade, the state will be back stronger than ever before. We are already seeing states attempting to diversify supply chains and trade routes amidst the COVID-19 pandemic in an effort to reduce dependence on geopolitical rivals. The future of globalisation will increasingly be 'gated'—and political trust will become an important factor in deciding who nations trade with and how they do it.[4] This trend also relates to how states have responded to the platform moment—by seeking to monopolise and control flows of data and technology. While China has long seen the acquisition of technology as a strategic national imperative and their corporations as an extension of state power,[5] this instinct is fast becoming the norm even in the USA and Europe. Today, states are racing to shape digital globalisation in accordance with their own value systems and for partisan gains.

It is also clear that the zeitgeist of techno-nationalism will not remain limited to states.

The demand for high-technology industries to be 'patriotic' and serve the interests of the state is growing. Businesses are increasingly—and overtly—entering geopolitical conflicts. Huawei is the most obvious case in point and its actions and investments are being discussed and debated across the world. But they are not alone and there are others that should also be examined to understand the breadth of the phenomena. Palantir technologies, for instance, has all but made it a business model to serve US national security interests and are the most prominent of Silicon Valley corporations with intimate ties with the US deep state.[6] Companies are shaping the international security environment in more subtle ways as well. Many are part of 'normative alliances', such as the Microsoft supported CyberPeace Institute,[7] that ostensibly seek to shape international norms and regimes. Although these are prima facie international and non-partisan efforts, it is conceivable that the economic and strategic interests of sovereigns will ultimately shape their research and advocacy.

This politics of nationalism—that has already weakened multilateral institutions and cooperation in other domains—has also crippled efforts to shape state behaviour in cyberspace and the use of emerging technologies more generally. The most important multilateral negotiations under the aegis of the United Nations have all but stalled,[8] and industry groups and civil society organisations are attempting to create a sometimes confusing and often overlapping patchwork of norms, regimes and institutions, prominent among them being the Paris Call for Trust and Security in Cyberspace[9] or the Global Commission for the Stability of Cyberspace[10] norms. Low entry barriers to develop and use cyber and digital tools have created standard multi-stakeholder cooperation problems—where the political capacity to enforce discipline on a myriad of states, businesses and non-state actors is non-existent.

Given these three structural preconditions—the platformisation of everything, the emergence of techno-nationalism and the weakening of multilateral institutions, all of which have been accelerated by the coronavirus outbreak—this essay will examine the relationship between emerging technologies, international security and India's security interests through three explorations. First, it will study how digital spaces will implicate the global balance of power and traditional security postures. It will then describe how supply chains and globalisation will change as states respond to this new moment. Next, it will study how communities and individuals will become front-line actors in the national security apparatus. And finally, this essay will seek to describe the key challenges for India as it navigates this new moment.

## Balance of Power and Conventional Security Postures

The first significant implication of emerging technologies on international security will be on the global balance of power and political–military doctrines and grand strategies. A note of caution: one should be wary of relying on technologically deterministic approaches when attempting to predict how emerging technologies will affect international security. Political and cultural norms will heavily influence the development and deployment of new technologies. China, for instance, is far less likely to be constrained by the ethics of genetic editing[11] than other Asian or Western democracies—particularly, should national security interests be at stake. We are seeing this trend play out in relation to mobile applications to track the coronavirus as well. East Asian countries such as Singapore and Taiwan have deployed such technologies rapidly,[12] while those in Europe are convening lengthy conversations around privacy implications before authorising such technologies. This adds a layer of complexity to forecasting—one that is exacerbated by two unique features of today's techno-social systems.

The first is how quickly emerging technologies are diffusing across a range of actors. North Korea—a nation largely disconnected from global supply chains—is capable of sophisticated cyber-espionage and cyber-attack operations.[13] The most aggressive digital recruiter was the Islamic State of Iraq and Syria (ISIS, now officially the Islamic State [IS])—deftly taking advantage of social media to bolster both its propaganda and outreach efforts.[14] A second related feature is the dual-use nature of most emerging technologies. The same capabilities that allow self-driving cars to operate will also enable drones to track, target and eliminate hostile individuals autonomously.[15]

At the same time, most of the advancements in such emerging technologies are taking place in the private sector. With businesses investing far more than governments in breakthrough technologies—and at a pace that is quicker than most regulatory regimes—it is difficult to identify which technology may have national security implications.

Taken together, it is nearly impossible to predict how political and technological developments will interact to produce international security outcomes. Still, just as the birth of the internet and communications technologies led to new military innovations, such as GPS-guided precision strikers and other 'network-centric' warfare methods,[16] a full suite of the fourth industrial revolution technologies—artificial intelligence (AI), big data, genomics, robotics, quantum computing—will alter the way states conduct conflict. Rather than attempting to anticipate the precise trajectory of these developments, it is more useful to identify two conceptual categories through which policymakers must assess the situation.

The first are the 'known unknowns', that is, conventional security arrangements that are expected to be disrupted. Emerging technologies will implicate first the 'big picture' security doctrines. How, for instance, will the use of AI in nuclear security command and control operations alter perceptions of risk?[17] Will the proliferation of cyber weapons change generating new 'first-use' pressures that nuclear security regimes long sought to mitigate?[18] Similarly, emerging technologies will also implicate traditional tactical and battlefield postures. How will drone swarms change warfare, for instance?[19] How, if at all, will autonomous weapons systems integrate humans into the decision-making loop?

These illustrations are linear extrapolations of trends that are already maturing rapidly. In a highly publicised event in August 2020, for instance, a human fighter pilot was bested by an algorithm in a simulated dogfight.[20] Although this was merely a demonstrator event, it is clear that the nature of war is going to change very quickly.

The proliferation of strategies relating to AI, cybersecurity and new weapons systems around the world indicate that the international community is responding to this reality. Most nations that are integrating advanced technologies into their military operations are updating and recalibrating existing doctrines and tactical approaches.

There is, however, a second cluster of developments that will require significant attention—the new arenas or the unknown unknowns. In other words, unintended or unexpected disruptive consequences of emerging technologies in the hands of malicious or sophisticated counter-system actors. In modern history, the 2016 Russian influence operations are the best demonstration of this risk—where the architecture of digital platforms was manipulated to undermine democratic processes.[21] These methods are being rapidly replicated by other malicious actors as well, most notably China, which is spreading misinformation about the origins of the coronavirus to deflect attention away from its own early failure to contain it.[22] How many more unintended vulnerabilities abound? What new risks, for instance, will the fusion of the digital and the biological create? Indeed, the COVID-19 outbreak has re-animated concerns around bio-engineering and weapons and has revealed that the international community is largely unprepared for systemic shocks.[23] Quantum computing is another area to watch—how will cybersecurity change when quantum computing overtakes even the most powerful supercomputer across a range of applications?

The change that these technological and political developments will have on the balance of power and military strategies will not always be visible at first blush. In many cases, it will be gradual, with new technological systems and new operational strategies emerging in traditional hotspots and conflict zones. China may, for instance, introduce autonomous naval vehicles to enforce its illegal claims on the South China Sea. The India–Pakistan border may see the introduction of unmanned defensive and asymmetric weapon systems. Insurgent groups will use drones for targeted assassinations and spectacles. But how will the world change if there is new, emerging technology–induced Pearl Harbour or Hiroshima? Such analogies are imperfect, but they do provide insight into how unanticipated attacks on critical military or civilian infrastructure, with significant fatalities or adverse economic consequences, could create new political incentives for war. Such events changed the course of history, will they do so again?

## Geo-economics of Emerging Technology

Even as emerging technologies continue to disrupt conventional security arrangements, one should not forget that war, conflict and competition will take place in an extremely interdependent world. The supply chains that carry human capital, innovations, technology and finance around the world are crucial to understanding conflict in the fourth industrial revolution. Geo-economic statecraft is not new—in 1990, strategist Edward Luttwak described it as the 'logic of conflict' being applied to the 'grammar of commerce'.[24] American control over the SWIFT system and the flow of capital, for instance, have long been instrumental in the relative success of its sanctions regimes against its various adversaries.[25]

Increasingly, trade and technology are being positioned as similar drivers of statecraft. The US–China trade war is only the first manifestation of this trend. It appears increasingly likely that major powers will soon begin insulating their technology systems or manipulating them for global strategic advantage. As this trend continues, there are a few notable ways in which it will change our understanding of globalisation, interdependence and economic security.

The first victim of this new practice of 'geo-technology' will be past assumptions about globalisation. Once it was understood that trade in goods and services would create positive-sum gains. Western markets would benefit from low prices, and emerging economies would manufacture their way to prosperity. But the complex nature of today's economy does not create the same conditions when it comes to the development of emerging technologies. Instead, states worry that one actor may 'manipulate' its role in the economic system to cause damage to the interests of others.

China's behaviour, specifically, has been singled out in the recent past as deserving special attention. The nature of the Communist Party's control over industry and China's central role in the topography of technology supply chains have allowed it to acquire technology through illicit means for many decades now. The sundry of official complaints and reports—especially from the USA[26] and the European Union (EU)[27]—all bear testament to the volume of forced technology transfer. As China steadily moved up the value chain, it also used its foreign investments abroad to a similar purpose. Huawei, for instance, is seen as an ambassador of Chinese interest in cyberspace. One should, however, be wary of singling out China. The USA has abused its position as an arbiter of networked interdependence as well. As the Snowden leaks revealed, its overwhelming control over global flows of data has allowed it to build among the most sophisticated intelligence-gathering capabilities at home with constitution-based caution around the rights of its own citizens and none for others.[28]

As the world's largest economies attempt to shape global technology flows in accordance with their own ideological, commercial and strategic interests, others are reassessing their interdependence with the digital world. Europe and India, especially, are increasingly concerned about the strategic implications of American and Chinese technologies in their markets and societies. Political leaders in both France and Germany have become increasingly vocal about developing 'European Champions' as alternatives to foreign technology platforms.[29] French President Macron even went as far as to call it a 'battle for sovereignty'.[30] New Delhi is similarly reassessing its technology policy—attempting to use tools such as data localisation, home-grown public digital goods and e-commerce policies to carve out its own digital propositions for the world. Most recently, Delhi banned TikTok and over 100 Chinese applications over security and sovereignty concerns following a border skirmish in the Himalayas.[31] Earlier, India also announced new foreign direct investment (FDI) restrictions that mandate government authorisation for *all* investments from China, motivated by fears of 'opportunisitic' takeovers of India's financial or technology sectors.[32] And it now seems inevitable that Chinese 5G vendors will be denied access to the Indian telecom market.[33]

This indeed dovetails into a broader trend of a new 'coupling' between economic and national security. Under the garb of this new trend, the Trump administration has gone so far as to declare a 'national security innovation base'—a catch-all term to net nearly all of America's entrepreneurial activity.[34] Amidst the COVID-19 pandemic, the USA is also pushing to create an alliance of 'trusted partners', dubbed the 'Economic Prosperity Network', to reshape the boundaries of global trade.[35] And taking a leaf out of India's policy playbook, the Trump administration has also decided to force TikTok out of the US market, either through regulatory restrictions or compelling its acquisition by an American firm.[36] With a range of other powers following suit—although to varying degrees and not always through official policy pronouncement—some basic norms of the multilateral economic order will have to be revisited. Where free trade was the norm and security interests were conditional, the 21st century is likely to see the needle shift the other way.

## Community and Social Consequences

The final—and perhaps, most worrying—trend relating to technology and international security will be the role of the citizen-consumer. In the information era, the neat distinctions between consumer and citizen are fast eroding. On a single digital platform, it is possible for an individual to engage in commerce and trade, to exercise free speech rights, and, more relevant to this essay, become a target of malicious digital operations. Three interrelated structural trends have exacerbated the risk to individuals and communities as they continue to adopt digital technologies.

The first is an already mature trend: surveillance as a service (SaaS). Surveillance was once largely the preserve of states and intelligence communities. In the information age, these capabilities have been truly democratised. More worryingly, most of them are commercially driven. Today, there exists a global, vast and shadowy data exchange market—with personal information being bartered and sold with little oversight. This environment created the conditions for l'affaire Cambridge Analytica and Russian manipulation of the American political process.

Despite the enactment of data protection laws—that are effective to varying degrees based on jurisdiction—SaaS is now a booming industry.[37] National governments, terrorist organisations, unethical businesses, and disgruntled organisations and individuals all compete in a rapidly maturing market for sensitive personal and behavioural information. More worryingly, most national governments are keen to make individuals even more vulnerable to this process by weakening encryption and privacy standards. The COVID-19 outbreak is only making it harder for civil society to push back against intrusive state surveillance. Just as states have accumulated massive powers to monitor their citizens under the garb of national security, health security has tilted the scales further. That even European nations, such as France, are urging multinationals to ease privacy rules to combat COVID-19 is a sign of things to come.[38]

A maturing market for surveillance has also acted as a force multiplier for the second—and still maturing—trend: disinformation as a service (DaaS).[39] The ability to profile unique individuals along with their behaviours and psychologies has allowed malicious actors to alter perceptions of what should ideally be shared realities. Like SaaS, the demand for such a service is genuinely multi-stakeholder—from military actors to political parties and feuding businesses and individuals. The introduction of AI systems into ordinary multimedia operations have also allowed actors to create and offer a full suite of disinformation services—from 'cheap fakes' or media that has been crudely manipulated to sophisticated and convincing 'deep fakes'. Indeed, the COVID pandemic has been accompanied by an 'infodemic as well',[40] with both state and non-state actors disseminating misinformation around the virus for geopolitical or ideological and political reasons.

The final trend is cybercrime as a service (CaaS)[41]—one that is accelerated by the interconnectedness of multiple devices, or the 'internet of things'. The kind that receives most attention is inevitably sophisticated cyber-espionage and theft operations—such as those that have plagued the US Office of Personnel Management[42] or large multinational firms such as Equinox.[43] But more worryingly for individuals are the 'petty' cybercrimes—those that affect the social, economic and financial well-being of individuals.[44] Most countries around the world simply do not have the criminal justice capacity to respond to individual crimes that may have minor repercussions systemically but significant implications for the individual or smaller businesses.

Like with SaaS and DaaS, a mature and thriving CaaS supply chain—from discovering vulnerabilities to delivering exploits and servicing the life cycle of a cyberattack—offers malicious actors a range of options based on cost and intent. Most such operations exploit individuals and institutions when they are at their most vulnerable—as the spike in coronavirus-related cybercrime is evidence.[45] Indeed, a series of low-value and distributed cybercrimes are as debilitating as single, large, sophisticated cyberattacks.

The citizen-consumer meanwhile is often and invariably exposed to new risks and has little claim to remedies. Governments are certainly struggling to frame new legal and constitutional paradigms for the relationship between individuals and digital technologies. Most jurisdictions see them as two separate entities despite years of gradual erasure of any meaningful difference between them.[46] And as they continue to try and reassert their sovereign jurisdiction on these spaces, they are fast eroding protections embedded within digital technologies, and by extension, protection for the individual and their rights. The global debates around encryption and privacy will bear witness to this. This has serious repercussions as emerging technologies increasingly implicate all aspects of our lives, with large technology platforms performing functions once limited to the domain of the state. Private platforms, on the other hand, are making decisions on censorship of speech of citizens and leaders and are even setting up 'courts' and other adjudication mechanisms. Few events highlighted each of these concern better than the recent US Antitrust hearings, where the CEOs of four major technology companies were grilled about issues as diverse as anonymity, political bias, abuse of market power and foreign interreference and national security.[47] Far from reassuring domestic and global audiences that technology would be accountable, however, the hearings point to the growing likelihood that citizens will be confronted with a new format of hierarchical control exerted by both the state and large corporations, with the latter being unaccountable to all but their stakeholders.

Taken together, digital and cyber technologies are double-edged tools for individuals. At one level, they create new opportunities for social mobility and economic growth for the individual. But a growing and increasingly diverse array of actors—be it states, corporations or rogue non-state organisations—are threatening to disrupt or co-opt the core infrastructure that underpins emerging technologies and their utility to individuals. These are non-traditional threats, and existing institutions have limited bandwidth or capacity to respond to them.

## India's Role in the New 'Code War'

The disruptions to conventional political–military doctrines, the re-emergence of geo-economic statecraft and new risks to individuals and communities all point to a new national security reality. Increasingly, 'code' is defining the very structure of our societies—and by extension, the means and methods to attack them. These trends have immense ramifications for India, which will be the first emerging economy to reach middle-income status amidst the fourth industrial revolution. Its growth in the coming decade then will require it to adapt to and adopt new and emerging technologies by design. This is already taking place—technologies such as Aadhaar and the India-Stack have already positioned India as a provider of what the United Nations calls 'digital public goods'. As the digitisation of its society and economy continues, New Delhi will have to learn to translate the lessons from its governance innovations into military and strategic doctrines as well. Four domains in particular merit attention.

For one thing, emerging technologies will add new pressures to an already ageing—and some would argue oversized—military–industrial force. National security in the fourth industrial revolution will compel the Indian government to make at least three crucial shifts.

First, the warfighter will require upskilling for their abilities to be effectively augmented by new technologies. Also, the state will have to shed its bias toward public sector defence manufacturing and incentivise the acquisition of private sector innovations and technologies. Finally, military doctrines will have to evolve from protecting physical borders alone to protecting civilian institutions and infrastructure.

Second, the deployment of emerging technologies will create new tactical pressures along borders with Pakistan and China. For one thing, new technologies—especially those available at low costs—tend to favour asymmetric actors. The twin vectors of mobile phones and affordable internet, for instance, have been manipulated by state-sponsored terrorist organisations to recruit and instruct young radicalised individuals in Kashmir. New Delhi must better understand how these risks will mutate as new technologies proliferate. Along the eastern border, on the other hand, India will have to learn to adopt asymmetric strategies against a China that will invariably possess greater technological sophistication for the foreseeable future.

Third, India will have to respond to new strategic pressures in the Indo-Pacific—especially those that emerge from China's technology propositions in the region. Indeed, just as India will rise as a power in the fourth industrial revolution, so will the Indo-Pacific mature as a construct. In this strategic geography, China is aggressively shaping the norms and institutions to manage politics, trade and security, including in the digital sphere. Through the 'Digital Silk Route', China is exporting data aggregating technologies, AI solutions and business models based on its own techno-authoritarian values. A digital Indo–Pacific order that is underwritten by Chinese digital infrastructure and technology propositions is naturally not in India's interests—for much the same reasons that compelled India to boycott the Belt and Road Initiative.

Fourth, the digitisation of global flows of ideas, people and innovation will require India to emerge as a stronger geo-economic actor—an aspect of statecraft it has traditionally been ineffective at. Indeed, as we have described earlier, the USA and China—arguably the most critical drivers of globalisation—are insulating their technology supply chains from vulnerability to each other. This phenomenon will lead to a fragmentation of well-integrated production lines and force states to make uncomfortable and suboptimal decisions about their economic partnerships. Simultaneously, digital trade barriers are on the rise around the world. Countries in the South Asian region are uncertain about regulating and creating local value from the digital economy, leading to a proliferation of measures such as data localisation, digital 'taxes' and restrictions on e-commerce. And finally, digital value chains no longer offer a reliable pathway for development to states in the developing world. In fact, with the onset of the fourth industrial revolution, 3D printing and automation will allow capital-rich nations to 're-shore' supply chains—depriving emerging economies of reliable development pathways. New Delhi will have to proactively shape international arrangements that ensure its access to flows of data and new technologies, and improve its ability to set norms, standards and rules that define these flows.

Finally, India must be wary of the impact of digital technologies on its social fabric—perhaps the most critical national security imperative of all. It is an unfortunate truth that India's digital public sphere is vitiated by misinformation, hate speech and a sundry list of 'social bads'. The potential of foreign actors to influence and undermine India's democratic institutions and processes adds another layer of risk and uncertainty to its social order. This risk is augmented by the fact that the rules shaping its digital public sphere are increasingly scripted by private actors.[48] India's diverse and unequal population presents many social cleavages that are already festering and ripe for manipulation. These risks to the social order will also be exacerbated by technologies such as AI that will 'encode' existing biases and inequities into societies. With many of these applications being shielded by IPR regimes, it may well be that private code will implicate public governance and social relations in ways that are not apparent or comprehensible to the ordinary citizen-consumer. Unless India creates new accountability frameworks to govern the effects of private platforms on its society, whether it is mandating explainability and transparency in the design of the technology itself or through oversight institutions, the most damaging effect of emerging technologies on India's society may well be their ability to undermine a citizen's trust in her communities, institutions and government.

In the 21st century, India must adopt an 'all of the society' approach to national security as it relates to new advancements in science and technology. In the year 2000, Lawrence Lessing prophetically wrote that in the future 'code is law'.[49] In other words, software would enforce, by design, certain legal relationships. It might be time to take this metaphor a little further and argue that code is life—and that technology now mediates nearly every aspect of our societal arrangements. This also means that it will increasingly be central to war and conflict. Not only will this new moment compel the Indian state to revisit strategies, doctrines and administrative arrangements, but it will also thrust upon it new international pressures and responsibilities. Primary among them will be to help secure the lives and livelihoods of its own citizens and provide replicable models for security for emerging technologies around the world.

19

# Education: A New Thrust

BRIGADIER SUKHJIT SINGH (RETIRED)

## Introduction

The current educational system, as followed in the nation, is still cast much in the mould of the 'Raj System'. The aim of education during the heyday of the Raj in India was, in essence, to seek to produce a reservoir of 'literate manpower', capable of providing material for the bureaucratic hierarchy required to govern the country. Upward mobility into the covenanted services of the government was available to such of those from amongst this select 'literate pool' as could absorb advanced studies or specialisation in certain fields.

The difference that is sought to be highlighted is between 'literacy' or 'the state and quality of being literate, or the ability to read and write' and 'education' or 'the imparting of knowledge and ability through formal training'. It will be readily accepted that the prevailing educational system in Indian colleges and institutions, is, in point of fact, producing a mass of unemployable people as opposed to a pool of educated manpower capable of development, elevation and higher expertise. The position in 2019, it would appear, was that 'a minimum of some eight million new job seekers enter the market every year. In 2017 only

5.5 million jobs had been created and the situation is worsening'.[1]

There appears a strange disconnect or paradox in this situation. Apparently, according to a recent survey some 48 per cent of Indian employers reportedly experienced difficulties in filling job vacancies due to talent shortage or inadequacies. One of the worst affected sectors, it would appear, is also one of the nation's strong points of the economy, namely the information technology sector where approximately 1,40,000 skilled technical trainees could not be recruited in 2018. One official report even stated that the more educated Indians are, the more likely they are also likely to remain unemployed. In March 2018, the Rajya Sahaba was informed by the then Minister of Skill Development that under the government's 'Skilling' Programme 4.13 million people had been trained, but only approximately 6,15,000 or 15 per cent of them had found employment.[2] The plight of the mass of students transiting through the portals of government or other private colleges and institutions of higher learning, with only a classical education qualification in hand, can well be imagined.

A brief examination of this problem as it currently obtains in one state of India, the Punjab, as we proceed would be instructive.

## Historical Survey of Education in India

In 1833, the Government of India was given a unitary form of organisation. Education, like every other subject, thus became a direct Central responsibility and the Provinces merely acted as agents of the Central authority. In 1870, a scheme for decentralisation was introduced, under which education became a 'provincial' subject with two limitations.

1. Certain fields such as 'legislation for Universities' continued to vest in the Government of India and in most other fields general powers and supervision were reserved with the Government of India whose sanction was required for major decisions.
2. The expenditure on education was to be met from the revenue assigned for the purpose (which later came to be called 'contract grants') and such additional funds as the Provinces might be able to raise themselves.

In 1902, a Universities Commission was appointed by Lord Curzon and in 1904, the Universities Act was passed. A vigorous policy of reform in every sector of education, supported by large financial grants of the Provinces, in addition to the 'contract grants', saw the education system in India progress rapidly till 1919, when the Government of India Act came into force. The next notable enactment was the post-war Plan of Educational Development in India, in 1944.

After the attainment of Independence in 1947, the role of the Government of India in the field of education came up for discussion when the Constitution was being framed. It was logical to follow that in this vital area of national development, and because of the vast size and local diversities of the nation, education became largely the responsibility of the state governments and local authorities. Entry 11 of List II of the Seventh Schedule to the Constitution of India, accordingly, made education a state subject, with certain other provisions of Entries 63, 64, 65 and 66 of List I and Entry 25 of List III being also applicable in such cases.[3]

Over the last two decades, there has been a great expansion in the number of colleges and in the numbers of students enrolling in the universities of the nation. This has created problems of adjustment and discipline, and a growing disillusionment with the public examination system where the dichotomy of a lack or correlation between the objects of teaching and the aims of examinations came into sharp focus. Memorising syllabi and subject contents, as opposed to reflective analysis and practical application of knowledge to problems, became endemic to the system of higher learning. Peripheral or 'tunnel knowledge' and narrow specialisation in subjects detracted from the production of a well-rounded, adjusted, educated human resource.

## Education in the Punjab

The tradition of learning has always been strong in the Punjab. As far back as 700 BC, educational centres such as the one excavated at Taxila flourished, which continued till about 200 AD. Thereafter, learning continued to be encouraged by the Muslims, the Hindus and the Sikhs in various establishments.

A modern system of education began in 1856 with the creation of a Department of Education under the first Director of Public Instruction, Lieutenant William

Dealfield Arnold. The first medical school, opened in 1869, was raised to the status of a college in 1961. Education in law and engineering was provided in 1870 and a school of art was set up in 1875.

In 1958–1959, there were two universities in the Punjab with some 76 degree standard colleges, out of which 12 were exclusively meant for girls. There were also five intermediate standard colleges with one exclusive college for girls. In addition, there were some 33 colleges for professional and technical education and 1 for special education. By the 1980s, the Punjab alone had four universities.

The largest number of universities today are of the affiliating and teaching type, in which university departments impart instruction at the postgraduate level and undertake research. These universities have a large number of degree colleges affiliated to them, giving undergraduate-level education. Agricultural universities in India are in the US pattern of land grant universities with stress on research and extension work. A substantial part of the funding of these agricultural universities comes from the Indian Council of Agricultural Research (ICAR).

The Radhakrishnan Commission (1948–1949) recommended a three-year integrated course at the Bachelor of Arts (BA) and Bachelor of Science (BSc) levels. A similar recommendation was made by the Secondary Education Commission (1952–1953). Most universities have adopted the three-year degree course, except for engineering and architecture, which are four-year degree courses, followed by one year of internship. The Bar Council of India has now recommended a five-year integrated law course.

## The Problem Area

The present system of education at the undergraduate level appears to suffer from the following inherent disadvantages:

1. All students, irrespective of academic ability, aptitude or desire have to complete undergraduate instruction at the level of BA/BSc to secure even marginal employment prospects. This has resulted in
   a. overcrowding in colleges,
   b. indiscipline, malpractices in securing pass marks and a deterioration in all academic standards and norms, and
   c. a waste of a young student's early formative employability.
2. A duplication of effort and a waste of productive years. In most cases, after graduation, many students opt for either vocational courses run by private institutions such as The British Institutes (BIET) in Mumbai or similar mushrooming enterprises. Alternatively, students accept employment in any sphere, even those totally unrelated to their graduation stream, seeking to thereby gain actual 'hands-on' experience.
3. Frustration and consequent inept instruction with compromises at every level of academic interaction in all colleges appear to be a common malaise, since the members of the college faculties simply cannot cope with the mass of humanity seeking passage through the portals of a BA/BSc passport to the wide world.

## The Syllabi

A perusal of a typical syllabus for undergraduate-level instruction in a Punjab college (the Nawab Jassa Singh Ahluwalia College, better known as the Randhir College, Kapurthala) is given in Table 19.1.

TABLE 19.1 *A Typical Syllabus for Undergraduate-level Instruction in a Punjab College*

| | | |
|---|---|---|
| (a) | Eligibility/Merit | Art class/40% |
| (b) | Syllabus | As laid down by the Punjab School Education Board's directive up to the undergraduate level. |
| (c) | Three-year degree (pass) | English, Sanskrit, Punjabi, Hindi, history, philosophy, economics, music, domestic science, geography, mathematics, physics, chemistry and physical culture |
| (d) | Honours classes | English, economics, arithmetic, music, Sanskrit, Punjabi and Hindi |
| (e) | Master of Arts (MA) Part I (English) | Classics in transition, medieval and renaissance literature, Elizabethan drama, Neoclassical literature |
| (f) | MA Part II | Romantic period, Victorian period, modern English period, American literature |
| (g) | MA Part I (Economics) | Micro-economic analysis, Macro-economic analysis, statistical and mathematical techniques, public finance or money, banking and finance |
| (h) | M.A Part II (Economics) | Economic development and theory, patterns and politics, international economics, Indian economics—development since Independence, public finance or money, banking and finance |

Source: Prospectus—Nawab Jassa Singh Ahluwalia Government College, Kapurthala, 1988–1989.

A perusal of the available subject options as set out in the preceding paragraphs would be sufficient to deter the most stouthearted middling students who comprise perhaps 80 per cent of the academic population. More likely as not, such a typical student from a largely rustic background has probably just managed to pass his Plus 2 examination with the last iota of personal effort and a large measure of his neighbour's answer paper. It is quite unrealistic and totally unproductive to subject such students to the esoteric realms of classical education and subjects such as Renaissance or Neoclassical literature. Such syllabi cannot but substantially contribute toward a rapid proliferation and augmentation of the existing, unmanageable semi-literate workforce, desperately seeking employment avenues.

## The Proposal

To ameliorate this situation, it is recommended that the following measures, initially even as an experimental measure, be considered:

1. Prescribe a pragmatic 'cut-off' percentage at the Plus 2 level. It is imperative that a 'weeding out' process be commenced at the Plus 2 level so as to create two streams in the student academic force. Classic higher education is to be imparted at the undergraduate level to those students of the academic fraternity who have displayed undoubted talent, ability and a desire to imbibe further knowledge at the Plus 2 level. The respective pass percentages of the students should be the ultimate arbiter. Equally, college-level instruction and degrees in vocational subjects should be made available to the residuary student body who fall

short of the 'cut-off' percentage. A realistic 'cut-off' percentage, certainly well in excess of the existing 40 to 45 per cent, would ensure that a worthwhile and relatively high-profile student potential is exposed to higher education and can attain respectable standards in this regard. The remaining student academic force would be equally benefitted, as within the same college-level exposure time frame, they too would graduate with vocational diplomas that would enable them to earn their livelihood in any milieu. Such a measure, if introduced in some colleges, would, it is felt, assist in the following:

a. Reducing the congestion that currently obtains in the basic BA/BSc courses as only those students who qualify within the cut-off percentage, would take these courses. The remaining students could then enter the vocational course stream.
b. Providing additional employment avenues among college faculties as various experts in vocational subjects would be required. Some adjustments or reassignments of existing faculty members may, however, become necessary.
c. Promoting student interest, incentive and better discipline. 'Student satisfaction' would be more pronounced since students would be exposed to areas of their personal interest and choice as opposed to dry prescribed texts in which they have no interest whatsoever.
d. Creating an 'employable pool' of vocationally trained young students who can be slotted into various openings in the commercial, industrial and professional work forces.

2. Commence vocational degree courses in selected colleges.

In certain selected colleges, possibly based on a rural or urban orientation, certain vocational degree courses could be offered. There appears to be no reason why a college too cannot offer a degree equivalent to a BA/BSc degree in any of the following vocational subjects:

a. office management and basic labour relations
b. library sciences
c. journalism and photography
d. basic hotel management, hospitality and catering
e. textile printing and design
f. commercial and art photography
g. environmental and ecological controls
h. fine arts
i. fashion/industrial design
j. social work/youth community work
k. basic cellular phone technology and maintenance
l. basic food technology, testing and preservation
m. basic electronic technology in TV, video and radio formats. Word processing, desktop publishing, CAD and spreadsheet operation
n. basic automotive mechanics
o. basic electrical repair, air conditioning, refrigeration and motor repair techniques
p. computer technology and maintenance
q. basic artificial intelligence and systems
r. ethical computer 'hacking' and codes
s. basic flight principles, drone technology and maintenance

t. basic studio audio recording technology and maintenance

3. Develop a result-oriented philosophy. Vocational degree subjects, as may be taught in selected colleges, should aim at a result-oriented approach. Where material utilisation is involved, such as journalism and photography, textile printing and design, printing technology, automotive mechanics, electrical motor maintenance and similar subjects, it should not be difficult to set up a college photographic centre that can also cater to the local populace on a quasi-commercial scale, a college printing press, a college vehicle servicing and repair shop, an electrical maintenance shop and a food preservation and testing centre. Students would learn not to shun manual labour and, most vitally, that they have acquired or are acquiring a marketable skill and expertise. Equally, students of other vocational subjects, such as fashion/industrial design, fine arts or other subjects, could organise exhibitions and shows or sale of items produced by the students to help defray the cost of materials consumed. By the same token, a college electronic centre or Word processor and desktop publishing facility could cater to the local needs while providing 'hands-on' experience for the students.
4. It may not be out of place to examine the introduction of the 'German model', suitably adapted to cater to the Indian environment, where a student, after completing his or her mandatory schooling till standard XII or other prescribed levels, can apply to a private company from a selected official list of such approved rural or urban companies, for a two- or

three-year training course. If accepted, the selected potential trainees, under the relevant legal and binding provisions of the vocational course selected, would sign contracts with the selected companies to undergo vocational training under the vocational training directives that guarantee a set and approved national standard in each subject. The government can supplement the trainees on the job learning with more broad-based education in his or her field of choice at an officially funded vocational school. Thus, hopefully, the trainee would spend three or four days at work in the sponsoring company and one or two days in the technical classroom, emerging thereafter with both technical and practical skills required in a global market. As an added insurance, the trainees could also receive official certificates of skill competency for passing the company's examinations designed and administered by industry groups. This would allow transfer of trainees to similarly oriented businesses should the training company not be able to retain the trainees beyond the initial contract period. Such a societal skill-oriented change could well help negate the existing Indian concept that vocational training is meant as a fallback option for those failing to enter the portals of 'higher education', thereby acting as a social hurdle to upward mobility.[4]

5. The alternative model could well be the 'apprentice cadre' model. This may well be likened to the ancient Indian model of the '*guru–sishya* (pupil)' system, where for example, an aspiring young goldsmith would attach himself to an established goldsmith and learn the trade first-hand from the 'master himself'.

> Of late, since about 2016, and with the introduction of the National Apprenticeship Promotion Scheme or NAPS, duly reformed in 2019 by the Central Apprenticeship Council, the perspective quota regime has been replaced by a percentage band from 2.5 per cent to 15 per cent within which employers can decide on the number of apprentices. This revision applies also to the small and medium enterprises sector, with units having four or more employees now being eligible to second apprentices either on their own or as a group of employers. To really succeed, the government and industry stakeholders must promote apprenticeships as a powerful learning tool and assist in leveraging third-party aggregators to create and set up tailored apprenticeships in specified skills or trades.[5]

Much of what has been discussed in the preceding paragraphs will also certainly eventually depend upon the New Educational Policy (NEP that has recently been announced by the government), which too, is acutely aware of the problem of 'skilling' so vast and diverse a student population. As is known, a new NEP is usually devised every few years. To this date, India has had three of them. The first one came along almost two decades after Independence in 1968. The second one was brought into effect in 1989 and was revised in 1992. After a wait of almost 30 years, the third batch of education policies was announced in September 2020. In what looks like a significant shift from the 1986 policy that dealt with the 10+2 structure of school education, the new NEP pitches for a '5+3+3+4' design corresponding to the age groups 3–8 years (foundational stage), 8–11 (preparatory), 11–14 (middle), and 14–18 (secondary). The NEP also states that students until class 5 should be taught in their mother tongue or regional language. Similarly, the NEP of 2020 has proposed to overhaul higher education in India, which includes, amongst other things: dismantling of the University Grants Commission (UGC) and the All India Council for Technical Education (AICTE), introduction of a four-year multidisciplinary undergraduate programme with multiple exit options, and discontinuation of the MPhil programme. The NEP also proposes phasing out of all institutions offering single streams, creating a multidisciplinary educational environment by 2040.

One final consideration may be called for at the very end of this essay. Namely the role of the National Cadet Corps in forging the contours of a modern young India and how best to dovetail it into the foregoing schema.

## The National Cadet Corps

The National Cadet Corps (NCC) can be termed as the 'Youth Wing of the Armed Forces'. Conceived in September 1946 under the chairmanship of late Pandit H.N. Kunzru, it took shape in 1948 after India attained Independence in 1947 through an Act of Parliament—Act No. XXXI of 1948 as the National Cadet Corps Act of 1948 with 13 Clauses. A total of 96 units of the Senior Division covering some 20,000 cadets were then raised. Today, it comprises some 1.3 million cadets in Senior, Junior and Girls Divisions. The aim of NCC training is essentially to develop individual character, comradeship, discipline and a secular outlook while encouraging young minds toward a possible career in the Armed Forces. Most educational institutions across India participate in NCC training. Here then is a ready reservoir of youth at various levels of education, who could, and should, benefit from the 'skilling programmes' enumerated earlier. It would consequently merit active consideration of the following:

1. Should NCC training be made compulsory and, if so, at what level of education?
2. Should 'skilling' commence at that particular level of educational instruction or even independently by affiliating NCC units to educational institutions imparting these skills?
3. What educational or other benefits or concessions can be offered to such NCC cadets who successfully complete 'skilling' training in higher educational levels or their selected careers?
4. Careful updating of the NCC Act of 1948 to reflect these contemplated changes.

## Summary

The following points are recommended:

1. A realistic and worthwhile 'cut-off' percentage for entry into classical undergraduate education subjects should be introduced at the conclusion of the Plus 2 level.
2. For students who do not qualify based on the requisite 'cut-off' percentage, vocational degree

subjects should be offered in colleges with attendant degree status.

3. All such vocational degree courses should be performance and result oriented.
4. An alternate model of 'skilling' could well be that of the 'apprentice-cadre' type.
5. Actively consider the compulsory inclusion of NCC training as part of this proposed schema.

## Conclusion

Education in the existing socio-economic context of the nation must not only be confined to a stereotyped imparting of knowledge and a familiarity with the 'Classics'. Preferably, the aim of the educational thrust should be to provide excellence in select student levels with regard to the 'Classics' and simultaneously provide a comprehensive range of courses in as many arts and skills as possible. It would thus cater to students of all calibres, diverse interests and aptitudes—apart from the select band of students admitted to the 'Classics' courses—who seek to pursue some form of higher learning and education. Hopefully, this range of vocational courses, would, in time, be also available to people of all ages who may wish to better their prospects or acquire additional practical skills.

The eventual aim should be to provide meaningful opportunities of study in the most appropriate form as a stepping stone to postgraduate qualification or for the practical gainful development of student talents to benefit both themselves and the society in general.

# EPILOGUE

As I have inferred in the Preface of this book, hopefully emphatically enough, this anthology's raison d'être is captured by its title, 'Securing India's Rise'. I am no hyper-nationalist nor am I driven by any polarising orientation having been born in a nation whose diversity and plurality are its strengths—an imperative we appear to be discarding since the past few years. I have always firmly believed that India has to not only exist but also rise—for its own interests as well as for the larger good of humanity. With that in mind, 19 renowned thinkers came together to proffer their invaluable thoughts for securing India's rise. It is my sincere hope that our humble endeavour will succeed in bringing to the notice of the readers of this book and beyond what goes into working toward and ensuring the ascent of India into a place of eminence and pride in the world. With all humility, I have no hesitation in stating that for me India is the world—for billions in India and abroad too it is so—and will continue to be so if we do not divert from the sacred path as exemplified by our founding fathers.

A nation's well-being and its future largely stem from the strength, growth and sustainability of the sinews of its Comprehensive National Power (CNP). Though there are many definitions of the much-used term 'CNP', the uncomplicated interpretation of it is that it is the simple amalgam of a nation's natural resources, its economic power, military strength, its diplomatic prowess, internal stability and cohesion, its technological advancement, its industrial growth, its population and demographic dividends, its agricultural output and, apart from other attributes, its educational and medical structures. Both military and non-military aspects contribute to making a nation's CNP of the desired order. It is thus crucial for all governments, while in power, to dedicatedly strive to enhance the nation's CNP employing all their genius and resources. All governments, both at the Centre and states, must thus work selflessly to not only increase the power of the State but also build the capacity of the State to serve its people, which comes in handy both in peace and war.

India's ancient civilisation is the repository of many treatises on human values, religion, statecraft, science, mathematics and many other subjects. Yet, the foundational bedrock of the modern Indian state is the Constitution of India adopted by the Constituent Assembly on 26 November 1949, which then came into force on 26 January 1950. India's Independence on 15 August 1947, after nearly 200 years of British rule, was indeed a momentous event in our civilisational history. It is an undeniable fact that after thousands of years of its existence, India became truly and politically one for the first time. That it had to bear alongside the bloody upheaval of the unfortunate partition of the country—resulting in the largest migration of people in human history, with over a million deaths in senseless fratricidal killings—was unfortunate.

The hallowed Constitution of India is a document which enshrines the right to liberty, fraternity and freedom of speech for all its people with equity and justice. Consequently, as a benchmark for governance, if elected governments scrupulously apply the yardstick of even-handedness, many of India's internal problems will cease to exist. However, in the anxious eagerness to win elections by means fair or foul, political dispensations, mixing religion with caste or other polarising temptations, do display a propensity for ignoring this rule, and this leads to adverse implications for internal cohesion and the much-needed unity of this vast and diverse country. Thus, the first cardinal rule to be practised for securing India's rise is a conscientious and totally faithful adherence to the Constitution of India, which embodies freedom of the human mind and spirit, justice, fair play, secularism and lofty loyalty to human values. We must not dilute the Idea of India, as bequeathed to us by the founding fathers of India's unique freedom struggle. This noble Idea of India is a matchless fusion of our glorious heritage and modern constitutional precepts.

By all parameters, India's economy, once resurgent and growing speedily between 2005 and 2015, is witnessing grave distress since the past two years or so, worsened now by the onset of the Wuhan-originated COVID-19 pandemic. During the previous government under the United Progressive Alliance (UPA) regime, the average growth rate of the Indian economy was 7.6 per cent—it was even higher in the first seven years of the UPA's rule, while it slowed down in its last three years. On the other hand, under the current National

Democratic Alliance (NDA) government, India's economy has been a cause of serious concern—from an average of 6.6 per cent till 2019 the growth rate fell to 4.4 per cent in 2019, a year before the pandemic. Even before the onset of the pandemic, which has severely affected the entire world, India's financial woes had, sadly, already appeared on the horizon. There are many differing schools of thought on the real causes of this downfall ranging from demonetisation to an ineffective implementation of GST and, of course, currently, the lockdown. To an ordinary citizen, such examples as the sorry state of the retrieval of huge non-performing assets, unnecessary spending on a few populist schemes by the government and lack of banking reforms seem to point out that the economy has been destabilised to a great extent.

A strong resurgent economy translates not only in the overall development of the nation but also in strengthening national security and in allocating adequate budgetary resources to the military defence of the country. Military capability takes inordinately long to establish and is symbolic of national power; it is linked to the fact that adequate resources are given to the nation's military which then converts them into the desired war-fighting capabilities. Keeping in mind the hostile environment prevailing in India's neighbourhood, especially the growing threat from China, India is spending far too less on its security needs. Our defence budget is a paltry 1.60 per cent of our gross domestic product (GDP). China's economy is nearly five times that of India, and in 2020 it had earmarked US$178 billion for its defence budget.

Though India does not have any extra-territorial ambitions like China, Indian defence spending should be around 2.5 to 3 per cent of its GDP in case it wishes to counter China's capabilities in the region—which may become a possibility only if India grows rapidly.

India has to take all measures to ensure that its growth multiplies substantially in the next two years, say, by 7 to 8 per cent to generate the scale and quality of jobs that our young people need and also to create economic conditions that are consistent with our long-term security needs.

India's weight in the Asian region and in the world, which contributes to the perception of India and, therefore, its heft in the world, depends also on the size of its markets. That size will increase only if India grows rapidly. The government will have to shape an economic policy which supports rapid growth. This will require solid work to restore fiscal balance and reduce the large fiscal deficit by fixing the banking system, which is under severe strain. The government must undertake sectoral reforms in many areas, all of which are likely to generate political opposition. Thus, India's political leadership will have to generate acceptance and cooperation between all sections of the society to encourage reforms which promote growth—a difficult task by all standards in the currently prevailing environment within the country. The nation already boasts the existence of adequate economic expertise; all that is required is synergising the wisdom of these scholars and economists for the greater good of the country. The government has to radically alter the poverty narrative within the country and economically lift millions of our people who are still unable to meet basic human needs.

In a true democracy, its armed forces take their legitimate orders from the elected government of the day. The roles and responsibilities of the armed forces of the union are clearly enunciated within the Constitution and in governmental instructions issued from time to time. In peacetime, defence planning has to be conscientiously undertaken so that the nation is fully prepared for all probable conflict situations across the entire spectrum of warfare. Defence planning must emerge from national security and military strategies and, thus, sound civil–military interaction following guidance from the political leadership is a sine qua non. However, since Independence, overall defence planning and serious interaction between bureaucracies and the civil as well as military leadership have remained lacking of the desired order. This is owing to our imperfect higher defence control structures and because the Ministry of Defence (MoD) conducts its business according to the 2nd Schedule of the 'Allocation of Business Rules and Transaction of Business Rules'. Even with the long-awaited appointment of the Chief of Defence Staff (CDS) in 2020, these Business Rules have not been altered and the Defence Secretary continues to be responsible for the overall defence of the union. It is felt that this long persisting anomaly should be rectified and the responsibility should be allocated to either the Raksha Mantri or the CDS. Besides, India requires a fully integrated MoD, wherein the military leadership remains fully in the loop of strategic defence planning and contributes towards decision-making regarding both external and internal security. The CDS should formally be inducted into all discussions held by the Cabinet Committee on security.

Since Independence, India's foreign policy, which has largely succeeded in serving national interests, has maintained a virtual consistency in its thrust commensurate with the nation's ideological world view. Adherence to strategic autonomy stemming from the country's time-honoured commitment to the principles of non-alignment and Panchsheel have underscored India's foreign policy. Indian diplomacy, at the bilateral and multilateral levels, has had its ups and downs but, unfortunately, it has been more reactive than initiative based. However, in the last few years, there have been many upheavals in the existing world order and Indian diplomacy will have to adapt to the new dynamics as they emerge. With many countries of the world being governed by military/quasi military governments, India may also consider using the instrument of military diplomacy to further national interests.

Overall, the dominance of the Western world, including that of the USA, has gradually diminished whilst China's global reach and influence, resulting in its assertiveness and unbridled ambitions, have reached a new high. Among the nations which China feels naturally to be in competition with and in confrontation are the USA at the global level and India at the regional one. The asymmetry between China and India, both in economic power and military capabilities, has grown over the years and till India narrows the gap considerably, China's bullying stance and its 'salami-slicing' tactics towards India are unlikely to cease. China's aggression and incursions witnessed since April 2020 in India's Eastern Ladakh region are a manifestation of the likely military conflict in waiting between the two Asian giants. Over the last few decades, employing brute force, including extermination of those Tibetans indulging in dissent, China has been able to integrate Tibet with the mainland. It perceives Tibet as the palm and Ladakh, Nepal, Sikkim, Bhutan and Arunachal Pradesh as the five fingers of that palm. The long-term ramifications of China's thinking must be factored in by the Indian security establishment.

As India gears up to combat a confrontationist China all across the Himalayan region, it must also shed its earlier strategic reticence and unequivocally support the provision of military muscle for the QUAD concept. Banning of Chinese apps and reducing imports from China, especially in the hi-tech telecommunications sector such as the controversial Huawei 5G deal, is a step in the correct direction taken by the Indian government. The nation has to be extra vigilant regarding importing equipment which may have embedded technologies.

India, the USA and many other nations need to analyse the economic, geopolitical and security ramifications of China's unabashedly ambitious Belt and Road Initiative (BRI), now over seven years in existence. Most smaller countries, though initially exuberant about China's soft loans—for building infrastructure connecting the maritime silk road and for connectivity between a large number of nations to multiply and ease trade between each other—are now definitely wary of Chinese 'debt-trap diplomacy'. As India watches the China–Pakistan Economic Corridor (CPEC) traversing the disputed territory of Gilgit-Baltistan and Pakistan Occupied Kashmir (POK) with concern, it will have to similarly keep the newly conceived China–Myanmar Economic Corridor within its gaze.

As the Indo–Pacific 'Great Game' intensifies into maritime rivalry, India will have to ensure its naval preparedness both on its eastern and western seaboards. The Indian Navy's operational requirement for a third aircraft carrier and additional submarines must be catered to so as to enable it to carry out its missions in the vast Indo–Pacific expanse. Fortunately, India is blessed with an advantageous maritime geography and can dominate both the Bay of Bengal and the Arabian Sea. The Andaman and Nicobar Islands confer on India the relatively easy strategic capability to augment China's 'Malacca Strait Dilemma' while dominating the sea-lanes towards China. Overall, by all indicators, non-military and military, China's not-so-peaceful rise and its defiance of established international norms must propel all other countries to synergise their resources to contain and manage China's evergrowing global ambitions. Its vastly superior information warfare capabilities and cyber and space challenges also need to be monitored and technologically negated.

Apart from China, India's foreign policy challenges also exist in its subcontinental neighbourhood. India's 'First Neighbourhood' policy requires reorientation and major re-energising as China, beyond any doubt, has made major inroads into India's traditionally warm relations with its neighbours. China's protégé Pakistan, on the verge of virtually becoming a Chinese colony, is most likely to continue displaying its traditional highly anti-India policies in all its politico-strategic formulations. Pakistan's strategic calculus will, in all likelihood, give further fillip to the use of cross-border terrorism, to the use of non-state actors as an extension of its state policy towards India and to stoke fires in India's Jammu and Kashmir (J&K). Pakistan's military collusion with China against India will only grow in span and substance in the coming years. India, consequently, will have to substantially increase its capabilities to thwart threats emerging from what could likely be a two-front war. As India retaliates strongly against Pakistan's mischief along the Line of Control and the international border as required, it will have to conceive of and implement a robust strategy to put an end to Pakistan's continuing machinations by exploiting that country's own integral fault lines. Thus, a firm message to Pakistan needs to be delivered with alacrity and the seriousness it deserves.

Notwithstanding China's deep pockets and wily strategies to wean away the smaller South Asian nations from India, we must ensure, by a multipronged approach, that we do not cede strategic or economic space to China. Implementation of projects we commit to undertake must be completed as scheduled as India does not, currently, carry a very high reputation in this regard! Further, India must restore its earlier friendly relations with Iran and commence oil imports from this nation while completing our commitments regarding the extension of the vital Chabahar port. Apart from cheaper oil imports, Iran is strategically important for India for the development of the Northern Highway emanating from this port towards Afghanistan and the

Central Asian republics. On the lines of the Changi port in Singapore, India getting naval access in Oman's port of Duqm is a welcome development.

The democratically elected government in Kabul requires financial, infrastructural and military support from India. India, without putting boots on the ground, must continue to assist in a variety of ways that troubled, violence-afflicted land. With the fundamentalist Pakistan-supported Taliban emerging as a major player in Afghanistan, India, the USA and, hopefully, Russia and Iran have their task cut out to ensure that a modicum of peace and harmony returns to Afghanistan.

Importantly, India will also have to step up its soft power forays in nations such as Nepal, Bangladesh, Sri Lanka, Bhutan, Myanmar, Vietnam and other countries of the Indo–Pacific rim. China's wily manoeuvres to create friction between India and Nepal, with whom we share age-old cultural and religious ties, need to be adequately checkmated. India cannot afford to lose its traditional space in Nepal to China.

As India endeavours to rebuild and further strengthen its traditional fraternal ties with the Arab world, it must keep a watchful eye on the discernible churning currently going on in the Islamic world—a couple of years back it would have been unimaginable to think of improvement in relations between any Arab nation and Israel! Meanwhile, India and Israel building closer ties is also an encouraging sign. The latter is a repository of technological advancements, especially in the fields of weaponry and even agriculture. Israel can vastly assist India in the our quest for self-reliance and indigenous production in diverse hi-tech areas.

India needs to equally ensure that its traditionally good relations with Russia are further strengthened. India has been sourcing state of the art military equipment and platforms from Russia, which has consistently supplied them to India since decades. Apart from being a willing military hardware supplier, Russia does have influence in the region and there is hardly any major geopolitical divergence between the two nations.

India's relationship with the USA has undoubtedly been ascendant since the turn of the century. The Manmohan Singh–George Bush bonhomie in the early years of the 21st century resulted in the signing of the nuclear accord between the nations. This was carried forward, spiritedly, by the warm personal relationship between PM Narendra Modi and President Donald Trump. The USA is now India's largest hi-tech arms supplier and it is hoped that the USA, under the new Biden administration, will supply critical technologies to the Indian armed forces as required apart from resolving trade and visa issues which crop up, off and on, between the two nations. US president-elect Joe Biden's policies towards China will be watched with interest not only in India but across the world.

Since some years there has been much discussion within the nation on the need for India to revisit its nuclear doctrine. India is committed to 'No First Use' (NFU) of strategic weapons under its nuclear doctrine whilst maintaining a posture of nuclear deterrence. Overall, India is also committed to 'universal, verifiable and non-discriminatory nuclear disarmament and for the elimination of nuclear weapons'. It may be recalled that former Indian Prime Minister Rajiv Gandhi had given a clarion call to the global community at the United Nations General Assembly (UNGA) in 1988 on these lines for a world free of nuclear weapons. Since 1998, India has moved a yearly resolution in the UNGA on 'Reducing Nuclear Dangers', which calls for immediate and urgent steps to reduce risks of unintentional and accidental use of nuclear weapons.

India's policy of Credible Minimum Deterrence is built on an assured second-strike capability. In addition, for India, whether strategic or tactical nuclear weapons are employed by any adversary is immaterial and will be met with Indian nuclear retaliation in full. As a responsible nuclear stakeholder, India, however, is only retaliatory in its nuclear response. Though it makes both sound military and diplomatic sense, India needs to keep its nuclear doctrine flexible depending on the threat emerging in a particular situation. Many Indian analysts opine that India's nuclear doctrine is weighted more towards a roguish Pakistan and not towards China, which is now the major challenge. Thus, difficult though it maybe, India's nuclear preparedness must take into account the threats from China and Pakistan, separately and in collusion. Meanwhile, it is strongly suggested that the safety, security, command and control systems and employment mechanisms of India's nuclear arsenal are given the highest priority and that foolproof preparedness is ensured. Further strengthening of India's nuclear responses, based on a TRIAD capability, must continue with vigour.

Since the turn of the century, India has been acutely conscious of the 'two-front war' challenge it faces from China and Pakistan. Though the nuances of this credible threat have been analysed in depth, and, equally, some preparations would have been made by the Indian armed forces, it still goes without saying that much more is essential in planning and build-up. The Chinese incursions in Eastern Ladakh this year, its sabre-rattling all across the Himalayan region in recent times and Pakistan's continuing and increasing ceasefire violations have proven, beyond doubt, that India has to be prepared to take on these two nations whose military collusion is almost assured. India may have to prioritise the two fronts, namely one to be classified as the primary front and the second as the secondary front. It may also consider a posture of deterrence against Pakistan and dissuasion against China.

Deterrence is a strategy intended to persuade an adversary from taking actions which may lead to serious reprisals and unacceptable damage against the adversary. Dissuasion, on the other hand, endeavours to advise against taking any action for larger reasons. However, compelling can force a client-state to take action on the instructions or influence of the mentor-state. Thus, India has to be wary of Pakistan being compelled to take some mischievous action against India on the instructions of China—this challenge has to be factored in by the Indian security establishment. A Pakistan on its knees for its financial survival will do anything against India at Beijing's bidding.

India, being largely a peace-loving, status-quoist country, now needs to wake up from its slumber and take necessary measures for not getting militarily surprised every now and then. Thus, it must put all its security organisations institutionally on a periodic strategic review, like the Blue Ribbon Commissions in the UK every 10 years. The institution of the CDS must look into these aspects with a long-term and ruthlessly candid perspective.

The art and science of intelligence—which, unquestionably, is the first line of defence for any country—its re-energising and progress in today's highly technology-driven world must also be put through periodic institutionalised reviews and course corrections. However, the Indian intelligence structure requires, for better coordination, the appointment of a Director National Intelligence (DNI). He/she should function directly under the National Security Adviser (NSA), who currently is overloaded with many macro-level strategic issues. The office of the DNI will be able to relieve the NSA of exclusively intelligence-related issues. India must vastly improve its covert acquisition and penetrative technical intelligence capabilities to be forewarned and, thus, forearmed. Apart from the attainment of critical technologies in intelligence gathering and analyses across multiple domains and counter-intelligence skills, India must work towards greater dexterity in aspects of information warfare and situational awareness.

In India, since Independence, civil and military harmony, which translates into effective decision-making as regards security matters, has not been of the desired order. Our political authorities are fully aware of the loyalty of the armed forces to the nation's democratic values, constitutional fidelity and their unique non-political orientation. Accordingly, the government must make full use of the talents and dedication of the senior military hierarchy in strategic affairs. As the relatively new office of the CDS endeavours to address this long-standing shortcoming, a most important task for him is to work with the government to issue a well-conceived and implementable national security strategic document. The armed forces must work with clarity and mission orientation on the short-term, mid-term and long-term perspectives. Additionally, inter-ministerial coordination in security aspects needs to be further synergised.

Apart from external security threats, India also confronts credible internal security challenges in J&K, its north-east region and from Left-wing extremism (LWE) in some states. As India gears up to meet these internal challenges it must comprehend the nuances of asymmetric conflicts and hybrid warfare, particularly because India's internal security challenges have a distinct external dimension. Though there is no clear-cut definition of hybrid warfare, it is generally accepted that it is a military strategy that employs and blends conventional warfare with diverse forms of irregular warfare, cyber warfare, lawfare, psychological warfare, covert operations, deniable actions, disinformation and fake news. Asymmetric warfare, as commonly understood, is between two adversaries whose military power and other combat resources are disparate and the weaker power employs unconventional methods to engage the more powerful adversary. Addressing internal security challenges also calls for factoring in the various parameters of such unconventional tactics and support from external sources.

The state of law and order, levels of terrorism and the overall security situation within J&K have had a roller-coaster ride, with Pakistan leaving no stone unturned to keep stoking the fires of terrorism and separatist tendencies inside the Kashmir Valley. The Modi government's decision to abrogate Article 370 and divide the erstwhile state into two Union Territories has further upset Pakistan and also provoked China. The latter's aggressiveness in Eastern Ladakh since April 2020 can also be linked to India's action which, by all standards, is India's internal decision. As India takes stern actions against Pakistan's attempts at infiltration and breeding terrorism inside J&K, it must reach out to the ordinary people of the region with added sensitivity and compassion. Meanwhile, strict vigilance has to be ensured on money laundering and financing of terror networks, the alarming increase in the number of Wahhabi mosques/'madrassas' and growing radicalism. The spread of the Islamic State's influence in the Valley, emanating from Afghanistan and/or Pakistan, must be strictly curbed. The government may consider sending a few learned Muslim clergy from the hinterland to tour the Valley and impress upon the common folk that their concept of Kashmiriyat/Sufism is closer to the secular ideals of India and at variance with the fundamentalist tenets of Pakistan.

The old saying that our north-east region as a frontier is a distant frontier no longer holds good. This region's strategic significance is crucial to the parent nation for it is encircled by five nations, namely Nepal, China, Bhutan, Myanmar and Bangladesh and connected to the rest of India by the narrow Siliguri Corridor. Each of the seven sisters (states) making up the north-east region has its own political and ethno-religious dynamics and has to be tackled differently. A host of historical, social and cultural issues have impacted this region and have thrown up diverse security challenges, both external and internal, aggravated by the geographical isolation of the region and severe economic disparity with the rest of the country.

India's 'Look East' policy, upgraded to 'Act East' policy by the Modi government, has to be taken seriously. Relevant actions—political and economic, and in the allocation of adequate resources—need to be taken for this pivot to contribute to the nation's strategies. Improvement in law and order and in the overall security situation, good governance at the grassroots level, containing age-old Chinese mischief, improvements in infrastructure, connectivity and foreign policy initiatives by Delhi to integrate economic opportunities of the north-east region with neighbouring nations are of the essence. It is also a fact that India is not yet fully geared to realise the immense all-round potential of its north-east region. India's Ministry of External Affairs, Ministry of Home Affairs and MoD must synergise their thought processes to conceive of and implement a cohesive long-term strategy for the north-east region. Meanwhile, border management, till the situation improves, must be consolidated under a single agency. The Border Security Force should look after the Indo–Bangladesh border, and the Sino–India and Indo–Myanmar borders should be placed under the Indian Army. It will be a prudent step towards national integration to recruit additional youth from the north-east region for the army, police and paramilitary forces.

Maoist insurgency referred to as Naxalism or LWE has been in existence in India since the 1960s. At one stage, it had engulfed almost one-third of the Indian hinterland from the north-east to the south-west, and it was referred to as the 'Red Corridor'. However over the years, LWE has steadily declined to 90 districts in 11 states. All state governments and the Centre have diligently worked to reduce Naxalism using a variety of security and civic actions. The Centre had formulated a National Policy and Action Plan in 2015, which has yielded good results. However, the Naxal guerillas are a highly motivated bunch of ideologically driven militants and spare no efforts to mislead and drive fear into the hearts of the locals by their violent actions. The Centre and affected state governments must work in unison to eliminate this long-standing malaise. By taking a multipronged approach which includes stern security measures against the Naxals and deployment of adequate number of Central Armed Police Forces units and the paramilitary, assisted by sharp intelligence at the grassroots level, drones UAVs and suchlike, and, above all, developmental initiatives in the areas affected, the problem will be considerably reduced. Many committees which have examined the LWE problem have recommended the enforcement of land reform laws to assist the tribals but surprisingly, this is one area where the state has failed. The Naxals continually strive to prevent governmental agencies from developmental work and destroy schools, hospitals, roads, culverts and post offices. Nevertheless, it is the task of the governments to bring the fruits of development to all people and zealously also endeavour to wean away the Maoists/Naxals from the misguided path they have been traversing since years.

The China-originated COVID-19 pandemic, which has caused unimaginable havoc and misery to the entire world, throws up many lessons for India, which need to be thoroughly analysed as the future may see worse manmade pandemics. Was this pandemic an inadvertent lapse originating in China's wet markets or its Wuhan-based laboratories or was it China's deliberate attempt at testing a biowarfare weapon—the jury is still out. Nevertheless, India, like the rest of the world, has to factor in the recurrence of such pandemics which may strike similar or even worse blows to humanity. India should play a leading role not only in medical research to prevent and contain such pandemics but also assist third-world nations in provisioning of medical aid.

A roadmap for ensuring the rise of a large and diverse nation like India can hardly be condensed into one anthology. I am personally grateful to the 19 exceptional Indians who have contributed their thoughts for India's growth and progress. In conclusion, I would like to state, in all humility, that this compilation of their views should be given serious attention by our establishment and all those who wish to witness India's rise.

Notwithstanding any current pitfalls or past mistakes made by the nation, India's rise is inevitable. However, all governments in India must remember the lessons of Indian history down the ages, where lack of unity within had crippled India's stability. An essentially diverse and large nation like India requires all its 1.3 billion people to march in unison and thus respect and celebrate its diversity and secularism. The country must never mix electoral politics with crucial macroeconomics and macro-strategic matters. Politicians who accentuate societal fault lines must be shunned by the people. We should never forget that all political dispensations and personalities are transient but the nation is eternal. All stakeholders must earnestly strive to strengthen our institutions independent of political influence. Our leadership, both in the states and at the Centre, has to recognise that India is bigger than the sum of all its parts. Only statesmen—lofty, visionary and selfless—must lead the nation for only the noble and self-sacrificing will be able to take this nation forward to its yet unattained glory.

My prayer is that in the coming years this ancient civilisation but relatively young nation, India, fulfills its dreams and the expectations of most in the world. I am sanguine it will!

# NOTES

## INTRODUCTION

1 The 'string of pearls' is a geopolitical gambit on the potential Chinese intentions in the Indian Ocean region (IOR). In the context of China, 'salami slicing' denotes its strategy of territorial expansion as in the South China Sea and the Himalayan regions.

## CHAPTER 1 LAW AND THE IDEA OF INDIA

1 Parts of this chapter were originally published as 'The Ideas of the Nation', *Open Magazine*, 20 March 2020 (https://openthemagazine.com/essays/ideas-of-the-nation). This chapter has been suitably edited for inclusion in this volume.

2 See https://www.washingtonpost.com/archive/entertainment/books/1991/03/03/mughals-mahatmas-and-brahmins/2d561e1e-2504-4d54-b5d7-27548c3dc55a/

## CHAPTER 2 POSITIONING INDIA IN A SHIFTING GEOPOLITICAL TERRAIN

1 It took the USA–India deal more than three years to come to fruition after going through several complex stages, including amendment of US domestic law, especially the Atomic Energy Act of 1954; a civil–military nuclear *Separation Plan* in India, an India–IAEA (The International Atomic Energy Agency) safeguards (inspections) agreement and the grant of an exemption for India by the Nuclear Suppliers Group, an export-control cartel that had been formed mainly in response to India's first nuclear test in 1974. The deal, as it stands, has placed permanent safeguards on those nuclear facilities that India has identified as 'civil' and permits broad civil nuclear cooperation, while excluding the transfer of 'sensitive' equipment and technologies, together with civil enrichment and reprocessing things even under UN agency safeguards.

## CHAPTER 3 NATIONAL SECURITY DECISION-MAKING PROCESS IN INDIA AND ITS TRAJECTORIES

1 See https://www.dnaindia.com/analysis/standpoint-here-is-why-india-s-armed-forces-urgently-need-a-complete-overhaul-2039560, accessed on 27 October 2020.

2 Lieutenant General Satish Dua in an interview with *The Hindustan Times*. See https://www.hindustantimes.com/india-news/weak-cross-service-cooperation-in-military-hit-decisions-says-lt-gen-dua/story-PC9cwBK8xrGrz1JX29VqKO.html#:~:text=The%20existing%20structure%20for%20cross,said%20Lieutenant%20General%20Satish%20Dua.&text=%E2%80%9CThe%20weak%20structure%20doesn't%20lead%20to%20effective%20decision%20making, accessed on 27 October 2020.

3 Text of the Indo–Sri Lanka Accord of 29 July 1987. See https://peacemaker.un.org/sites/peacemaker.un.org/files/IN%20LK_870729_Indo-Lanka%20Accord.pdf, accessed on 27 October 2020.

4 See Chapter 1, 'Operation Pawan' in General V.P. Malik's *India's Military Conflicts and Diplomacy: An Inside View of Decision Making*, New Delhi, HarperCollins, p. 16.

5 Lieutenant General Depinder Singh in *The IPKF in Sri Lanka*, South Asia Books, p. 146.

6 Brigadier Satish K. Issar, VSM (Retd), *General S.M. Shrinagesh: Soldier, Scholar, Statesman*, New Delhi, Vision Books, 2009.

7 Andrew Gyorgi, 'The Geopolitics of War: Total War and Geo-strategy', *The Journal of Politics*, Vol. 5, No. 4 (1943) : pp. 347–362.

8 Detailed allocation of work and staff between the Department of Defence and the newly created DMA was issued vide MoD Order No. 38(1)/2020-D (O&M) dated 9 January 2020.

## CHAPTER 4 INDIA AND THE MARITIME DIMENSION

1 K.M. Panikkar, *India and the Indian Ocean:* An *Essay on the Influence of Sea Power on Indian History*, London: George Allen & Unwin, 1945, p. 82.

2 George K. Tanham, *Indian Strategic Thought: An Interpretive Essay*, Santa Monica: RAND, 1992, p.13.

3 Paul M. Kennedy, *The Rise and Fall of British Naval Mastery*, London: The Ashfield Press, 1983, p. 17.

4 *The New Indian Express*, 17 February 2020, available at https://www.newindianexpress.com/nation/2020/feb/17/approval-for-third-aircraft-carrier-may-not-come-soon-indicates-cds-rawat-2104718.html, accessed on 25 June 2020.

5 *Business Standard*, 11 May 2020, https://www.business-standard.com/article/economy-policy/bipin-rawat-defends-lower-spending-says-military-plays-limited-role-120051100025_1.html, accessed on 25 June 2020.

6 Angus Maddison, 'The World Economy: Historical Statistics', Development Centre Studies, New York: OECD Publishing, 2003, p. 261.

7 Arun Prakash, 'Evolution of the Indian Navy', in *The Handbook of Indian Defence Policy*, edited by Harsh Pant, New Delhi: Routledge, 2016, pp. 145–159.

8 Captain A.T. Mahan, 'The Persian Gulf and International Relations', in *National Review*, September 1902, p. 249, cited in Jon Tetsuro Sumida, *Inventing Grand Strategy and Teaching Command: The Classic Works of Alfred Thayer Mahan Reconsidered*, Washington: Woodrow Wilson Centre Press, 1999, p. 93.

9 Indian Navy, Integrated HQ, Ministry of Defence (Navy), *Ensuring Secure Seas, Indian Maritime Security Strategy*, 2015, Chapter, 2.

10 Gurmeet Khurana, 'The Indo-Pacific Concept: Retrospect & Prospect', CIMSEC, available at http://cimsec.org/indo-pacific-concept-retrospect-prospect/34710, accessed on 25 March 2020.

11 Ministry of External Affairs, available at https://www.mea.gov.in/Speeches-Statements.htm?dtl/29943/Prime+Ministers+Keynote+Address+at+Shangri+La+Dialogue+-June+01+2018, accessed on 23 March 2020.

12 The nine-dash line refers to the undefined and vaguely located demarcation line used by the People's Republic of China and Taiwan (Republic of China) for their claims of the major part of the South China Sea.

13 Halford J. Mackinder, 'The Geographic Pivot of History', *The Geographical Journal*, Vol. 23, No.4 (April 1904): pp. 421–437.

14 David Brewster, *India and China at Sea*, New Delhi: OUP, 2018, pp. 10–34.

15 'Indian Maritime Security Strategy', Chapter V.
16 'Indian Maritime Security Strategy', Ministry of Defence, Government of India, Chapter V.

## CHAPTER 5 FACING CHINA'S CHALLENGES ROBUSTLY

1 Government of India, Ministry of External Affairs Annual Report 2019–20 (New Delhi: 2020), p.15, available at http://www.mea.gov.in/Uploads/PublicationDocs/32489_AR_Spread_2020_new.pdf, accessed on 26 September 2020 and Government of India, Ministry of Defence Annual Report 2018–19 (New Delhi: 2018), pp. 4–5, available at https://mod.gov.in/dod/sites/default/files/MoDAR2018.pdf, accessed on 26 September 2020. However, with the killing of 20 Indian soldiers at Galwan on 15 June 2020 by China's troops the government of India has once again revived the 'expansionist' China discourse.
2 On China's military developments, see Peng Guangqian, Zhao Zhiyin, and Luo Yong, *China's National Defense* (Singapore: Cengage Learning Asia, 2010); David Shambaugh, *Modernizing China's Military: Progress, Problems, and Prospects* (Berkeley: University of California Press, 2002); Richard D. Fischer, Jr, *China's Military Modernization: Building for Regional and Global Reach* (Westport: Praeger, 2008); Richard Bitzinger and James Char, eds, *Reshaping the Chinese Military: The PLA's Roles and Missions in the Xi Jinping Era* (London: Routledge, 2019); and the United States Department of Defence annual report on the PLA, 'Military and Security Developments Involving the People's Republic of China 2020', 1 September 2020, available at https://media.defense.gov/2020/Sep/01/2002488689/-1/-1/1/2020-DOD-CHINA-MILITARY-POWER-REPORT-FINAL.PDF, accessed on 26 September 2020.
3 This is based on Srikanth Kondapalli, 'Is India Ready? China Steps Up Military Build-up in Tibet as America Passes Law of Reciprocal Access', *Financial Express*, 14 January 2019, available at https://www.financialexpress.com/defence/is-india-ready-china-steps-up-military-build-up-in-tibet-as-america-passes-law-of-reciprocal-access/1443394/, accessed on 26 September 2020.

4 See https://maritimeindia.org/chinas-anti-ship-ballistic-and-cruise-missiles/, accessed on 27 October 2020.

5 See https://www.financialexpress.com/defence/is-india-ready-china-steps-up-military-build-up-in-tibet-as-america-passes-law-of-reciprocal-access/1443394/, accessed on 27 October 2020

6 It is a hybrid constellation consisting of around 30 satellites in three kinds of orbits: Geostationary Earth Orbit (GEO), Inclined Geo-Synchronous Orbit (IGSO) and Medium Earth Orbit (MEO). It offers accurate positioning, navigation and timing, as well as short messaging communication, international search and rescue, satellite-based augmentation, ground augmentation and precise point positioning and so on.

7 See http://www.xinhuanet.com/english/2018-09/06/c_137449885.htm, accessed on 27 October 2020.

8 R.V. Kumar, *Chinese Air Force Threat*, New Delhi: Manas Publications, 2003, p. 152. See chapter nine for the operational conditions of the Chinese Air Force in Tibet, pp. 145–164.

9 See Andrew Small, *The China–Pakistan Axis: Asia's New Geopolitics*, London: Random House, 2015, and Ghulam Ali, *China–Pakistan Relations: A Historical Analysis*, Oxford: Oxford University Press, 2017, pp. 203–209.

10 'PN allowed to negotiate purchase of Chinese frigates', *The News*, 21 February 2003, in FBIS-CHI-2003-0221, 24 February 2003.

11 See Vipin Narang, 'Posturing for Peace? Pakistan's Nuclear Postures and South Asian Stability', *International Security*, Vol. 34, No. 3 (January 2010): p. 58.

12 See 'China's Missile Exports and Assistance to Pakistan' available at http://www.nti.org/db/china/mpakpos.htm, accessed on 6 January 2005, and https://citeseerx.ist.psu.edu/viewdoc/download?doi=10.1.1.1033.2290&rep=rep1&type=pdf, accessed on 27 October 2020.

13 For the declassified documents, see William Burr, ed., 'China, Pakistan, and the Bomb: The Declassified File on U.S. Policy, 1977–1997', National Security Archive Electronic Briefing Book No. 114, 5 March 2004, available at http://www.gwu.edu/~nsarchiv/NSAEBB/NSAEBB114/index.htm, accessed on 26 September 2020. See also Anil K Joseph, 'China Concerned over Proliferation', PTI, 17 February 2004,

available at http://in.rediff.com/news/2004/feb/17pak.htm, accessed on 26 September 2020, and 'China Was Involved in Pak Nuke Programme: Report', 16 February 2004, available at http://in.rediff.com/news/2004/feb/16pak2.htm, accessed on 26 September 2020.

14 'Pakistani PM Hails Chashma Nuclear Power Project', *Xinhua*, 28 December 2005, available at http://pk.china-embassy.org/eng/zbgx/t228923.htm, accessed on 26 September 2020.

15 'Dhaka Considering Chinese offer of F-7 MB Jets', *Daily Star*, 28 December 1999; 'MiG Deal Made with Absolute Transparency, says PM', *Independent*, 23 March 2000; 'Bangladesh to Acquire Eight Chinese Fighter Planes', *Daily Star*, 8 April 2000.

16 On China's environment issues, see Liu Junhui and Wang Jia, *China's Environment*, Singapore: Cengage Learning Asia, 2011, and Kristen A. Day, ed., *China's Environment and the Challenge of Sustainable Development*, Armonk, NY: ME Sharpe, 2005.

17 See https://www.mea.gov.in/Speeches-Statements.htm?dtl/2395/, accessed on 3 November 2020.

18 Akhilesh Pillamarri, 'Project Mausam: India's Answer to China's "Maritime Silk Road"', *The Diplomat*, 18 September 2014, available at http://thediplomat.com/2014/09/project-mausam-indias-answer-to-chinas-maritime-silk-road/, accessed on 27 September 2020.

19 See 'H.E. Ambassador Le Yucheng's address at the Media and Think Tank Reception', 4 March 2015, available at http://www.fmprc.gov.cn/mfa_eng/wjb_663304/zwjg_665342/zwbd_665378/t1242679.shtml, accessed on 27 September 2020.

20 See Yang Siling, '一带一路': 印度的回应及对策' [The One Belt and One Road Strategy: India's Response and Countermeasures], 亚非纵横, No. 6 (2014): pp. 51–60.

21 Xu Juan and Wei Ling, '印度对21 世纪' 海上丝绸之路' 倡议的认知*' [India's Perception of 21st Century Maritime Silk Road], 南亚研究季刊, Vol. 3, No. 158 (2014): pp. 1–6.

22 See Siegfried Wolf, *The China-Pakistan Economic Corridor of the Belt and Road Initiative: Concept, Context and Assessment*, Springer, 2019.

23 China's foreign ministry spokesman denied China violating India's sovereignty and termed these as 'commercial' in nature.

See '中国对印参与'一带一路'有耐心' [China Has Patience with India's Participation in the 'Belt and Road Initiative'], 参考消息网, 17 April 2019, available at http://column.cankaoxiaoxi.com/2019/0417/2377591.shtml, accessed on 27 September 2020.

24 'Official Spokesperson's Response to a Query on Media Reports Regarding Possible Cooperation with China on OBOR/BRI', 5 April 2018, available at https://www.mea.gov.in/media-briefings.htm?dtl/29768/Official+Spokespersons+response+to+a+query+on+media+reports+regarding+possible+cooperation+with+China+on+OBORBRI, accessed on 27 September 2020. See also the reply of the Minister of State for External Affairs to the Lok Sabha on 'Question No.849 One Belt and One Road Initiative', 26 June 2019, available at https://mea.gov.in/lok-sabha.htm?dtl/31484/QUESTION+NO849+ONE+BELT+AND+ONE+ROAD+INITIATIVE, accessed on 27 September 2020.

25 Sutirtho Patranobis, 'Sushma Swaraj Lays Silk Road for PM Modi's China Visit in May', *The Hindustan Times*, 1 February 2015, available at http://www.hindustantimes.com/india-news/india-committed-to-settle-boundary-row-early-swaraj-tells-china/article1-1312494.aspx, accessed on 27 September 2020.

26 'China Eyes Consensus with India on Building New Silk Road', *China Daily*, 18 September 2014, available at http://www.chinadaily.com.cn/world/2014xisco/2014-09/18/content_18623473.htm, accessed on 27 September 2020; and Ananth Krishnan, 'China Wants India to Play Key Role in "Silk Road" plan', *The Hindu*, 10 August 2014, available at http://www.thehindu.com/news/international/world/china-wants-india-to-play-key-role-in-silk-road-plan/article6301227.ece, accessed on 27 September 2020; and Ananth Krishnan, 'China Asks India to Put Aside "Maritime Silk Road" Concerns', *India Today*, 12 February 2015, available at http://indiatoday.intoday.in/story/china-india-asean-sushma-swaraj-maritime-silk-road-concerns/1/418576.html, accessed on 27 September 2020.

27 At one time, China also accused India of violating its sovereignty claims in the South China Sea when an Indian company was involved in drilling for energy resources in the

Vietnam-held areas of the region. However, the South China Sea case is different as there are a number of claimants; besides, the July 2016 judgment of the Permanent Court of Arbitration overruled any 'historical claims' to the artificial reefs in the region. In the case of Jammu and Kashmir, neither the Pakistani nor the Chinese constitution has any provisions regarding Kashmir, while the Indian Constitution specially mentions the Instruments of Accession in 1947.

28 William C. Pacatte, 'Competing to Win:A Coalition Approach to Countering the BRI', *CSIS*, 19 December 2019, available at https://www.csis.org/analysis/competing-win-coalition-approach-countering-bri, accessed on 27 September 2020.

## CHAPTER 6 INDIA'S ECONOMIC CHALLENGES AND COUNTERING CHINA

1 China's economy picked up speed in August as a strong industrial sector and stock market, better business confidence, and home and car sales combined to make it the first economy globally to emerge from the COVID-19 slump. See https://www.bloombergquint.com/global-economics/china-s-covid-19-rebound-lost-momentum-in-july-as-consumers-wary, accessed on 27 September 2020.

2 See https://www.businesstoday.in/sectors/jobs/india-unemployment-rate-hits-26-amid-lockdown-14-crore-lose-employment-cmie/story/401707.html, accessed on 27 September 2020.

3 See https://www.theglobaleconomy.com/India/capital_investment/, accessed on 27 September 2020.

4 'It is expected that the shift in economic power that we have seen in recent decades will continue. Our model projects that China's share of world GDP in PPP [purchasing power parity] terms will increase from 16.5% in 2014 to a peak of around 20% in 2030 before declining to around 19.5% in 2050. India's share of world GDP in PPP terms could increase steadily from just under 7% in 2014 to around 13.5% in 2050. Our model suggests that India could overtake the EU [European Union] and the US in terms of share of world GDP in PPP terms by 2044 and 2049 respectively. Given the rise of India and China, our model suggests that the US and the EU's share of world GDP in PPP

terms will face a steady decline from around 33% in 2014 to only around 25% by 2050. This shift of global economic power to Asia may occur somewhat more quickly or slowly than this, of course, but the general direction of change and the historic nature of this shift are clear. In many ways, it is a return to the pre-Industrial Revolution era when China and India dominated world GDP in large due to their great populations, and relatively efficient agricultural sectors at that time.' See https://www.pwc.com/gx/en/issues/the-economy/assets/world-in-2050-february-2015.pdf, accessed on 27 September 2020.

5 Gross domestic savings (per cent of GDP) in India was reported at 34.2 per cent in 2010 and declined to 27.99 per cent in 2019, according to the World Bank collection of development indicators, compiled from officially recognised sources. See https://tradingeconomics.com/india/gross-domestic-savings-percent-of-gdp-wb-data.html, accessed on 27 September 2020.

6 See https://www.financialexpress.com/economy/farm-wages-growth-fell-to-a-four-quarter-low-in-q3-fy-20/1789235/, accessed on 27 September 2020.

7 'India's top 1% of the population now holds 73% of the wealth while 67 crore citizens, comprising the country's poorest half, saw their wealth rise by just 1%. The growing divide undermines democracy and promotes corruption and cronyism,' said Oxfam India CEO Nisha Agrawal.See https://www.oxfamindia.org/blog/15-shocking-facts-about-inequality-india?gclid=Cj0KCQjw1qL6BRCmARIsADV9JtZPGmki-WCnkvePTJfAE0Fi5sDXU70eodTNmmQsiL0VaXht8_erZ5kaAlm_EALw_wcB, accessed on 27 September 2020.

8 '140 million hectare of land is used as agricultural area, as of 2012-13. Over the years, this area has been fragmented into smaller pieces of land.... the number of marginal land holdings (less than one hectare) increased from 36 million in 1971 to 93 million in 2011. Marginal and small land holdings face a number of issues, such as problems with using mechanisation and irrigation techniques.' See https://www.prsindia.org/policy/discussion-papers/state-agriculture-india, accessed on 27 September 2020.

9 See https://economictimes.indiatimes.com/news/politics-and-nation/demographic-time-bomb-young-india-ageing-

much-faster-than-expected/articleshow/65382889.cms, accessed on 27 September 2020.

10 See https://www.thehindubusinessline.com/opinion/all-you-wanted-to-know-about-minimum-support-price/article7342789.ece, accessed on 27 September 2020.

11 See https://www.businesstoday.in/current/economy-politics/india-forex-reserves-climb-to-record-53819-billion-in-week-ended-august-7/story/413158.html, accessed on 27 September 2020.

12 See https://www.hindustantimes.com/india-news/in-video-conversation-with-rahul-rajan-suggests-65k-crore-aid-for-poor/story-CtrtvW6HErR16L9m1t9wHP.html, accessed on 27 September 2020.

13 See https://economictimes.indiatimes.com/news/economy/policy/rahul-gandhi-in-conversation-with-abhijit-banerjee-india-needs-a-bigger-stimulus-package-like-us-japan-to-revive-economy/videoshow/75549770.cms, accessed on 27 September 2020.

14 See https://www.screener.in/screens/2551/Cash-Rich-Companies/, accessed on 6 October 2020.

## CHAPTER 7 REVISITING INDIA'S NUCLEAR DOCTRINE

1 Emma Anderson, 'Iran Takes a Step Back from the Nuclear Deal after US Air Strike', *Politico.com*, 5 January 2020, available at https://www.politico.eu/article/iran-takes-step-back-from-nuclear-deal-after-us-airstrike/, accessed on 28 September 2020; 'North Korea Withdraws from the Nuclear Treaty', *The Guardian*, 10 January 2003, available at https://www.theguardian.com/world/2003/jan/10/northkorea1, accessed on 28 September 2020.

2 Anna Fifield, 'In Japan and South Korea, Bewilderment at Trump's Suggestion They Build Nukes', *Washington Post*, 28 March 2016, available at https://www.washingtonpost.com/world/asia_pacific/in-japan-and-south-korea-bewilderment-at-trumps-suggestion-they-build-nukes/2016/03/28/03eb2ace-f50e-11e5-958d-d038dac6e718_story.html, accessed on 28 September 2020. The falling of Asian 'nuclear dominoes' owing to unreliable US treaty commitments was predicted in Bharat Karnad, *India's Nuclear Policy*, Westport, CN, &

London: Praeger, 2008 [South Asian edition published by Pentagon Press, New Delhi], pp. 29–32.

3 Bharat Karnad, 'Habit of Free Riding', *Seminar*, Issue No. 599, 2009, available at http://www.india-seminar.com/2009/599/599_bharat_karnad.htm, accessed on 28 September 2020. That US security pledges mean nothing and such reliance will cost the country dearly in terms of lost sovereignty and restricted foreign and defence policy freedom are discussed at length in Bharat Karnad, *Why India Is Not a Great Power (Yet)*, New Delhi: Oxford University Press, 2016, pp. 187–219.

4 Karnad, *Why India Is Not a Great Power (Yet)*, pp. 585–586. For the case why India needs all-azimuth nuclear forces, with high-yield thermonuclear weapons and intercontinental ballistic missiles, sized in relation to the Chinese Second Artillery Strategic Forces (SASF) see Bharat Karnad, *Nuclear Weapons and Indian Security: The Realist Foundations of Strategy*, second edition, New Delhi: Macmillan India Ltd., 2005 [2002], pp. 614–647.

5 'Nuclear Weapons: Who Has What at a Glance', Arms Control Association, July 2019, available at https://www.armscontrol.org/factsheets/Nuclearweaponswhohaswhat, accessed on 28 September 2020.

6 Karnad, *Nuclear Weapons and Indian Security*, pp. 561–577.

7 Even the fairly level-headed Pakistani diplomat and former ambassador to India Ashraf Jehangir Qazi has written about extending the coverage of Pakistani nuclear weapons to the supposedly genocide-facing Kashmiris in Jammu and Kashmir post the abrogation of Article 370. 'Is It Genocide?', *The News*, 7 December 2019, available at https://www.thenews.com.pk/print/579611-is-it-genocide, accessed on 28 September 2020. It took a bit more sober-minded junior colleague of his and former Foreign Secretary, Riaz Mohammad Khan, to point out a few days later that Pakistani nuclear first use can be considered only if an Islamabad frustrated by India's fait accompli in Kashmir and the international community's acceptance of it leads to Inter-Services Intelligence's (ISI's) reviving terrorist actions against India, triggering Indian conventional hostilities, and Pakistan's option then of starting a nuclear exchange. See

his 'India, Kashmir & Deterrence', *Dawn*, 9 December 2019, available at https://www.dawn.com/news/1521226/india-kashmir-deterrence, accessed on 28 September 2020. This, of course, is the usual nuclear 'flashpoint' scenario that Pakistan has flogged. The Pakistan Foreign Minister Shah Mahmood Qureshi on 19 December 2019 in his seventh letter dated 12 December 2019 to the UN Secretary General warned of a 'grave situation' due to India's 'deployment and testing of missiles of various ranges and capabilities' as prelude to a 'false flag' attack on Pakistan over Kashmir. See 'India Has Deployed Missiles: Pak to UN', *Times of India*, 20 December 2019.

8 Defence Minister Rajnath Singh, in one such ill-advised exchange, hinted at the government dumping the No First Use (NFU) policy. Imran Ahmed Siddiqui and G.S. Mudur, 'No First Use Not Cast in Stone, Says Rajnath Singh', *The Telegraph*, 17 August 2019, available at https://www.telegraphindia.com/india/no-first-use-not-cast-in-stone-says-rajnath-singh/cid/1698270, accessed on 28 September 2020.

9 Bharat Karnad, 'Scaring-up Scenarios: An Introduction', in Gurmeet Kanwal and Monika Chonsoria, eds, *Pakistan's Tactical Nuclear Weapons: Conflict Redux*, New Delhi: Centre for Land Warfare Studies and Knowledge World, 2014. On the taboo, refer George H. Quester, *Nuclear First Strike: Consequences of a Broken Taboo*, Baltimore: Johns Hopkins University Press, 2005.

10 Seymour M. Hersh, *The Samson Option: Israel, America and the Bomb*, London: Faber & Faber, 1991.

11 A study using Palit's description as an analytic template found that India–Pakistan 'wars' indeed met the metrics of riots, in that they are limited in time, intensity of violence (limited, force-on-force engagements) and geographic space. See Bharat Karnad, 'South Asia: The Irrelevance of Classical Deterrence Theory', *India Review*, Vol. 4, No. 2, April 2005, and Bharat Karnad, 'Key to Peace in South Asia: Fostering 'Social' Links between the Armies of India and Pakistan', *The Round Table: The Commonwealth Journal of International Affairs*, Issue 338, April 1996.

12 Bharat Karnad, *Staggering Forward: Narendra Modi and India's Global Ambition*, New Delhi: Penguin India, 2018, pp. 333–334.

13 This option was detailed nearly two decades ago in Karnad, *Nuclear Weapons and Indian Security*, pp. 541–544.

14 The late Manohar Parrikar as defence minister first hinted in 2016 that India was not permanently bound to NFU. See 'Why Bind Ourselves to 'No First Use' Policy, Says Parrikar on India's Nuke Doctrine', *The Hindu*, 10 November 2016, available at https://www.thehindu.com/news/national/Why-bind-ourselves-to-%E2%80%98no-first-use-policy%E2%80%99-says-Parrikar-on-India%E2%80%99s-nuke-doctrine/article16442100.ece, accessed on 28 September 2020.

15 Why NFU is a liability and India's original strategy of massive retaliation a fraud is discussed at length in Karnad, *Nuclear Weapons and Indian Security*, pp. 433–438.

16 In 2015, a senior US Department of Defence official feared the 'rapid closing of the capability gap'; three years later, the US Pacific Command chief, Admiral Harry Harris, declared in Congressional testimony that 'China's impressive military buildup could soon challenge the United States across almost every domain'. See 'People's Liberation Army versus the US Military', *GlobalSecurity.org*, available at https://www.globalsecurity.org/military/world/china/pla-v-us.htm, accessed on 28 September 2020.

17 For authoritative accounts of the development of the Chinese Bomb and the nuclear-powered submarine, see the twin studies by John Lewis and Xue Litai, *China Builds the Bomb*, Palo Alto, CA: Stanford University Press, 1988, and *China's Strategic Seapower: The Politics of Force Modernization*, Palo Alto, CA: Stanford University Press, 1995.

18 Avery Goldstein, *Deterrence and Security in the 21st Century: China, Britain, France and the Enduring Legacy of the Nuclear Revolution*, Palo Alto: Stanford University Press, 2000.

19 See the posts on my 'Security Wise' blog at www.bharatkarnad.com during the Ladakh confrontation. Also, Bharat Karnad, 'A Cowering Response to China's Provocations May Lose India More Territory', *Bloombergquint.com*, 28 May 2020, available at https://www.bloombergquint.com/opinion/india-china-tensions-cowering-response-to-chinas-provocations-may-lose-india-more-territory, accessed on 28 September 2020. For a more detailed argument that India needs to reorient its

nuclear forces majorly to 'aggressively blunt the China threat', see Karnad, *Staggering Forward*, pp. 340–349.

20 On cyber war with China, see Karnad, *Staggering Forward*, pp. 349–353. On the growing economic disparity, refer to 'India Has Only Fallen Further behind in the First 5 Years of Modi', Bloomberg, *Business Standard*, 28 April 2019, available at https://www.business-standard.com/article/economy-policy/from-economy-to-defence-india-under-modi-slips-further-behind-china-119042800117_1.html, accessed on 28 September 2020.

21 James S. Johnson, 'China's Vision of the Future Network-Centric Battlefield: Cyber, Space and Electromagnetic Asymmetric Challenges to the United States', *Comparative Strategy*, Vol. 37, Issue 5, 2018.

22 Ananth Krishnan, 'Time to Teach India "Bitter Lesson Greater than 1962", Says Chinese Media', *India Today*, 5 July 2017, available at https://www.indiatoday.in/world/story/china-india-sikkim-border-issue-doklam-standoff-1022452-2017-07-05, accessed on 28 September 2020. Regarding PLA beefing up its strength in Tibet, see Saibal Dasguptga, 'China Deploys New Weapons in Tibet Military Exercise', *Times of India*, 7 January 2020.

23 Yifei Zhang, 'Does Sun Tzu's The Art of War Influence China's Military Behavior? A Case Study of the 1962 Sino-India War', Iowa State University, Digital Repository, 2014, available at https://lib.dr.iastate.edu/cgi/viewcontent.cgi?article=4709&context=etd, accessed on 28 September 2020.

24 For an analysis of 'incentive' and 'opportunity' as drivers of 'strategic surprise', see Klaus Knorr, 'Strategic Surprise: The Incentive Structure' and Patrick Morgan, 'The Opportunity for a Strategic Surprise', in Klaus Knorr and Patrick Morgan, eds, *Strategic Military Surprise: Incentives and Opportunities*, New Brunswick, NJ, and London: Transaction Books, 1983.

25 Karnad, *Staggering Forward*, pp. 78–153.

26 Sameer Lalwani and Heather Byrne, 'Great Expectations: Asking Too Much of the US–India Strategic Partnership', *Washington Quarterly*, Vol. 42, Issue 3, Fall 2019, available at https://www.stimson.org/sites/default/files/file-

attachments/LalwaniByrne_42-3.pdf, accessed on 28 September 2020.

27 For strategic utility of nuclear wargames, see Jeffrey Appleget, Jeffrey Kline and James J. Wirtz, 'Do Wargames Impact Deterrence?' in Beatrice Heuser, Tormod Heier and Guillaume Lasconjarias, eds, *Military Exercises: Political Messaging and Strategic Impact*, Rome: NATO Defence College, February 2018.

28 It is a line ritually repeated by incoming service chiefs of staff, most recently the new Chief of Army Staff, General M.M. Naravane. See Shaurya Karanbir Gurung, 'Nukes a Deterrent, No Other Role: Army Chief General Naravane', *Economic Times*, 5 January 2020, available at https://economictimes.indiatimes.com/news/defence/india-has-carried-out-operations-against-pakistan-on-two-to-three-occasions-without-nuclear-portion-army-chief-general-naravane/articleshow/73089865.cms, accessed on 28 September 2020; and by serving and former National Security Advisers. Refer to Shivshankar Menon, 'Narendra Modi's Foreign Policy Failures Laid Bare', *The Wire*, 3 November 2018, available at https://thewire.in/books/review-bharat-karnad-narendra-modi-foreign-policy, accessed on 28 September 2020.

29 Henry Kissinger, *Nuclear Weapons and Foreign Policy*, New York: Council on Foreign Relations and Harper & Brothers, 1957.

30 Karnad, *Why India Is Not a Great Power (Yet)*, pp. 388–392; Karnad, *Staggering Forward*, p. 346. Regarding earth-dirt as insulation against radioactivity, T.K. Jones, US Deputy Under Secretary of Defence in the Reagan administration, said this when alarms were raised about possible nuclear war with the Soviet Union: 'Dig a hole [put a roof] ... throw three feet of dirt on top ... It's the dirt that does it...' See Robert Scheer, *With Enough Shovels: Reagan, Bush, & Nuclear War*, New York: Random House, 1982.

31 The consequences for China's economy of an attack or threat of nuclear strike on the Three Gorges Dam are detailed in Karnad, *Why India Is Not a Great Power (Yet)*, pp. 332–333.

32 'Shanghai: Industry, Economics and Policy', *China Briefing*, 20 August 2019, available at https://www.china-briefing.com/

news/shanghai-industry-economics-policy/, accessed on 28 September 2020.

33 Karnad, *Why India Is Not a Great Power (Yet)*, p. 332.

34 There are already a couple of tunnel missile complexes on the north-eastern front with China. See Karnad, *India's Nuclear Policy*, pp. 101–102. Tunnel complexes in mountains to make Indian missiles survivable and invulnerable to surprise attack was first proposed in Karnad, *Nuclear Weapons and Indian Security*, pp. 631–635.

35 Refer to Menon, fn28.

36 Richard Reeves, *Infamy: The Shocking Story of the Japanese American Internment in World War II*, New York: Picador, paperback, reprint, 2016; J. Samuel Walker, *Prompt and Utter Destruction: Truman and the Use of Atomic Bombs against Japan*, Third edition, Chapel Hill: University of North Carolina Press, 2016.

37 Karnad, *Staggering Forward*, pp. 344–349.

## CHAPTER 8 INDIA—PAKISTAN: THE WAY FORWARD

1 Rustam Shah Mohmand, 'Does Kashmir Really Matter to Most Pakistanis?', *The Express Tribune*, 3 September 2015, available at https://tribune.com.pk/story/949567/does-kashmir-really-matter-to-most-pakistanis/, accessed on 29 September 2020.

2 P.N. Dhar, *Indira Gandhi, the 'Emergency', and Indian Democracy*, New Delhi, Oxford University Press, 2001 edition, p. 195.

3 'A Possible Outline of A Solution', *Outlook*, 14 May 2014, full text available at https://www.outlookindia.com/website/story/a-possible-outline-of-a-solution/290718, accessed on 29 September 2020.

4 See http://www.satp.org/satporgtp/countries/india/document/papers/parliament_resolution_on_Jammu_and_Kashmir.htm, accessed on 29 September 2019.

5 'Surgical Strikes: Pakistan Rejects India's Claims', *Al Jazeera*, 30 September 2016, available at https://www.aljazeera.com/news/2016/09/pakistan-denies-india-carried-surgical-strikes-160929165646369.html, accessed on 29 September 2020.

6 Shaun Gregory, 'Analysis: South Asia's Nuclear Brinkmanship', BBC News, 29 May 2002, available at http://news.bbc.

co.uk/2/hi/south_asia/2013471.stm, accessed on 29 September 2020.

7 Ayesha Siddiqa, 'Read the Full Court Order to Understand Pakistan's Game in Jailing Hafiz Saeed, *The Print*, available at https://theprint.in/opinion/read-the-full-court-order-to-understand-pakistans-game-in-jailing-hafiz-saeed/368610/, accessed on 29 September 2020.

8 See https://www.usatoday.com/story/news/politics/onpolitics/2018/01/01/trump-lashes-out-against-pakistan-first-tweet-2018/994066001/, accessed on 29 September 2020.

9 'Pakistan listed 9th largest arms importer in the world by SIPRI', *The Express Tribune*, 13 March 2018, available at tribune.com.pk/story/1657844/3-pakistan-listed-9th-largest-arms-importer-world-sipri/, accessed on 29 September 2020.

## CHAPTER 9 INDIA AND THE TWO-FRONT WAR

1 *Firstpost*, 'Bipin Rawat Warns of Two-Front War: India Will Have to Work on Its Strategy, Prepare for Worst Case Scenarios', available at https://www.firstpost.com/india/bipin-rawat-warns-of-two-front-war-india-will-have-to-work-on-its-strategy-gear-up-for-worst-case-scenarios-4020115.html, accessed on 8 March 2020.

2 Franz-Stefan Gady, 'Ajai Shukla on the Current and Future State of India's Military', available at https://thediplomat.com/2019/09/ajai-shukla-on-the-current-and-future-state-of-indias-military/, accessed on 8 March 2020.

3 Pravin Sawhney, 'End of the Two-Front War Chimera', Tribune India News Service, available at https://www.tribuneindia.com/news/archive/end-of-the-two-front-war-chimera-652383, accessed on 10 March 2020.

4 'A Comprehensive Response Strategy to a Collusive and Collaborative Threat from China and Pakistan—USI', available at https://usiofindia.org/events/a-comprehensive-response-strategy-to-a-collusive-and-collaborative-threat-from-china-and-pakistan/, accessed on 10 March 2020.

5 'Challenge of a Two-Front Threat—USI', available at https://usiofindia.org/publication/usi-journal/challenge-of-a-two-front-threat/, accessed on 10 March 2020.

6 Sujan Dutta, 'IA Puts Mountain Strike Corps Aimed at China in Cold Storage', *The Print* (blog), 12 July 2018, available at https://theprint.in/defence/indian-army-puts-mountain-strike-corps-aimed-at-china-in-cold-storage/82319/, accessed on 29 September 2020.
7 See https://economictimes.indiatimes.com/news/defence/pakistan-moves-20000-soldiers-to-gilgit-baltistan-loc/articleshow/76718059.cms, accessed on 29 September 2020.
8 See https://www.globalfirepower.com/countries-listing.asp, accessed on 14 March 2020.
9 'Imbalance of Power', available at https://www.cnas.org/publications/reports/imbalance-of-power, accessed on 14 March 2020.
10 *The Indian Express*, 'Op Parakram Most Punishing Mistake: Ex-Navy Chief Indian Express', available at http://archive.indianexpress.com/news/op-parakram-most-punishing-mistake-exnavy-chief/871149/, accessed on 14 March 2020.
11 *The Guardian*, 'U.S. Embassy Cables: India "Unlikely" to Deploy Cold Start against Pakistan', 30 November 2010, available at https://www.theguardian.com/world/us-embassy-cables-documents/248971, accessed on 29 September 2020.
12 Arjun Subramaniam, 'Closing the Gap: A Doctrinal and Capability Appraisal of the IAF and the PLAAF', in Pushan Das and Harsh V. Pant, eds, *An Indian Military in Transformation?*, pp. 35–43. Observor research Foundation.
13 Indian Navy, *Ensuring Secure Seas: Indian Maritime Security Strategy*, 2015, available at http://indiannavy.nic.in/sites/default/files/Indian_Maritime_Security_Strategy_Document_25Jan16.pdf, accessed on 29 September 2020.
14 Indian Navy, *Ensuring Secure Seas*.
15 Aneela Shahzad, 'View of India's Maritime Strategy and Its Implications for Pakistan' , available at https://journal.cscr.pk/stratagem/index.php/stratagem/article/view/44/71, accessed on 18 March 2020.
16 Claude Arpi, 'The Sumdorong Chu Incident: A Strong Indian Stand', *Indian Defence Review* (blog), available at http://www.indiandefencereview.com/the-sumdorong-chu-incident-a-strong-indian-stand/, accessed on 4 May 2013.

17 Rajeswari Pillai Rajagopalan, 'India Is Still Losing to China in the Border Infrastructure War', available at https://thediplomat.com/2018/09/india-is-still-losing-to-china-in-the-border-infrastructure-war/, accessed on 18 March 2020.

18 Subir Bhaumik, 'More Troops on Sino-India Border', *BBC News*, 23 November 2010, available at https://www.bbc.com/news/world-south-asia-11818840, accessed on 29 September 2020.

19 PTI, 'Army Gets Govt Nod to Raise Corps along China Border', *Livemint*, 19 November 2013, available at https://www.livemint.com/Politics/DufIjGF03QZZzUnhhTz0CP/Army-gets-final-nod-for-raising-corps-along-China-border.html, accessed on 29 September 2020.

20 Anit Mukherjee and Yogesh Joshi, 'From Denial to Punishment: The Security Dilemma and Changes in India's Military Strategy Towards China', *Asian Security*, Vol. 15, No. 1 (2018): pp. 25–43.

21 Dinakar Peri, 'Third Regiment of T-72 Tanks to Be Moved to Ladakh Soon', *The Hindu*, 19 July 2016, , available at https://www.thehindu.com/news/national/Third-regiment-of-T-72-tanks-to-be-moved-to-Ladakh-soon/article14497629.ece, accessed on 29 September 2020.

22 Vinod K. Bhatia, 'Airpower across the Himalayas: A Military Appreciation of Chinese and IAFs', S. Rajaratnam School of International Studies.

23 *Business Standard News*, 'Ambala, Hasimara IAF Bases Being Readied for Rafale Jets', available at https://www.business-standard.com/article/economy-policy/ambala-hasimara-iaf-bases-being-readied-for-rafale-jets-117100100163_1.html, accessed on 18 March 2020.

24 Abhishek Bhalla, 'BrahMos with Su-30s to Boost Firepower to Combat Chinese Threat in Indian Ocean Region', *India Today*, available at https://www.indiatoday.in/india/story/indian-ocean-region-navy-iaf-brahmos-su30-squadron-china-threat-1637869-2020-01-17, accessed on 18 March 2020.

25 'A Comprehensive Response Strategy to a Collusive and Collaborative Threat from China and Pakistan—USI', available at https://usiofindia.org/events/a-comprehensive-response-strategy-to-a-collusive-and-collaborative-threat-from-china-and-pakistan/, accessed on 29 September 2020.

26 'China Military Power, 2019', available at https://www.dia.mil/Portals/27/Documents/News/Military%20Power%20Publications/China_Military_Power_FINAL_5MB_20190103.pdf, accessed on 29 September 2020.

27 Eric Heginbotham, Michael Nixon, Forrest E. Morgan, Jacob L. Heim, Jeff Hagen, Sheng Tao Li, Jeffrey Engstrom, et al. 'The U.S.–China Military Scorecard: Forces, Geography, and the Evolving Balance of Power, 1996–2017.' RAND Corporation, 2015, available at https://www.rand.org/pubs/research_reports/RR392.html, accessed on 29 September 2020.

28 'China Military Power, 2019'.

29 Jeffrey Engstrom, 'Systems Confrontation and System Destruction Warfare: How the Chinese People's Liberation Army Seeks to Wage Modern Warfare', RAND Corporation, 2018, available at https://www.rand.org/pubs/research_reports/RR1708.html, accessed on 29 September 2020.

30 Sandeep Unnithan, 'The New Strike Strategy', *India Today*, available at https://www.indiatoday.in/magazine/the-big-story/story/20190916-the-new-strike-strategy-1595666-2019-09-06, accessed on 26 March 2020.

31 Ashley J. Tellis, 'Troubles, They Come in Battalions: The Manifold Travails of the IAF—Carnegie Endowment for International Peace', available at https://carnegieendowment.org/2016/03/28/troubles-they-come-in-battalions-manifold-travails-of-indian-air-force-pub-63123, accessed on 28 March 2020.

32 *The Indian Express*, 'New Report on IAF: It Can't Protect North-Eastern and Western Frontiers Simultaneously', 28 March 2016, available at https://indianexpress.com/article/explained/new-report-on-iaf-it-cant-protect-eastern-and-western-frontiers-simultaneously/, accessed on 29 September 2020.

33 Tellis, 'Troubles, They Come in Battalions'.

34 Rediff.Com India News, '68 per Cent of Army's Equipment Is in Vintage Category', available https://www.rediff.com/news/report/sixty-eight-per-cent-of-armys-equipment-is-in-vintage-category/20180313.htm, accessed on 29 March 2020.

## CHAPTER 10 INDIA'S RELATIONS WITH WEST ASIA AND ENERGY SECURITY

1 See https://in.reuters.com/article/india-citizenship-protests-iran/irans-khamenei-asks-india-to-stop-attacks-on-muslims-after-deadly-riots-idINKBN20S1UY, accessed on 28 October 2020.
2 Henry Kissinger, *World Order: Reflections on the Character of Nations and the Course of History*, Penguin, 2015, p. 207.
3 Francis Fukuyama, *Identity: The Demand for Dignity and the Politics of Resentment*, Farrar, Straus and Giroux, 2018, p. x.
4 Fukuyama, *Identity*, p. 182.
5 Zbigniew Brzezinski, *Power and Principle: Memoirs of the National Security Adviser, 1977–1981*, Farrar Straus & Giroux, 1983.

## CHAPTER 11 THE SHIFTING BORDERS OF CONFLICT

1 This essay elaborates on the author's presentation at the Border Security Force's K.F. Rustamji Memorial Lecture, 2019, delivered on 22 May 2019.
2 See, for instance, Ajai Sahni, 'Social Science and Contemporary Conflicts: The Challenge of Research on Terrorism', in *Faultlines: Writings on Conflict & Resolution*, volume 9, New Delhi: ICM-Bulwark Books, July 2001, pp. 131–157.
3 Lester Brown, *World without Borders*, New York, Random House, 1972.
4 Hannah Arendt, Lecture at Bard College, New York, 11 December 1968, available at https://www.youtube.com/watch?v=EMUae5HXgOQ, accessed on 20 May 2019.
5 Walter Lippman, *U.S. Foreign Policy: Shield of the Republic*, Boston: Little, Brown, and Company, 1943, p. 51.
6 Robert Strausz-Hupe, Willaim R. Kinlner, James E. Dougherty, and Alvin J. Cottrell, *Protracted Conflict*, New York: Harper Colophon, 1963, p. 2.
7 Strausz-Hupe et al., *Protracted Conflict*, p. xi.
8 Strausz-Hupe et al., *Protracted Conflict*, p. 132.
9 Qiao Liang and Wang Xiangsui, *Unrestricted Warfare*, New Delhi: Natraj Publishers, 2007.
10 Liang and Xiangsui, *Unrestricted Warfare*, p. x.
11 Liang and Xiangsui, *Unrestricted Warfare*, p. x.

12 Liang and Xiangsui, *Unrestricted Warfare*, p. 191.
13 Liang and Xiangsui, *Unrestricted Warfare*, p. 11.
14 Liang and Xiangsui, *Unrestricted Warfare*, p. xi.
15 The 9/11 Commission Report, p. 172, available at https://www.9-11commission.gov/report/911Report.pdf, accessed on 30 September 2020.
16 Erin Duffin, 'Total Budgetary Cost in the U.S. of the War on Terror by Category FY 2001–2020', 27 November 2019, available at https://www.statista.com/statistics/1075849/total-us-war-costs-war-terror-category/#statisticContainer, accessed on 20 May 2019.
17 Liang and Xiangsui, *Unrestricted Warfare*, pp. 36–43.
18 Samuel Brazys and Alexander Dukalskis, 'Why U.S. Universities Are Shutting Down China-Funded Confucius Institutes', *The Washington Post*, 11 January 2019, available at https://www.washingtonpost.com/news/monkey-cage/wp/2019/01/11/u-s-universities-have-shut-down-confucius-institutes-heres-what-you-need-to-know/, accessed on 20 May 2019.
19 Liang and Xiangsui, *Unrestricted Warfare*, p xv.
20 Liang and Xiangsui, *Unrestricted Warfare*, p. 36.
21 Walter B. Wriston, 'Bits, Bytes, and Diplomacy', *Foreign Affairs*, September–October 1997, pp. 172, 174.
22 Liang and Xiangsui, *Unrestricted Warfare*, p. 153.
23 Liang and Xiangsui, *Unrestricted Warfare*, p. 32, 36.
24 Liang and Xiangsui, *Unrestricted Warfare*, p. 19.
25 See, for instance, Ly Hay Newman, 'What Israel's Strike on Hamas Hackers Means for Cyberwar', *Wired*, 6 May 2019, available at https://www.wired.com/story/israel-hamas-cyberattack-air-strike-cyberwar/, accessed on 20 May 2019.
26 Liang and Xiangsui, *Unrestricted Warfare*, p. 36.
27 The strategy is best described in Mohammad Yousaf and Mark Adkin, *The Bear Trap: Afghanistan's Untold Story*, Lahore, Jang Publishers, 1992, esp. pp. 1, 3.
28 See, for instance, Brynjar Lia, *Architect of Global Jihad: The Life of Al Qaeda Strategist Abu Mus'ab Al-Suri*, Oxford, Oxford University Press, June 2009.
29 See, for instance, Joanne Zuhl, 'How Trump Incites Violence with Stochastic Terrorism', *Real Change*, 23 October 2019, available at https://www.realchangenews.org/2019/10/23/

how-trump-incites-violence-stochastic-terrorism, accessed on 20 May 2019.

30 'Conspiracy Theories: 'When Social Trust Has Been Eroded, People Don't Know What to Believe', interview with Chip Berlet, *Civicus*, available at https://www.civicus.org/index.php/media-resources/news/interviews/4091-conspiracy-theories-when-social-trust-has-been-eroded-people-don-t-know-what-to-believe, accessed on 20 May 2019.

31 'China May Have Found a Way to Keep India in the Dark over Trade Deficit', *Economic Times*, 15 April 2019, available at https://m.economictimes.com/news/economy/foreign-trade/china-may-have-found-a-way-to-keep-india-in-the-dark-over-trade-deficit/articleshow/68884958.cms, accessed on 20 May 2019.

32 'China May Have Found a Way to Keep India in the Dark over Trade Deficit'.

33 *Impact of Chinese Goods on Indian Industry*, 145th Report of the Parliamentary Standing Committee on Commerce, Rajya Sabha Secretariat, July 2018, p. 3, available at http://164.100.47.5/committee_web/ReportFile/13/97/145_2018_7_13.pdf, accessed on 20 May 2019.

34 *Impact of Chinese Goods on Indian Industry*, p. 15.

35 *Impact of Chinese Goods on Indian Industry*, p. 15.

36 'Indian Mobile Phone Market: Emerging Opportunities for Fulfilling India's Digital Economy Dream, A Joint report by IAMAI & Enixta Innovations', undated, available at https://www.ccaoi.in/UI/links/fwresearch/Indian%20Mobile%20Phone%20market%20IAMAI%20Report.pdf, p. 23, accessed on 20 May 2019.

37 'Indian Mobile Phone Market', p. 8.

38 'Indian Mobile Phone Market', p. 8.

39 Dan Charles, 'Farmers Got Billions from Taxpayers in 2019, and Hardly Anyone Objected', National Public Radio, 31 December 2019, available at https://www.npr.org/sections/thesalt/2019/12/31/790261705/farmers-got-billions-from-taxpayers-in-2019-and-hardly-anyone-objected, accessed on 20 May 2019.

40 Vincent P. Luchsinger and John Van Blois, 'Spin-offs from Military Technology: Past and Future', *Journal of Technology Management*, Vol. 4, No. 1, 1989: pp. 21–29.

41 William O'Neill, *The Pursuit of Power*, Oxford: Blackwell, 1983, pp. 280–287.
42 Bob Work, Deputy Secretary of Defence, 'Third Offset Strategy Bolsters America's Military Deterrence', US Department of Defence, 31 October 2016, available at https://www.defense.gov/News/Article/Article/991434/deputy-secretarythird-offset-strategy-bolsters-americas-military-deterrence/, accessed on 20 May 2019.
43 Kai-Fu Lee, *AI Super-Powers: China, Silicon Valley, and the New World Order*, New York: Houghton Mifflin Harcourt, 2018, p. 19. See also Evan Feigenbaum, *China's Techno Warriors*, Stanford: Stanford University Press, 2003.
44 Adam Segal, 'When China Rules the Web', *Foreign Affairs*, Vol. 97, No. 5, September–October 2018, p: 12.
45 Segal, 'When China Rules the Web'.
46 The World Bank, 'Research and Development Expenditure (% of GDP)', available at https://data.worldbank.org/indicator/GB.XPD.RSDV.GD.ZS, accessed on 20 May 2019.
47 Liang and Xiangsui, *Unrestricted Warfare*, p, 95.
48 Liang and Xiangsui, *Unrestricted Warfare*, p. 191.
49 Liang and Xiangsui, *Unrestricted Warfare*, p. 14.
50 Liang and Xiangsui, *Unrestricted Warfare*, p. 15.
51 Ofer Fridman, *Russian 'Hybrid Warfare': Resurgence and Politicisation*, London: Hurst, 2018, p. 91.
52 Liang and Xiangsui, *Unrestricted Warfare*, p. 153.

## CHAPTER 12 NON-TRADITIONAL NEIGHBOURHOOD CHALLENGES IMPACTING INDIAN SECURITY

1 See https://sites.google.com/site/cabinetmissionplan/Cabinet-Mission-Plan-May16, accessed on 1 October 2020.
2 Tilak Devasher, *Pakistan: Courting the Abyss*, Noida: Harper Collins India, 2016.
3 Figures taken from various World Bank documents.
4 Ashfak Bokhari, 'Forgotten Water Policy Initiatives', *Dawn* 13 June 2016, available at http://www.dawn.com/news/1264521/forgotten-water-policy-initiatives, accessed on 1 October 2020.

5 *Economic Survey of Pakistan 2013–2014*, Government of Pakistan, p. 250, available at https://edepot.wur.nl/76463, accessed on 28 October 2020.

6 'Is the Glass Half Empty or Half Full? Issues in Managing Water Challenges and Policy Instruments', *IMF*, June 2015, available at https://www.imf.org/external/pubs/ft/sdn/2015/sdn1511.pdf, accessed on 1 October 2020.

7 Shaheen Akhtar, 'Emerging Challenges to Indus Waters Treaty: Issues of Compliance and Trans-boundary Impacts of Indian Hydro-Projects on the Western River', *Focus,* Vol. 28, No. 3, 2010, cited in Daanish Mustafa, Majed Akhter and Natalie Nasrallah, *Understanding Pakistan's Water–Security Nexus*, United States institute of Peace, 2013, available at https://www.usip.org/sites/default/files/PW88_Understanding-Pakistan's-Water-Security-Nexus.pdf, accessed on 1 October 2020.

8 Anwar Iqbal, 'Water Scarcity May Threaten National Economy: IMF', *Dawn*, 9 June 2015 http://www.dawn.com/news/1187036/water-scarcity-, accessed on 1 October 2020.

9 FAO, AQUASTAT database, 2013, www.fao.org/nr/water/aquastat/data. Cited in Mustafa, Akhter and Nasrallah, *Understanding Pakistan's Water–Security Nexus*.

10 National Seminar on 'Water Conservation, Present Situation and Future Strategy', Cited in *PILDAT*, 'Construction of Kalabagh Dam', March 2011, available at http://www.pildat.org/Publications/publication/Conflict_Management/ConstructionOfKalabaghDamBackgroundPaper.pdf, accessed on 1 October 2020.

11 Simi Kamal, 'Pakistan's Water Challenges: Entitlement, Access, Efficiency, and Equity', in *Running on Empty: Pakistan's Water Crisis*, edited by Michael Kugelman and Robert M. Hathaway, Washington DC: Woodrow Wilson International Center for Scholars, 2009.

12 'Arabian Sea Eating Up 100 Acres of Sindh Land Daily', *The News*, 28 September 2015, , available at https://www.thenews.com.pk/print/14892-arabian-sea-eating-up-100-acres-of-sindh-land-daily, accessed on 1 October 2020.

13 Caleb Mills, 'Water Shortages: China's Unrecognized Threat', *Geopolitical Monitor*, 6 June 2018, available at https://

www.geopoliticalmonitor.com/water-shortages-chinas-unrecognized-threat/, accessed on 1 October 2020.

14 Paul A. Davies and R. Andrew Westgate, 'China Faces Serious Water Supply Problems', available at https://www.globalelr.com/2018/06/china-faces-serious-water-supply-problems/, accessed on 28 October 2020.

15 Jim Yardley, 'Beneath Booming Cities, China's Future Is Drying Up', *The New York Times*, 28 September 2007, available at https://www.nytimes.com/2007/09/28/world/asia/28water.html, accessed on 1 October 2020.

16 Yardley, 'Beneath Booming Cities'.

17 Benn Abbs, 'The Growing Water Crisis in China, *Global Risks Insights*, 10 August 2017, available at https://globalriskinsights.com/2017/08/shocks-china-growing-water-crisis/, accessed on 1 October 2020.

18 Mills, 'Water Shortages'.

19 Abbs, 'The Growing Water Crisis in China'.

20 Yoichi Funabashi, 'Water: China's Achilles Heel', *The Japan Times*, 9 September 2019, available at https://www.japantimes.co.jp/opinion/2019/09/09/commentary/japan-commentary/water-chinas-achilles-heel/#.XlIQDGgzbIV, accessed on 1 October 2020.

21 Bilal Hussain, 'China, India, Pakistan: Moving Beyond Water Wars', *The Diplomat*, 6 October 2016, available at https://thediplomat.com/2016/10/china-india-pakistan-moving-beyond-water-wars/, accessed on 1 October 2020.

22 Zhang Hongzhou, 'China–India: Revisiting the "Water Wars" Narrative', *The Diplomat*, 30 June 2015, available at https://thediplomat.com/2015/06/china-india-revisiting-the-water-wars-narrative/, accessed on 1 October 2020.

23 Figures taken from various World Bank documents.

24 'Education Emergency' is assessed to be equivalent to an estimated lost yield to the economy on the scale of a flood every year; 'Education Emergency in Pakistan', *Dawn*, 9 March 2011, available at http://www.dawn.com/news/611831/education-emeregency-pakistan, accessed on 1 October 2020.

25 'Pakistan Vision 2025', Ministry of Planning, Government of Pakistan, available at http://www.pc.gov.pk/wp-content/

uploads/2015/05/Pakistan-Vision-2025.pdf, accessed on 28 October 2020.

26 *Economic Survey 2014–15*, Government of Pakistan, available at http://www.finance.gov.pk/survey_1415.html, accessed on 1 October 2020.

27 William Easterly, 'The Political Economy of Growth Without Development: A Case Study of Pakistan', available at https://williameasterly.files.wordpress.com/2010/08/9_-easterly_thepoliticaleconomyofgrowthwithoutdevelopmentpakistan.pdf, accessed on 1 October 2020.

28 A.H. Nayyar, 'Insensitivity to the Religious Diversity of the Nation', in *The Subtle Subversion: The State of Curricula and Textbooks in Pakistan*, edited by A.H. Nayyar and Ahmad Salim, Islamabad: Sustainable Development Policy Institute, 2004, available at https://www.hurights.or.jp/archives/pdf/asia-s-ed/v07/10Pakistan.pdf, accessed on 28 October 2020..

29 See https://www.metransparent.com/old/texts/subtle_subversion_pakistan.pdf, accessed on 3 November 2020.

30 Pervez Hoodbhoy, 'Can Pakistan Work? A Country in Search of Itself', *Foreign Affairs*, November/December 2004, available at https://www.foreignaffairs.com/reviews/review-essay/2004-11-01/can-pakistan-work-country-search-itself, accessed on 1 October 2020.

31 'Divisive Curricula', *Dawn*, 1 April 2016, available at http://www.dawn.com/news/1249173/divisive-curricula, accessed on 1 October 2020.

32 Figures taken from various World Bank documents.

33 Oxford Poverty and Human Development Initiative, 'Pakistan Country Briefing', Multidimensional Poverty Index Data Bank, OPHI, University of Oxford, June 2015, available at www.ophi.org.uk/multidimensional-poverty-index/mpi-country-briefings/, accessed on 1 October 2020.

34 'Pakistan Vision 2025'.

35 World Economic Forum, 'The Global Competitiveness Report, 2015–16', available at http://www3.weforum.org/docs/gcr/2015-2016/Global_Competitiveness_Report_2015-2016.pdf, accessed on 1 October 2020.

36 Stephen Cohen, ed., *The Future of Pakistan,* New Delhi: OUP.

37 Figures taken from various World Bank documents.

38 Shahid Javed Burki, 'Historical Trends in Pakistan's Demographics and Population Policy', in *Reaping the Dividend, Overcoming Pakistan's Demographic Challenges*, edited by Michael Kugelman and Robert M. Hathaway, Washington DC: Woodrow Wilson International Center for Scholars, 2011.

39 Rabbi Royan and Zeba A. Sathar, 'Overview: The Population of Pakistan Today', in *Capturing the Demographic Dividend in Pakistan*, edited by Zeba A. Sathar, Rabbi Royan and John Bongaarts, Islamabad: The Population Council, 2013, available at http://www.popcouncil.org/uploads/pdfs/2013_CapturingDemoDivPak.pdf, accessed on 1 October 2020.

40 Rashid Amjad, 'Why Has Pakistan Not Reaped Its Demographic Dividend?', in Sathar, Royan and Bongaarts, *Capturing the Democratic Dividend*.

41 'Pakistan Vision 2025'.

42 'The Issue of Malnutrition of Children in Pakistan', *Daily Times*, 18 July 2016, available at http://dailytimes.com.pk/editorial/18-Jul-16/the-issue-of-malnutrition-of-children-in-pakistan, accessed on 1 October 2020.

## CHAPTER 13 COMBATING LEFT-WING EXTREMISM

1 *The Times of India*, 10 July 2017.

2 Ministry of Home Affairs Annual Report, 2018–2019, p. 9.

3 See https://www.satp.org/terrorism-assessment/india-maoistinsurgency, accessed on 2 October 2020.

4 *The Times of India*, 5 December 2019.

5 *Millennium Post*, 24 April 2019.

6 *The Indian Express*, 27 August 2019.

7 *Dainik Jagaran*, 11 November 2019.

8 *The Indian Express*, 3 May 2019.

9 Indrajit Sharma, Chhattisgarh: 'Sukma: Diminishing Influence', *South Asia Intelligence Review*, Volume 18, No. 27, 30 December 2019.

10 *The Times of India*, 29 August 2019.

11 Rahul Noronha and Amitabh Srivastava, 'The Tribal Uprising', *India Today*, 9 July 2018.

12 *South Asia Intelligence Review*, Vol. 18, No. 32, 3 February 2020.

13 Sharma, Chhattisgarh: 'Sukma'.
14 Report by UK-based Centre for Economics and Business Research.
15 See https://economictimes.indiatimes.com/news/economy/indicators/indias-richest-1-holds-over-40-of-national-wealth-oxfam-report/videoshow/73447727.cms?from=mdr, accessed on 2 October 2020.
16 Mark Gruenberg, Uphill Battle, *The Millennium Post*, 26 February 2020.
17 See https://www.transparency.org/country/IND, accessed on 2 October 2020.
18 'Development Challenges in Extremist Affected Areas', Report of an Expert Group to Planning Commission, 2008, p. 29.
19 Report of the Expert Group on Prevention of Alienation of Tribal Land and Its Restoration, Ministry of Rural Development, Government of India, April 2006, p. 75.
20 Development Challenges in Extremist Affected Areas, p. 15.
21 *The Times of India*, 20 December 2018.
22 Deepak Kumar Nayak, 'Maoists: No Takers', *South Asia Intelligence Review*, Vol. 18, No.12, 16 September 2019.
23 Prakash Singh, *The Naxalite Movement in India*, third Impression, Rupa Publications India Pvt. Ltd, 2016, p. 252.

## CHAPTER 15 EMERGING SECURITY SCENARIOS AND ROLE OF INTELLIGENCE

1 Office of the Director of National Intelligence, *Global Trends 2030*.
2 Marc Goodman, *Future Crimes: Everything Is Connected, Everyone Is Vulnerable and What We Can Do About* It, Doubleday, 2015, p. 18; also cited in Vikram Sood, *The Unending Game: A Former R&AW Chief's Insights into* Espionage, Penguin Viking, 2018, p. 207.
3 Sood, *The Unending Game*, pp. 202–203.
4 Ray Kurzweil, *The Singularity Is Near: When Humans Transcend* Biology, Penguin USA, 2006, pp. 332–335.
5 Sood, *The Unending Game*, pp. 241–260, Chapter 11, 'Keeping Intelligence Relevant'.

## CHAPTER 16 INDIAN JOURNALISM: THE FOURTH PILLAR OF OUR DEMOCRACY?

1 See https://www.enfieldsouthgate-labour.org.uk/2019/02/06/top-7-john-pilger-quotes/, accessed on 28 October 2020.

2 Noam Chomsky, *Media Control: The Spectacular Achievements of Propaganda*, Seven Stories Press, 2002, p. 37.

## CHAPTER 17 COVID-19: GLOBAL CHALLENGES AND INDIAN RESPONSES

* Parts of this chapter were originally published as 'The Legal Hole in Battling Covid-19', *Hindustan Times*, 19 March 2020 (https://www.hindustantimes.com/analysis/the-legal-hole-in-battling-covid-19/story-soVFHssIu68NoIoHs5LgDI.html) and 'India's Fight against Health Emergencies: In Search of a Legal Architecture', Observer Research Foundation, 31 March 2020 (https://www.orfonline.org/research/indias-fight-against-health-emergencies-in-search-of-a-legal-architecture-63884/). This chapter has been suitably edited for inclusion in this volume.

1 The reason this piece has been written in the midst of a yet evolving pandemic is to give the readers a sense of the what the thinking was at that point in time about the world and even the challenges that India faced. I am sure once all this is behind us more insightful and scholarly pieces will be written about how the world dealt with COVID-19 and if those approaches were correct.

2 See https://foreignpolicy.com/2020/03/18/un-diplomacy-lockdown-coronavirus-diplomats-headquarters/, accessed on 4 October 2020.

3 See https://www.unog.ch/80256EDD006B8954/(httpAssets)/6D16C7B1933F0937C125815D00349763/$file/BWS%20brochure.pdf, accessed 4 October 2020.

4 See http://nhsrcindia.org/sites/default/files/Task%20Force%20on%20Public%20Health%20Act_2012_approach%20paper.pdf, accessed on 4 October 2020.

5 See https://indiankanoon.org/doc/1077116/, accessed on 4 October 2020.

## CHAPTER 18 A NEW FRONTIER: DIGITAL INSECURITY AND INDIA

1 Samir Saran is President, Observer Research Foundation. Akhil Deo is a Masters candidate at the Hertie School of Governance.

2 Samir Saran, *Navigating the Digitization of Geopolitics*, Observer Research Foundation, 22 Jan 2020, available at https://www.orfonline.org/expert-speak/navigating-the-digitisation-of-geopolitics-60612/, accessed on 4 October 2020.

3 Marshall Mcluhan, *Understanding Media: The Extensions of Man*, Chapter 1, New York: Mentor, 1964, available at https://web.mit.edu/allanmc/www/mcluhan.mediummessage.pdf, accessed on 4 October 2020.

4 Samir Saran, 'Order at the Gates: Globalisation, Techphobia and The World Order', *Valdai Club*, 27 April 2020, available at https://valdaiclub.com/a/highlights/order-at-the-gates-globalisation-techphobia-/, accessed on 4 October 2020.

5 See generally, Manoj Joshi, 'Invest, Acquire, Dominate: The Rise and Rise of China Tech', ORF Occasional Paper No. 223, Observer Research Foundation, 2019.

6 Rosalie Chan, Here's What You Need to Know about Palantir, the Secretive $20 Billion Data-Analysis Company Whose Work with ICE Is Dragging Amazon into Controversy, *Business Insider*, 19 July 2019, available at https://www.businessinsider.in/enterprise/mobile/heres-what-you-need-to-know-about-palantir-the-secretive-20-billion-data-analysis-company-whose-work-with-ice-is-dragging-amazon-into-controversy/articleshow/70298697.cms, accessed on 4 October 2020.

7 See https://cyberpeaceinstitute.org/who-we-are, accessed on 4 October 2020.

8 Arun Sukumar, 'The UN GGE Failed. Is International Law in Cyberspace Doomed as Well?', *Lawfare*, 4 July 2017, available at https://www.lawfareblog.com/un-gge-failed-international-law-cyberspace-doomed-well, accessed on 4 October 2020.

9 'The 9 Principles', *Paris Call*, available at https://pariscall.international/en/principles, accessed on 4 October 2020.

10 Norms, *Global Commission on the Stability of Cyberspace*, available at https://cyberstability.org/norms/, accessed on 4 October 2020.

11 Sui-Lee Wee, 'China Uses DNA to Track Its People, with the Help of American Expertise', *New York Times*, 21 February 2019, available at https://www.nytimes.com/2019/02/21/business/china-xinjiang-uighur-dna-thermo-fisher.html, accessed on 4 October 2020.

12 Yasheng Huang et al., 'How Digital Contact Tracing Slowed Covid-19 in East Asia', *Harvard Business Review*, 15 April 2020, available at https://hbr.org/2020/04/how-digital-contact-tracing-slowed-covid-19-in-east-asia, accessed on 4 October 2020.

13 Michelle Nichols, 'North Korea Took $2 Billion in Cyberattacks to Fund Weapons Program: U.N. Report', Reuters, 5 August 2019, available at https://www.reuters.com/article/us-northkorea-cyber-un/north-korea-took-2-billion-in-cyberattacks-to-fund-weapons-program-u-n-report-idUSKCN1UV1ZX, accessed on 4 October 2020

14 Brenden I. Koerner, 'Why ISIS is Winning the Social Media War', *Wired*, April 2016, available at https://www.wired.com/2016/03/isis-winning-social-media-war-heres-beat/, accessed on 4 October 2020

15 See generally, Maaike Verbruggen, 'The Role of Civilian Innovation in the Development of Lethal Autonomous Weapon Systems', *Global Policy*, Vol. 10, No. 3, 2019, pp. 338–342.

16 See generally, Clay Wilson, 'Network Centric Operations: Background and Oversight Issues for Congress', RL32411, Congressional Research Service, 2007.

17 See generally, Andrew Futter, 'Cyber Threats and Nuclear Weapons: New Questions for Command and Control, Security and Strategy', Occaisional Paper, RUSI, 2016.

18 See generally, Annegret Bendiek and Tobias Metzger, Deterrence Theory in the Cyber-Century: Lessons from a State-of-the-Art Literature Review', Working Paper RD/EU/Europe, 2015/02, SWP Berlin, 2015.

19 Zachary Kallenborn, 'The Era of the Drone Swarm Is Coming, and We Need to Be Ready for It', Modern War Institute at West Point, 25 October 2018, available at https://mwi.usma.edu/era-drone-swarm-coming-need-ready/, accessed on 4 October 2020.

20 Patrick Tucker, 'An AI Just Beat a Human F-16 Pilot in a Dogfight—Again', *Defense One*, 20 August 2020, available at https://www.defenseone.com/technology/2020/08/ai-just-beat-human-f-16-pilot-dogfight-again/167872/, accessed on 4 October 2020.

21 'Report of the Select Committee on Intelligence: United States Senate on Russian Active Measure's Campaigns and Interference in the 2016 U.S. Election', Volume 2: 'Russia's Use of Social Media with Additional Views, Report 116-XX', 1st Session, 116th Congress, October 2019, available at https://www.intelligence.senate.gov/sites/default/files/documents/Report_Volume2.pdf, accessed on 4 October 2020.

22 Venessa Molter and Graham Webster, 'Coronavirus Conspiracy Claims: What's behind a Chinese Diplomat's COVID-19 Misdirection', Stanford Cyber Policy Centre, 31 March 2020, available at https://fsi.stanford.edu/news/china-covid19-origin-narrative, accessed on 4 October 2020.

23 Max Brooks, 'The Next Pandemic Might Not Be Natural', *Foreign Policy*, 20 April 2020, available at https://foreignpolicy.com/2020/04/20/coronavirus-pandemic-bioterrorism-preparedness/, accessed on 4 October 2020.

24 Edward N. Luttwak, 'From Geopolitics to Geo-Economics: Logic of Conflict, Grammar of Commerce', *The National Interest*, Vol. 20, 1990: pp. 17–23.

25 Henry Farrell and Abraham Newman, 'America's Misuse of Its Financial Infrastructure', *The National Interest*, 15 April 2019, available at https://nationalinterest.org/feature/america's-misuse-its-financial-infrastructure-52707?page=0%2C, accessed on 4 October 2020.

26 Sean O'Connor, 'How Chinese Companies Facilitate Technology Transfer from the United States', Staff Research Report, US–China Economic and Security Review Commission, 2019.

27 'EU Steps Up WTO Action against China's Forced Technology Transfers', *News Archive*, European Commission, 20 December 2018, available at http://trade.ec.europa.eu/doclib/press/index.cfm?id=1963&utm_source=dlvr.it&utm_medium=facebook, accessed on 4 October 2020.

28 'The NSA Files', *The Guardian*, available at https://www.theguardian.com/us-news/the-nsa-files, accessed on 4 October 2020.
29 Kenneth Prop, 'Waving the Flag of Digital Sovereignty', *Atlantic Council*, 11 December 2019, available at https://www.atlanticcouncil.org/blogs/new-atlanticist/waving-the-flag-of-digital-sovereignty/, accessed on 4 October 2020.
30 Prop, 'Waving the Flag of Digital Sovereignty'.
31 Sankalp Phartiyal and Aditya Karla, 'India Widens China App Ban to Cover More from Xiaomi, Baidu', Reuters, 5 August 2020, available at https://in.reuters.com/article/india-apps-ban/india-widens-china-app-ban-to-cover-more-from-xiaomi-baidu-idINKCN2511FN, accessed on 4 October 2020.
32 'The Great Wall against China: Understanding India's New Foreign Investment Rules, *The Week*, 23 April 2020, available at https://www.theweek.in/news/biz-tech/2020/04/23/the-great-wall-against-china-understanding-india-new-foreign-investment-rules.html, accessed on 4 October 2020.
33 Amy Kazmin and Stephanie Findlay, 'India Moves to Cut Huawei Gear from Telecoms Network', *Financial Times*, 25 August 2020, available at https://www.ft.com/content/55642551-f6e8-4f9d-b5ba-a12d2fc26ef9, accessed on 4 October 2020.
34 Doug Palmer, 'Trump's National Security Strategy Shines Spotlight on China', *Politico*, 18 December 2017, available at https://www.politico.com/newsletters/morning-trade/2017/12/18/trumps-national-security-strategy-shines-spotlight-on-china-055167, accessed on 4 October 2020.
35 Humeyra Pamuk and Andrea Shalal, 'Trump Administration Pushing to Rip Global Supply Chains from China: Officials', Reuters, 4 May 2020, available at https://www.reuters.com/article/us-health-coronavirus-usa-china/trump-administration-pushing-to-rip-global-supply-chains-from-china-officials-idUSKBN22G0BZ, accessed on 4 October 2020.
36 Shishir Gupta, 'Donald Trump Cites India to Ban 'National Security Risk' Chinese TikTok, *Hindustan Times*, 7 August 2020, available at https://www.hindustantimes.com/india-news/donald-trump-s-ban-on-tiktok-leans-on-india-says-

risks-are-real/story-9qr2rA5DoLv5T4EJCLnNsI.html, accessed on 4 October 2020.

37 'The Global Surveillance Industry', *Privacy International*, 16 February 2018, available at https://privacyinternational.org/explainer/1632/global-surveillance-industry, accessed on 4 October 2020.

38 Alex Hern, 'France Urges Apple and Google to Ease Privacy Rules on Contact Tracing', *The Guardian*, 21 April 2020, available at https://www.theguardian.com/world/2020/apr/21/france-apple-google-privacy-contact-tracing-coronavirus, accessed on 4 October 2020.

39 Joe Uchill, 'Disinformation as a Service Crosses Borders with Ease', *Axios*, 3 October 2019, available at https://www.axios.com/disinformation-misinformation-service-online-1da509b2-d535-4ab0-bd51-3ae2fc344e31.html, accessed on 4 October 2020.

40 Samir Saran, 'An Old Scourge in a New, Uncertain Age', Observer Research Foundation, 20 March 2020, available at https://www.orfonline.org/research/an-old-scourge-in-a-new-uncertain-age-63351/, accessed on 4 October 2020.

41 Keman Huang et al., 'Cybercrime-as-a-Service: Identifying Control Points to Disrupt', Working Paper CISL# 2017-17, Sloan School of Management, MIT, 2017.

42 Branded I. Koerner, 'Inside the Cyberattack That Shocked the US Government', *Wired*, 23 October 2016, available at https://www.wired.com/2016/10/inside-cyberattack-shocked-us-government/, accessed on 4 October 2020.

43 'Equifax Data Breach', Electronic Privacy Information Centre, available at https://epic.org/privacy/data-breach/equifax/, accessed on 4 October 2020.

44 Samir Saran, 'Cyber (In)Security: Looking Back at 2017', ORF Special Report 53, Observer Research Foundation, 2017.

45 'COVID-19 Cyberthreats', Interpol, available at https://www.interpol.int/en/Crimes/Cybercrime/COVID-19-cyberthreats, accessed on 4 October 2020.

46 See note 37.

47 Nikhila Natrajan, 'The Epic Big Tech Hearing: Five Highlights', Observer Research Foundation, 1 August 2020, available at https://www.orfonline.org/expert-speak/the-

epic-big-tech-hearing-five-highlights/, accessed on 4 October 2020.

48 Samir Saran, 'Social Media Platforms Can't Be a Law unto Themselves', Observer Research Foundation, 19 August 2020, available at https://www.orfonline.org/expert-speak/social-media-platforms-cant-be-a-law-unto-themselves/, accessed on 4 October 2020.

49 Lawrence Lessig, *Code: And Other Laws Of Cyberspace*, Basic Books, 1999.

## CHAPTER 19 EDUCATION—A NEW THRUST

1 Christophe Jaffrelot and Vihang Jumle, 'The Problem of Skilling India', *The Indian Express*, 7 September 2018, available at https://indianexpress.com/article/opinion/columns/the-problem-of-skilling-india-unemployment-joblessness-modi-government-5973808/, accessed on 28 October 2020, p. 7.

2 Jaffrelot and Jumle, 'The Problem of Skilling India'.

3 'Review of Education in India, 1947–61', National Council of Educational Research and Training (NCERT), Ministry of Education, New Delhi, 1961, and *Universities Handbook India 1983–84*, Association of Indian Universities.

4 Anil Sasi, 'If You Are Missing Skills', *The Indian Express*, 2017.

5 Rajesh Agarwal, 'The Apprentice, Rebooted', *The Indian Express*, 28 August 2019, p. 6.

# ABOUT THE EDITOR AND CONTRIBUTORS

## Editor

Lieutenant General Kamal Davar is a retired Indian military officer and security expert. He served as the first Director General of the Defence Intelligence Agency and the Deputy Chief of the Integrated Defence Staff. He is an alumnus of the National Defence Academy, Khadakwasla; he also holds an MSc in defence studies from University of Madras, and a doctorate in security studies from Chaudhary Charan Singh University, Meerut.

## Contributors

Dr Shashi Tharoor is a third-term Member of Parliament from Kerala. He is a former Under Secretary-General of the United Nations and a former Minister of State for Human Resource Development and for External Affairs. He is the best-selling author of twenty-one books, both fiction and non-fiction.

Among the many awards he has won are the Pravasi Bharatiya Samman, the Commonwealth Writers' Prize and the Crossword Lifetime Achievement Award. For his book *An Era of Darkness* he won the Sahitya Akademi Award. He is currently the Chairperson of the Departmentally Related Standing Committee on Information Technology in the Lok Sabha.

Ambassador Shyam Saran is a former Foreign Secretary of India and has served as the Prime Minister's Special Envoy for Nuclear Affairs and Climate Change. After his retirement from service, he headed the Research and Information System for Developing Countries, a prestigious think tank. He has also been Chairman of the National Security Advisory Board. He is currently Life Trustee of the India International Centre, Member of the Governing Board of the Centre for Policy Research and the Institute of Chinese Studies, New Delhi, among other institutions. He has recently published a book titled *How India Sees the World*. He was awarded the Padma Bhushan in 2011 for his contribution to civil service in India. He was also conferred the Order of the Rising Sun, Gold and Silver Star by the Emperor of Japan for promoting India–Japan relations.

General V.P. Malik (Retired) was the Chief of the Army Staff of the Indian Army from 1997 to 2000. He commanded the army during Operation Vijay to successfully defeat Pakistan's intrusion in the Kargil sector in 1999. Post retirement he was a Member of the National Security Advisory Board for two terms.

He has authored two books, *Kargil: From Surprise to Victory* and *India's Military Conflicts and Diplomacy: An Inside View of Decision Making*.

Admiral Arun Prakash (Retired) is a renowned and distinguished war-decorated naval-aviator. He rose to be India's 18th Chief of the Naval Staff and was the Chairman of the Chiefs of Staff Committee. Prior to this, he commanded the Eastern Naval Command, the National Defence Academy, the Andaman and Nicobar Command and the Western Naval Command. He has served twice as Member of the National Security Advisory Board and has been Chairman of the National Maritime Foundation. Currently, he holds a Distinguished Chair at the Naval War College, Goa.

Srikanth Kondapalli is Professor in Chinese Studies at Jawaharlal Nehru University, New Delhi. He has also been the Chairman of the Centre for East Asian Studies at the university for many years. He has a PhD in Chinese studies, is a scholar of the Chinese language and was a postdoctoral Visiting Fellow at People's University of China (now known as Renmin University of China), Beijing, from 1996–1998. He is actively associated with many universities in China and Taiwan. He is the author of many articles and monographs on China besides two books, *China's Military* and *China's Naval Power in 2001*. Professor Kondapalli has received the prestigious K. Subramanyam Award in 2010 for Excellence in Research in Strategic and Security Studies.

Mohan Guruswamy is a Distinguished Fellow at the United Service Institution of India, New Delhi, and a Visiting Professor at the Administrative Staff College of India, Hyderabad. He has held senior positions in industry and the government. He is the author of several books on policy issues, the latest being *Chasing the Dragon: Will India Catch-up with China?* A Harvard graduate, he is a frequent commentator on matters of current interest in the print and electronic media. He is also a participant in several ongoing Track 2 dialogues with China and Pakistan.

Bharat Karnad is Emeritus Professor of National Security Studies at the Centre for Policy Research, New Delhi. He has authored many books including *Staggering Forward: Narendra Modi and India's Global Ambition*, *Why India Is Not a Global Power (Yet)* and *Nuclear Weapons and Indian Security*. He was a Member of the National Security Advisory Board and the Nuclear Doctrine Drafting Group. He has been a Visiting Scholar at Princeton University, USA, and has been associated with many other universities and think tanks abroad, including the Henry L. Stimson Center, Washington. He has also been associated with the Indian Ministry of Defence with regard to its nuclear studies.

Ambassador Sharat Sabharwal is a career diplomat who joined the Indian Foreign Service in 1975 and served for over 37 years in various important appointments. He was India's Deputy Commissioner to Pakistan from 1995 to 1999 and, subsequently, the High Commissioner to

Pakistan from 2009 to 2013. He is now a Distinguished Fellow with the Ananta Centre, New Delhi.

Lieutenant General D.S. Hooda (Retired) is an infantry officer. He served the Indian Army for 40 years and acquired vast experience in counter-insurgency operations while serving in the north-east and Jammu and Kashmir (J&K). He rose to be the Northern Army Commander and was responsible for handling the troubled borders with Pakistan and China and counter-terrorist operations in J&K. The successful surgical strikes of September 2016 in Pakistan were launched under his leadership.

Ambassador K.C. Singh joined the IFS in 1974 after obtaining his master's degree in English literature and a bachelor's degree in law. Has served in Indian missions in Cairo, New York and Ankara besides also serving as Deputy Secretary to the President of India. He has held important posts in the Ministry of External Affairs and subsequently was India's ambassador to the United Arab Emirates and Iran. He retired from service after serving as Secretary (Economic Relations). He is a well-respected columnist, a renowned analyst appearing on various media platforms and is associated with many think tanks.

Dr Ajai Sahni is an internationally renowned expert on terrorism and counter-insurgency operations. He is the Executive Director of the Institute for Conflict Management, the South Asia Terrorism Portal and Khalistan Extremism Monitor. He is the publisher and editor of *South Asia Intelligence Review* and the Project Director of IMPACT. He has participated in many advisory projects for the national and state governments. He has also authored many books including (with K.P.S. Gill) *Terror and Containment: Perspectives on India's Internal Security*, and *The Global Threat of Terror: Ideological, Material and Political Linkages* among others.

Tilak Devasher is a former Special Secretary, Cabinet Secretary, Government of India. He is currently a Member of the National Security Advisory Board and a Consultant with the Vivekananda International Foundation, New Delhi. He is the author of three widely acclaimed books on Pakistan:—*Pakistan: Courting the Abyss*, *Pakistan: At the Helm* and *Pakistan: The Balochistan Conundrum*. He specialises in security issues primarily pertaining to India's neighbourhood.

Prakash Singh is a very distinguished police officer who has not only served in most of the turbulent theatres of the country but has also headed the Uttar Pradesh police force; he was later the Director General of the Border Security Force. A prolific writer, he has authored 6 books and over 350 articles and has spearheaded the implementation of police reforms in the country. He has also been a Member of the National Security Advisory Board. Currently, he is Chairman of the India Police Foundation; he is also associated with the Vivekananda International Foundation and the Joint Special Operations University, USA. For his contribution to national security, he was awarded the Padma Shri in 1991.

Lieutenant General Syed Ata Hasnain (Retired), PVSM,UYSM,SM,VSM and Bar is a former Corps Commander of Strike Corps and subsequently of the Srinagar-based Corps. He is an alumnus of King's College London and Royal College of Defence Studies, UK, and Daniel K. Inouye Asia–Pacific Center for Security Studies, Hawaii, USA. One of India's distinguished military thinkers, General Hasnain is an expert on the dynamics of the proxy war in Jammu and Kashmir and a much sought after speaker and participant both in India and abroad on various seminars and meetings whilst also being a prolific writer on strategic issues.

Vikram Sood is a distinguished career intelligence officer and has headed India's external intelligence agency, the Research and Analysis Wing (R&AW). A prolific writer on intelligence, security and strategic issues, Sood has also authored two books, *The Unending Game: A Former R&AW Chief's Insights Into Espionage* and *The Ultimate Goal: A Former R&AW Chief Deconstructs How Nations Construct Narratives*. He is currently Adviser to a leading think tank, the Observer Research Foundation.

Seema Mustafa commenced her journalism career with *The Pioneer* and later worked with *The Patriot*, *Indian Express*, *The Telegraph*, *India Today*, *Economic Times* and *Asian Age* among others. She has also worked with the electronic media as National Affairs Editor in NewsX. She was the only Indian journalist to cover the wars in Beirut and later in Iraq, Iran and Darfur. Mustafa has also covered many communally violent events and internal disturbances within the country. She has been the recipient of the prestigious Prem Bhatia Award for her coverage of the Kargil War in 1999. She is currently the Editor-in-Chief of *The Citizen*, an acclaimed digital news portal.

Manish Tewari is a lawyer and currently a Member of Parliament from Punjab. He has previously served as a Union Minister of State. He is a member of many important parliamentary committees and of the government. He also writes widely on strategic and current affairs. He has also authored three books: *Decoding a Decade: The Politics of Policy Making*, *The Fables of Fractured Times* and *Tidings of Troubled Times*. He is currently also the National Spokesperson of the Indian National Congress.

Samir Saran is the President of the Observer Research Foundation, one of Asia's leading think tanks. He also curates the Raisina Dialogue, India's annual flagship platform on geopolitics and geo-economics and chairs CyFy, India's annual conference on cyber security and internet governance. He spearheads the foundation's efforts to foster new international partnerships and globalise its platforms. He is also an eminent member of many international think tanks. He has recently co-authored two books, *The New World Disorder and*

*The Indian Imperative* with Shashi Tharoor and *Pax Sinica: Implications for the Indian Dawn* with Akhil Deo.

Akhil Deo is a masters candidate in international affairs at the Hertie School, Berlin. He was formerly a Junior Fellow with the Technology and Media Initiative at Observer Research Foundation. He has co-authored *Pax Sinica: Implications for the Indian Dawn* with Samir Saran.

Brigadier Sukhjit Singh (Retired) is a distinguished soldier and an alumnus of The Doon School, Joint Services Wing and the Indian Military Academy. He was commissioned in The 14th Prince of Wales's Own Scinde Horse in 1954. He is a graduate of the Defence Services Staff College, Wellington, and the Joint Services Command and Staff College, UK. Brigadier Singh participated in the 1962, 1965 and 1971 conflicts and was awarded the Mahavir Chakra for gallant leadership in the 1971 operations. After taking an early retirement from the army, he has been active in Punjab in the fields of heritage, conservation, education and wildlife conservation. He has served on the Board of Governors of the Punjab Public School, Nabha, and is a Member of the Governing Body of the Pushpa Gujral Science City, Punjab. He has been associated with the Sainik School, Kapurthala, which is located in the Kapurthala Palace, the former home of Brigadier Singh's family.